ANYWHERE BUT
Saudi Arabia!

ONCE

EXPERIENCES OF A RELUCTANT EXPAT

Anywhere but Saudi Arabia!
Experiences of a Once Reluctant Expat

Published by
Barzipan Publishing
www.barzipan.com

ISBN 978-0-9567081-3-7

Printed and bound by Short Run Press, Exeter

CIP Data: A catalogue record for this book is available from the British Library.

ANYWHERE BUT

Saudi Arabia!

EXPERIENCES OF A ONCE RELUCTANT EXPAT

KATHY CUDDIHY

Barzipan
Publishing

Introduction

With this memoir, my old friend Kathy Cuddihy brings alive what life was like for a young family of expatriates in mid-1970s Riyadh and how her initial reservations about living in Saudi Arabia were gradually replaced by enthusiastic enjoyment of life there. Kathy has great zest for life and this comes across in her writing. My husband and I arrived with our small children at exactly the same time as Kathy and Sean. Those were pioneering days when the state was still young and many of the comforts of life considered essential by us Westerners weren't yet obtainable, and accomplishing the simplest of tasks was often beset by obstacles. But that was not to say that it was a miserable time for us: friendships for life were forged in those days and everyday frustrations were made bearable by the amusing incidents we regularly encountered and the warmth with which we were welcomed by our hosts. All these aspects of life come across clearly in Kathy's lively writing.

Like Kathy, I went to Riyadh in 1976 with great trepidation, fearing there would be too little for a woman to do, that I would be reduced to coffee mornings and housewifery: like her I said to my husband "I'll go anywhere with you, as long as it's not Riyadh". And like her I completely changed my mind, and we extended our contract year after year, returning joyfully after a long break, as Kathy and Sean did.

Kathy remembers with surprising clarity the minutiae of life over 40 years ago and her book brings back to my mind the look and feel, even the smells of the place in those days. I was reminded of the chaos at Customs which greeted the newcomer at old Riyadh Airport. The city then was one big building site with little of architectural merit. How different it all is now: returning after a long gap, I was unable to recognise anything of the city of the 1970s, other than the wonderful *suqs*. Then rubbish collection was non-existent and bags were chucked over the compound walls – though the contents were usually devoured by passing goats. The electricity would often fail, plunging one into sweltering darkness. Not so these days. However, not everything has changed for the better and the shocking story with which this book starts gives the reader a jolt. Persevere, though, and you will find how many positive things Kathy has to say in tribute to a country and its people whom she grew to love.

She describes the gradual change in her feelings for life in Riyadh. She makes new friends, (both expatriate and Saudi), finds work opportunities and takes up new interests. The realisation that she is in fact having a good time slowly dawns. After their initial two-year contract was over, Kathy was able to say to her husband, "We have a great life here," and it was her decision as much as his that they should stay on for a bit.

This is an account written with the lightest of touches. Kathy has a very good eye for the ludicrous, the sort of incongruous clashes of culture which we all experienced. For those who lived through those hard but often hilarious early years, this book will bring back some of the details of life which they may have forgotten, (as I had), while those who are now living in Riyadh will be amazed to hear of a way of life and an emerging city which has completely disappeared.

Ionis Thompson
Honorary Secretary, Society of Arabian Studies
London, June 2012

Chapter One

A sharp knock interrupted our concentration. Tarek, our Sudanese driver, wasn't expected for another half hour, so who could this be?

As Marlen, my Filipina maid, started to open the warehouse door, three members of Saudi Arabia's religious police, the *mutawwa*, forced their way in. When she shouted a warning to me, the leader slapped Marlen's face with a force that knocked her to the ground. I speed-dialled my husband at work.

"You need to get here as fast as you can," I said to Sean. "We're being raided!"

Sean had long been dreading this call. In the heightened conservative atmosphere of post-war Riyadh, it was almost inevitable that one day his non-conformist wife would get into trouble with ultra-conformist zealots.

"Tarek's got my car," Sean said, clearly distressed. "I'll take a taxi and ask him to meet us at the warehouse."

"Just hurry. They've hit Marlen and now they're heading in my direction."

"I've already left the office," he assured me. "Stay on the phone so I know what's happening."

The men strode purposefully toward me, their long, wispy beards swaying to and fro, their distinctive short *thobes* swishing to the rhythm of the tattoo made by dusty sandals on rough concrete. In an attempt to delay the unavoidable, I walked quickly up and down the aisles. Keeping Sean updated, I glanced over my shoulder and saw the stalkers following at the same pace. We formed a tidy line of pursued and pursuers.

Satisfied that Sean was now only minutes away, I got off the phone and focused on surviving the imminent confrontation unscathed. Once clear of the aisles, I came to a halt. The commander of the assault made a sudden, aggressive move. Thinking he was going to hit me like he had Marlen, I smacked his outstretched arm. This unexpected behaviour stopped the man in his tracks but I knew the action would not bode well for me.

Another *mutawwa* sniffed my water bottle. He was looking for incriminating signs of *sadiki*, the locally-brewed alcohol. It was time for a phone call that would bring a halt to this nonsense. I pretended to speak to Saudi Arabia's Crown Prince.

"Hello, Prince Abdullah. It's Kathy… Fine, fine, thank you. How are you?… I have a problem. I'm in my warehouse and the *mutawwa* have just barged in… OK, thank you. I'm grateful for anything you can do."

I had hoped this ruse might take some steam out of the raiders. Not so.

"We answer to no one except the King," the leader stated in a canny show of oneupmanship. His English was certainly more accomplished that his PR skills.

Throwing caution to the wind – and no doubt digging a deeper hole for myself – I replied, "You should be working for God. You're supposed to be setting a religious example, not chasing innocent women around a warehouse."

Outside, the cavalry had arrived. Sean, Tarek, Mohammed the warehouse manager, and Ibrahim, from the office of my royal business partner, unsuccessfully tried to convince the *mutawwa* brigade that I ran a legally registered business, not the immoral enterprise they suspected. Our team gained a small victory in dissuading the *mutawwa* from handcuffing Marlen and me before removing us to their office. Sean insisted on coming with us rather than following in his own car.

"Do you think I should call the Canadian Embassy?" I asked Sean from the back of the Chevy Suburban. Incredibly, no one had confiscated my phone.

"I suppose it wouldn't hurt," he replied. "The more people who know what's happening, the better."

The lunchtime absence of my usual Embassy contacts gave me a moment of panic. The switchboard finally put me through to a newly-arrived consular officer. Omer El Souri was reassuringly professional. He asked pertinent questions and promised to alert the necessary officials.

When we arrived at a villa that served as the neighbourhood *mutawwa* station, Marlen and I were told to wait in the hot Suburban while Sean gave a statement in the air-conditioned office. Although she made no complaints and the unwarranted attack left no physical evidence, Marlen's quiet comment "*No one* has ever hit me" revealed her emotional bruising. My own outrage at Marlen's ill-treatment roused my defiance. These people would not get the better of us, I vowed.

Twenty minutes later Sean came out to tell us we would be taken to another location to be searched by women.

We arrived at a massive, walled structure in an unfamiliar part of the city. This looked far more imposing than what we expected for a female *mutawwa* office. Where *were* we?

The driver ordered Sean out of the vehicle. The Suburban moved forward a few feet and a large sliding gate slammed shut, separating us from Sean both physically and visually. As a female guard led Marlen and me towards another gate, the leader of the raid reappeared. His hot breath whispered directly into my ear, "You'll be here for at least two weeks."

* * * *

Our escort brought us to what appeared to be a reception area. The bored young woman behind the counter looked up from her novel.

"Give. All." Her manicured finger made a lazy circuit in the direction of our possessions: handbags, phone, jewellery.

From the clutter on her desk, she unearthed a pen and an official form.

"You get paper. Everything back when you leave," she assured us as she scribbled a list of the items.

My spoken Arabic was good but my reading and writing skills were limited; the untidy room and her inefficient manner made me insist on printing detailed descriptions in English. She was too lethargic to disagree.

The guard then guided us along an unkempt outdoor path to the next stop. On the way we met two business-like, unescorted females. Writer's curiosity overcame me. I brought our little group to a halt and began chatting with the women. One of them was a psychologist and the other was the head of the facility: a women's prison. Hmm. Saudi prisons had an unsavoury reputation. I'd had a secret yearning to see the allegedly dire conditions for myself, not as an invited journalist researching a story but as an undercover inmate. Now that my wish was about to be granted, I prayed the negative accounts had been exaggerated.

A discreet nod from the warden brought the conversation to an end and spurred our guard to push us toward a free-standing room. She signaled for me to enter – for a strip search! My protests went unheeded; this was a non-negotiable event.

Having passed inspection, Marlen and I were then taken to the main building. Marlen held onto my arm, afraid we would be separated. Giving her hand a reassuring squeeze, I quickly scanned our surroundings. The dark, narrow hallway had a disturbingly Dickensian feel to it. The sight of a huge circular tray piled high with rice, topped with whole chickens and bordered with fresh oranges reassured me.

"Look, Marlen, you won't have to cook lunch today." I hoped my quip would take her mind off the uncertainties of our fate. She rewarded me with a weak smile.

A short corridor off our main route revealed another encouraging sight: two toilet cubicles.

"Let's make a quick stop here, Marlen."

"Ma'am, I don't need to go."

"Force yourself. We don't know when there will be another opportunity. This hole in the floor might be better than what's coming."

"You no stop now," our guard commanded sharply. "We go interrogation. Then you go toilet."

Interrogation? That sounded ominous – and not bladder friendly.

"Let's go, Marlen. Now."

Faced with a potentially messy alternative, the guard gruffly acquiesced.

* * * *

In a large, white-tiled space that reminded me of an Irish butcher shop, a black-clad woman handed me a long width of opaque black gauze and told me to veil. Only recently had I yielded to wearing the *abaya*, the neck-to-ankle nylon cloak that covers regular clothes. The veil was still a step too far.

After an inept effort to place the gauze over both my face and hair, one of the wardens took the cloth and wrapped it firmly around my head, rendering me almost sightless. My theatrically flailing arms periodically met unsuspecting bodies and momentarily distracted me from anxiety over the looming interrogation. Marlen stayed behind as I was taken to a separate area.

We hadn't done anything wrong, so what confessions were the police hoping to extract? Before I could dwell on the crude methods they might employ, the guard and I had arrived. The partitioned room ensured that the female prisoners and the male authorities had no physical contact.

"Sit." The guard's beefy hands pushed down on my shoulders, just in case the verbal instruction hadn't been clear.

I immediately loosened the veil and uncovered my face in order to properly see my two interrogators on the other side of the glass: a glaring *mutawwa* and a distinguished-looking civil policeman. The *mutawwa* have no powers of imprisonment, so civil police have to validate any arrests.

"Good afternoon. I need to ask you a few questions," the policeman stated in perfect English.

His cordial manner and an absence of anything that might be construed as torture tools restored my confidence.

"Good afternoon," I replied. "Your English is infinitely better than my Arabic but I wonder if you would mind conducting this… interview… in Arabic. Just to avoid any misunderstandings." I smiled, hoping to remove from the request any possible offense.

The policeman's face expressed mild surprise. Not many Western women spoke Arabic. No doubt curious to see how I would cope, he immediately agreed. After establishing the name of my sponsor and other basic details, he explored the nitty-gritty of the charges.

"You have been accused of wearing provocative, skin-tight clothing," my interrogator said with a frown.

I gave a hearty laugh and raised one leg in the air to show him unstylish baggy pants.

"I've never worn skin-tight clothing in my life. I'm not about to start at my age – which is a respectable fifty-three," I added pointedly.

My gratuitous display of leg, even covered leg, made the *mutawwa's* lips quiver rapidly, as though he was involved in a conversation with himself.

"You're here to observe. Do not say a single word," the policeman warned his companion. He made a few notes then continued, "Did you go home to remove your excessive makeup?" My interrogator's voice sounded puzzled as he looked at my makeup-free face.

"I was raided in my warehouse. These… gentlemen… haven't let me out of their sight. If I were going to go home first, it would be to clean up and change my clothes. And maybe *put on* some makeup."

The policeman frowned as he wrote his notes.

"It says here," he said sternly, "that you had men in the warehouse with you. Is that true?"

"I wish there had been men there," I responded wistfully. "They could have lifted all the heavy boxes." For maximum effect, I said in English, "I was in a warehouse, not a whorehouse."

Our unusual situation wasn't simply a conflict of East versus West or Muslim versus non-Muslim. At the heart of most run-ins with the religious police was the fundamental issue of tradition versus change. Saudi Arabia's natural progress brought the Kingdom both physical and social advances. Orthodox Muslims, however, believe that the only acceptable path is the one laid down by the Prophet Mohammed. In Riyadh, home of the ultra-conservative Wahhabi sect of Islam, the interpretation is particularly strict. The *mutawwa* take seriously their role to protect society from what they perceive as corrupting influences and a deterioration of the status quo. The problem is that some *mutawwa* become extreme in the delegation of their duties. As a result, innocent individuals might be accosted and even end up going to prison. Marlen and I were now part of this unfortunate minority.

The civil policeman completed the interrogation and then passed me the pages written in Arabic.

"I just need you to sign your statement, please," he said.

"Ah, now that's a problem. I'm sure your record is accurate but I'd prefer not to sign anything I can't read and don't understand. Don't worry, though. I'll write a statement in English and then we can both sign it."

"How long will it be?" The policeman looked concerned.

"I'm a writer. I could make it any length at all. This one will just be a *short* story."

The quick précis satisfied the policeman. The guard led me back to the room where Marlen waited nervously. Now it was her turn. The policeman, evidently convinced there had been no wrongdoing on our parts, asked her only a few questions.

I assumed I had done a sterling job pleading our innocence. It shocked us to learn that we would be kept in jail until the report was filed and then ruled upon by a judge. The huge engine of Saudi bureaucracy moved slowly at the best of times. The *mutawwa*'s menacing prediction might be true after all. We were experiencing at first-hand the vagaries of the Saudi legal system and the sometimes unprincipled power of the religious police. This was turning into more of an adventure than I'd anticipated or desired.

* * * *

Our jailers led us through a warren of corridors.

"Should we put them upstairs or downstairs?" I heard one guard ask the other. The irrational thought that one of these locations might be death row flashed through my mind. I didn't dare volunteer a preference.

They settled on a large pen on the ground floor. Instead of conventional cells, a floor-to-ceiling chain-link barrier separated the enclosure from the rest of the prison. Initially we saw no other women, nor did we hear any sound except the old lock clicking noisily with the turn of the key. The guard motioned for us to enter. I steeled my reflexes not to look back when the wire door banged shut.

Marlen and I stood in a spacious open area with, of all things, a small television. No one was watching it. The poor standard of Saudi TV evidently couldn't even tempt bored prisoners! We saw three doorless rooms to the left of us and another room on the back wall. The entire right wall had what appeared to be bathroom and kitchen facilities.

Having no idea where to go, we moved toward the first room on the left. A young woman with a kind face patted the mattress of her lower bunk, inviting us in. Hesitantly, we entered a dim, windowless chamber that had three bunkbeds. Seven faces observed our arrival. The bottom bunk across from us held a very large, scar-faced black woman whose bulk sprawled along the full length of the bed. A thin but equally scary-looking woman perched on a narrow corner at the end. Two young girls and a small boy huddled beside a timid woman in the other lower bunk.

The looks in their eyes ranged from idle curiousity to open hostility. In this restricted space full of black and brown inmates, it suddenly occurred to me I was potentially 'white meat'. My survival instinct warned me to quickly establish myself as a friendly victim before they had time to suspect me of being some sort of spy – or whatever other ideas frustrated inmates might conjure up.

"*Sabah al-khair*," I said politely, hoping to create a good first impression.

The responses to my greeting were mumbled and unenthusiastic. This definitely had the makings of A Tricky Situation. I wasn't familiar with prisoner protocol but surely we women had *some* common ground. I chose family, not least because I had an ample Arabic vocabulary in this topic.

"So," I said, targeting the big mama who seemed to be the leader. It was best, I reasoned, to win her over as soon as possible. "Do you have any children?"

No response. Just a glare. Unfazed, I moved my focus to our non-hostile 'bedmate' and repeated the question.

"No," she replied. "I'm not married. What about you? Do you have children?"

Progress.

"Yes, I have two children, a boy and a girl. My son is in the film business. When I get out of here, I'm going to ask him to make a movie about this whole thing. We could call it something like Jail Birds." The intended play on words didn't translate well into Arabic but the improbability of the idea resulted in incredulous looks from previously impassive faces.

"The only question," I continued, warming to the subject, "is which actresses are we going to get to play all of us?"

Now I had their attention. Impulsively, I turned to Big Mama.

"You," I said, pointing at her with feigned self-assurance, "for you, we're going to get Madonna."

Stunned silence. Then a gasp. Then a giggle from a dark corner of the room. And then a throaty laugh from Big Mama herself. I had broken the ice. With this seal of approval everyone now felt comfortable enough to introduce themselves and exchange arrest stories with us.

All the women had been accused of prostitution. Two of the Sudanese had been at home with their mistress washing windows. When an electrician came to repair a faulty circuit breaker, cruising *mutawwa* saw the man enter the house and immediately raided this apparent den of iniquity. They imprisoned the two maids for being 'alone' with a man who wasn't their husband. Statements from the other women were no less preposterous.

The three-year-old boy belonged to Charuni, the timid – or intimidated – woman. The two girls were economic hostages: the *mutawwa* had arrested their father. He argued that he couldn't go to jail because his wife was out of the country and he had no one to care for his daughters. The *mutawwa* relieved him of this worry by putting the girls in jail until he could pay his fine.

"But you," one of my new friends said in astonishment, "how could they possibly charge *you* with prostitution? You're too old!"

Evidently there was no room for tact in these confines.

* * * *

"Come," said Sesen, the gentle Eritrean who had first welcomed us, "we'll show you around."

The neighbouring room was crammed with apathetic African women, mostly from Sudan and Ethiopia. The majority of the listless inhabitants of the third cell were Filipinas. A miscellany of hapless women crowded the final cell of the detention area. Of the possibly 60 inmates, mine was the only Western face.

I talked with many of the women. Some were too despondent to relate the circumstances of their arrest; others welcomed the chance to voice their frustrations. Time and again the wretched stories emphasised the injustice of their imprisonment. Only one woman had committed what the rest of the world would recognise as a jailable offense: she had murdered her employer. The mitigating circumstances, however, were overwhelming. The Filipina had been kept as a slave. For almost three years she had not been allowed to leave the house or communicate with anyone. She received no pay, minimal food, and frequent physical and verbal abuse. One day she snapped and plunged a kitchen knife into her Saudi employer's chest. Being in jail surrounded by supportive women was definitely a step up for this poor soul.

The bathroom area, which took up nearly half of the right-hand wall, was reassuringly clean. A row of doored cubicles faced a long trough in which the women washed themselves and their clothes.

"This looks pretty good," I said, as though I were the local hygiene inspector, "but where are the towels… and the soap? And how do you dry your hair?"

I immediately realised how ridiculous I sounded. Where did I think I was, a five-star hotel?

"The prison has a small shop but we have no money to buy supplies," one of the women replied.

"What about clean underwear? A change of clothes?" I asked. This situation was fast losing its appeal.

"You have to be lucky enough to have someone bring clothes. For most of us, our families or employers don't know where we are. If they are in the country illegally, they are afraid to look for us."

Suddenly shampoo and hair dryers seemed painfully superficial.

The final room, the kitchen, was as spotlessly clean as the other rooms. Its sole piece of furniture was a picnic table. We had missed lunch; I'd have to wait for dinner to test my theory that everyone ate sitting on the floor in the communal area at the centre of the enclosure.

When we got back to our room, I asked the women what they did all day to keep busy. To me, inactivity was an unfamiliar state of being.

"Do?" responded Charuni. "What do you mean 'do'? We're in jail, alone and forgotten. There's absolutely nothing to 'do'.

This did not sound good. A lack of stimulation for any length of time would drive me stir crazy.

"Listen up, girls. Doing nothing is not healthy. Tonight we're going to have a party."

"A party?" several voices responded in disbelief.

"A party. Who knows how to belly dance?" A couple of the women raised their hands. "OK. You can teach Marlen and me."

Marlen was as surprised as the others at the plan but she nodded her consent with good grace. She felt less anxious now that we had remained together. Also, she had bonded with several of the Filipinas.

"Maybe the other women would like to join us?" I suggested.

The promise of a temporary distraction from their monotonous existence, no matter how unlikely, brought genuine smiles to their faces.

"And tomorrow morning," I announced, "we're going to have an exercise class." More questioning glances but no voiced dissent.

"You won't be here tomorrow," Sesen said matter-of-factly. "You're a white woman, a Westerner. You will leave soon."

The other women nodded in agreement. It's true that I had a potent armory of external forces: a devoted husband, an influential Saudi business partner and an embassy, all of whom presumably were working to gain our release. This security sustained me in these otherwise bleak circumstances and allowed me to enjoy the luxury of hope.

Then Zeneb, the formerly fearsome Big Mama, reached under her mattress and pulled out a dirty scrap of paper and a dull stub of a pencil.

"We trust you," she said. "When you get out, can you please phone people to let them know where we are?"

"Of course," I said. My throat got a lump in it when I heard this hearbreaking request.

I wrote names and phone numbers and carefully put the paper in my pocket. Then, not wanting to waste any of their precious – and forbidden – paper supply, I wrote my name and number in Arabic on a lower part of the wall behind the bunks. I wasn't sure what I could do to help but they had my contact information if they needed it.

By now my adrenalin had exhausted itself. The day's excitement had taken its toll.

"Would anyone mind if I had a nap?"

Despite considerate invitations to take a prized lower bunk, I hoisted myself onto an upper mattress. There were no sheets or blankets. Sesen insisted that I take the room's one pillow. A brick would have been softer and cleaner but the gesture was too generous to ignore. I couldn't have fallen asleep faster if my head had rested on goose down.

* * * *

"Wake up, ma'am. Wake up. It's time to go." Marlen's hand shook my shoulder.

Go? I didn't know where I was let alone where I was supposed to go. With relief in her voice, Marlen explained that we were being released. Good news but I couldn't suppress a twinge of regret at the thought of not being able to attend the party we'd planned. Then a profound wave of sadness swept over me: I'd miss this eclectic collection of decent women.

What had begun as an unexpected opportunity to research the reality of a Saudi prison had ended as participation in an episode of human tragedy.

A guard waited for us in the central area. Her sharp eyes caught me touching my trouser leg to make sure I had the paper with the phone numbers.

"What do you have in there?" she demanded.

My heart sank. Would my carelessness get the women in trouble? The tension in the room was tangible. I reached into my pocket and pulled out... the receipt for my belongings. The guard carefully checked the paper and returned it, seemingly disappointed not to have found damning evidence. I thanked God for a small miracle.

As Marlen and I headed toward the wire door we had entered only six hours previously, Zeneb's sizeable frame appeared in front of me. She enveloped me in her tree trunk-like arms to give me the mother of all bear hugs. The other cell mates followed suit. I wasn't crying when I went into prison but I couldn't stop the tears as I left.

* * * *

Outside the prison walls, I spotted Sean anxiously waiting for us to appear. He'd spent a stressful few hours worrying about our fate and trying to hasten a normally sluggish process. Omer El Souri, the conscientious consular representative who had taken my original call, was on hand to supervise the completion of the paperwork and the return of our belongings. Once Sean assured himself that Marlen and I were unharmed, we headed home.

The impact of the day's events was beginning to sink in. With a shiver, I realised how easy it could have been for this story to have a different ending.

"Well, Kathy, your arrest has caused quite a bit of excitement in the city," Sean said, breaking the somber silence in the car. "Even the Deputy Governor has heard the news. He's furious at what's happened. It doesn't seem possible for you to lead a low-key existence, does it?" Sean threw me a quick sideways glance. "It's kind of ironic to think that one of your main concerns about moving to Riyadh was that you'd be a bored housewife."

Chapter Two

Creative inspiration stubbornly eluded me. Staring absently out the high-rise window for an extended period had been futile; I just couldn't focus on the job at hand. After six weeks of maternity leave, I was still adjusting to the regimented requirements of office life. It was an ongoing struggle to redirect my thoughts from new parenting duties to the equally demanding tasks of corporate writing and editing. The ringing phone interrupted my flagging concentration.

"There's been a development," my husband Sean announced after the usual chitchat. "An overseas position has become available. It could be interesting."

His voice sounded pleased but controlled. This was typical of Sean. In contrast to my somewhat quirky personality, Sean's character was steady and reliable. Because he carefully considered the consequences of his words and actions he seldom had to dig himself out of sticky situations like I did.

"Fantastic! Where?" I asked excitedly. This news evaporated my earlier feeling of inertia.

"I'll tell you tonight," he responded vaguely.

No amount of cajoling could squeeze additional information from him. I knew from experience the more I pushed, the more he would torment me with resistance.

Throughout the afternoon my imagination bubbled with possibilities. I prayed that this time we would be on our way. We both worked at the head office of Bechtel, a large, international engineering and construction management company with projects all over the world. Bechtel had moved us from Labrador, Canada, where we had met, to San Francisco nearly two years previously. To our repeated disappointment, the company hadn't been successful in coordinating a foreign transfer for Sean, one of the company's many engineers. Several times the paperwork had been almost complete, only to have the project or Sean's position cancelled or postponed at the last minute. Now, finally, it looked as though the long wait was over.

At last, 5 p.m. came. During the 15-minute walk from the office to our apartment, Sean remained agonizingly mute on the subject of the potential posting. At home, Tara, our two-month-old daughter, and Oscar, our Labrador retriever desperate for a walk, distracted us from the hot topic. An hour later, immediate responsibilities attended to, I poured us each a glass of red wine and prepared to savour the moment.

"Talk," I said, moving closer to Sean on the couch.

"Well," he began slowly, "Bechtel has made me an offer, a good offer. One that looks pretty certain not to fall through."

"Eureka!" I shouted, throwing my arms around his neck. "When do we leave?"

"Don't you even want to know where we might be going?" Sean asked.

"My darling, I trust you completely." At least, I thought I did. Why did he have that funny look on his face?

"Calm down, Kathy. We have to discuss this."

Easygoing Sean, who usually had a twinkle in his celery green eyes, wasn't smiling. His lack of enthusiasm made my energetic display seem… inappropriate. Something was wrong. With diminishing confidence, I tried to reclaim the celebratory mood that had all but evaporated.

"We agreed that we wouldn't consider hot or cold war zones or postings above the tree line," I said. "And, despite its financial lure, Saudi Arabia is also out because it would be unfair to impose my liberated nature on such a traditional society. But that still leaves a whole lot of territory in the world. Why not just give me a few packing guidelines and let me be surprised? It'll be like a magical mystery tour."

"If we accept this assignment there will be enough surprises," Sean warned.

Suddenly I remembered Sean had said the offer didn't seem to have any likelihood of falling through.

"Why do I have this horrible feeling that I'm not going to like what I hear?" I asked apprehensively. "What trick has Bechtel pulled out of its hard hat? They don't want you to go to Siberia, do they?"

"No," Sean replied uncomfortably, "it's not Siberia."

"Oh, God, no. You can't be serious," I gasped in disbelief. "You're not considering…not…"

"I'm afraid so. It's Saudi or nothing for the foreseeable future."

Bechtel had already been awarded the design contract for Riyadh's new airport. Now they were negotiating a contract for the project management phase. In the meantime, engineers were being sent to Riyadh to liaise with various user agencies and to support the design team in San Francisco.

Although eager to live almost anywhere abroad, Sean and I had excluded Saudi Arabia from our list of preferred destinations. The little-known kingdom might have tempted a romantic or intrepid traveller but a desert outpost perhaps wasn't the ideal place to raise a young family. Besides, surely the sizeable financial incentives Bechtel offered to relocate to Saudi Arabia signalled difficult working and living conditions.

"I have a few days to think about it," Sean said calmly. "You can be the one who decides."

"That's clever," I snapped, "putting the ball in my court. The stories I've heard in the office are that there's not much to do there if you're unemployed… and most women are unemployed."

"Sweetheart, I know it's a disappointment – for both of us. We can wait for another opportunity, if that's what you'd feel more comfortable doing. I really think, though, that Riyadh might not be too bad." Sean wandered over to the large living room window and gazed at the panorama of San Francisco's famed bay and cityscape. "You have a new baby to keep you busy. You'll make new friends. I really think you'll adapt. Just think, you'll have all sorts of free time that you don't have now. Maybe you could take up…"

"Don't say it," I warned, wagging my finger at his back. "I don't want to 'take up' anything. I just want to live in an environment that has some semblance of normality, not a place with little more than sand, oil and palm trees."

Oscar lay at my feet with his head between his paws, his intelligent brown eyes gazing up at me. His tail thumped briefly, as though he supported these sentiments.

"Well, all the other women will be in the same position. It's not as though you'll be the only one."

"That's heartening." I folded my arms across my chest. "Why do I feel that Fate is shoving me down a road I don't want to travel? My instinct is rebelling." Then, in a more conciliatory tone, I added, "Let's see what we can find out about the place. Maybe I'm overreacting, but if reality is as bad as rumour, we give this assignment a wide berth. Agreed?"

Sean nodded and gave me a reassuring hug, relieved perhaps that my sometimes impulsive nature hadn't influenced me to instantly spurn the offer. While he, too, would have preferred a more appealing destination, it didn't make sense to refuse to go to Saudi Arabia without justification.

On the strength of our discussion, Sean requested full details of the conditions. The compensation package was impressive. In addition to a generous, tax-free salary, we would be given tickets home to Canada plus a paid R&R annually, free housing, a company car, free private schooling and a cash bonus upon completion of each contract year.

"My God," I breathed in astonishment. "Now I'm really suspicious about the assignment. What is so wrong with Riyadh that the company is offering so much? They don't expect you to do anything criminal, do they?"

"It's just a job, Kathy," Sean replied patiently, "but it's a demanding job in a tough environment. Obviously the client, the Saudi government, pays for all these incentives in the long run. They're in a hurry to create a modern, quality infrastructure with a minimum of delay. Their thriving economy allows them to seek top talent at any price."

Throughout our decision-making process, these benefits undeniably made us pause – no doubt as they were intended to do.

* * * *

Getting any information about Saudi Arabia, fact or fiction, proved more difficult than we anticipated. A pronounced lack of Saudi-related reading material hindered our quest. The few Bechtel families already in Riyadh had not sent any particulars on local conditions. We consulted almost everyone we came across in the hope of collecting valid data. Our generally unsuccessful efforts revealed that many people didn't know where to look for the place on a map; a few had not even heard of the country.

When I phoned my mother in Canada to tell her our news, she offered some curious clues about enigmatic Arabia.

"Well," she said, calling on her astonishing storehouse of intriguing trivia, "I've read that oil-rich shaikhs ride through the desert in flashy Cadillacs. They live lavishly and everyone else struggles to survive on a diet of dates and an occasional sheep. If that weren't bad enough, the men are allowed to have several wives – at once." She reflected for a few seconds, unable to decide on the gravity of this cultural oddity. "I guess there's no crime in that, except they keep all the females locked up in harems. It doesn't sound like your type of place, Kathleen."

"Thanks for sharing that, Mom. This sure helps to make our decision a whole lot easier," I said glumly.

My mother's bizarre observations began to look relatively tame compared to some of the details we were gathering. A recurring rumour stressed that Saudi authorities imposed infinite constraints on both nationals and foreigners. This official stance stemmed in part from the vigilance of a strong monarchy that continually guarded against intrigue in a politically unstable region. The country's strict adherence to Islam, however, was the overriding influence. Unfamiliar with Arab customs on the one hand and religious fervour on the other, we found the rationale behind some of the rulings difficult to comprehend or accept.

We kept hearing disturbing stories about women's lack of rights. It seemed absurd, for example, that women were not permitted to drive cars. The Saudi Consulate confirmed this incredible fact. They admitted that it wasn't illegal for women to drive but driving without a Saudi license was illegal, and women weren't given Saudi licenses; nor did the authorities accept international driving licenses or licenses from other countries in the names of women.

The outlook wasn't any better concerning women working. An elusive Kuwaiti businessman lived in the apartment next door to us. One morning we happened to take the elevator together. When I quizzed him, he reluctantly confirmed this inconceivable reality.

"Because the two holiest sites in Islam, Makkah and Medina, are in

Saudi Arabia, the government feels an obligation to rigorously uphold Islamic tradition. Ideally, women should stay at home to raise the children and be good wives." He pushed back a lock of his shiny black hair. "Career choices for women are pretty much restricted to teaching and medicine."

Since I had no training in either, I faced unemployment. This might not have been so bad if I'd at least been able to drive. Having to depend on men for such basic needs and pleasures as grocery shopping and visiting friends made the prospects seem particularly grim. It wasn't hard to figure out why Saudi Arabia rated high on the index of hardship postings – and places that Independent Women should energetically avoid.

The only good news was that we'd be able to bring Oscar. Saudis considered all dogs except salukis unclean – and unwelcome. However, they didn't prohibit guard or guide dogs. Oscar's muscular bulk belied his gentle nature but presumably customs would find him menacing enough not to quibble.

On Saturday afternoon we walked to Ghirardelli Square, a couple of miles from our apartment, to consider our options. We found an outdoor café and ordered cups of the famous Ghirardelli hot chocolate. Our heart-to-heart talk brought us to a mutual conclusion: Saudi Arabia was closer in attitude to the Middle Ages than the Space Age.

"It just doesn't seem to be a fun place, does it?" I said despondently. Tara gurgled contentedly in her stroller, oblivious to our dilemma.

With a half-hearted smile, Sean tried to put a more agreeable spin on some of the daunting, inescapable realities.

"Maybe the driving isn't such a big deal. After all, you don't drive a car in San Francisco."

"That's different," I replied testily. "It's my choice. Give me such a practical argument for why I won't be allowed to work. What on earth will I do? I'd have to hang around the house and be a – let me grab the table for support – *housewife*! I don't want to be forced to stay home and get fat and idle. The idea of having no stimulating goals each day terrifies me. I don't want to exist, I want to live."

By all accounts, relocation to Riyadh would mean a temporary halt to many of the liberties that the Western world in general and Western women in particular take for granted. On top of all this, we had heard that

Saudi society did not condone mixed public gatherings. I couldn't think of anything more tedious than being forced to spend all my time with women. Sean wasn't thrilled with the custom, either.

"If I have to work in a male-only environment all day, I'd like the freedom to enjoy mixed company socially." His brow furrowed at the thought of such an infringement on his private life.

"Just be glad you can get out of the house and go to work," I retorted unsympathetically.

We weren't inclined to bind ourselves to a two-year contract but neither could we dismiss the idea of a unique experience. We returned home with nothing resolved.

* * * *

We tried not to let any tension creep into our routines on this last evening before Sean had to refuse or accept the transfer. Sean played on the floor with Tara while I set the table for dinner. Abruptly, I abandoned all pretence of nonchalance.

"How often does a person get an opportunity to live in a mysterious land with a totally unfamiliar culture?" I heard myself saying. "Besides, the financial uplifts would make us seriously solvent."

Sean looked up warily, knowing better than to break my flow.

"As I see it," I continued, "we have two possibilities: we can live in our safe, comfortable but increasingly costly cocoon or we can take a risk that comes cushioned with attractive compensations. I think we have to abandon our pampered perceptions of an ideal lifestyle. Maybe it's time to resurrect our spirit of adventure." After a pregnant pause, I gave my decision. "Let's accept the offer."

"You're sure?" Sean responded hesitantly.

"Of course I'm not sure," I said, trying to relieve my turmoil by pacing. "How can anyone be sure about bounding into the unknown? Especially when the unknown appears so bleak. We're probably crazy. I'm putting my faith in the wisdom of Zen: leap and the net will appear. If the net *does* appear, this could be a fascinating interval in our lives. If the net *doesn't* appear… I guess we're screwed. Either way, we can't know until we take the leap. Go ahead; tell your boss we'll go. But only for two years. Not a minute longer."

* * * *

World oil prices were spiralling upward. Saudi Arabia, a primary producer, sat on immense proven reserves. As a result of recent political manoeuvres, the country was reaping the benefits of a vast increase in revenue.

"It makes me think of the Wild West," I sighed as we walked home from work one evening. "Instead of a gold rush, people are probably running through the streets in a frenzy of oil fever. This truly is the last frontier."

"I doubt it's as exciting as you're imagining," Sean said, "but the restrictions are real, We'll be a minority culture and we'll be expected to exercise tolerance, tact and patience." He looked at me pointedly.

"I know, I know. Don't worry. I'll be good," I said, all too aware of my shortcomings. I couldn't quell the little caution signals my brain kept flashing. Saudi Arabia's controlled society and my inclination to rebel against constraints didn't sound like a wise pairing. I feared that if my outspoken, independent nature had a run-in with the Kingdom's conservative rules, the outcome might be unpleasant. They stone women to death, for goodness sake. Could I trust myself to stay out of trouble for two whole years?

The more immediate concern focused on basic packing requirements. What on earth should we include in our limited shipment? Planning an intelligent inventory was impossible: we couldn't find anyone who had lived in Riyadh. Bechtel eventually put us in touch with a couple of employees who had just returned from the Kingdom's Eastern Province, but they had gone on single-status assignment for relatively brief periods of time. They could supply no details pertinent to women and babies or to families wishing to set up home in a desert oasis. We were on our own. Not even the Saudi Consulate gave much assistance.

"Would you believe it? The Consulate won't give a straightforward response to any of my enquiries, no matter how mundane." I had just got off the phone with them and now I was phoning Sean in frustration. "I asked about the temperature range in Riyadh and they practically refused to acknowledge that the place even *has* weather! They said it would be best if we experienced 'the situation' for ourselves! I'm beginning to feel there's a conspiracy of silence. Maybe this transfer isn't such a good idea after all."

"Don't start with the cold feet again, Kathy," Sean said firmly. "The movers come in a few days. We're committed. Keep thinking 'adventure' and look on the bright side: it can only get better."

"Don't be so sure," I replied with a sense of foreboding. "Something tells me Saudi Arabia has 'situations' we can't even begin to imagine."

Chapter Three

Sean had to report for work in Riyadh almost immediately. Tara and I took advantage of a free ticket half way around the world to visit family in Canada and Ireland.

Finally, after a month of travel, Tara and I arrived in London, the last leg of the journey. We made our way to the offices of Saudia, Saudi Arabia's national airline. With efficiency and charm, the Saudi gentleman behind the counter confirmed our reservations.

"You're absolutely certain I won't have to bring baby food or diapers on board?" I insisted. "It's not a problem for me to do so but the less I have to carry, the better."

Instinct urged me to make sure everyone understood my requirements.

"Please, Madam, don't worry," the roguishly handsome clerk said. He smoothed his sleek black hair and gave me a look that excluded everyone else. Then, in silky tones, he continued, "I recognise your voice. You're the lady who has already called twice about this matter. Believe me, you will be astonished on the flight. Saudia prides itself on looking after families. That's a special Arab trait, you know, a devotion to the family." His velvet brown eyes almost invited me to be part of *his* family.

Mr Wonderful seduced me into what proved to be a false sense of security. This was my first encounter with the sometimes frustrating Arab trait of not wanting to cause possible offense or hurt feelings by saying 'no'.

The following day, at Heathrow airport, instead of a gorgeous, I'll-do-anything-for-you agent, I encountered an officious British check-in representative.

"No, Madam," the gaunt, bespectacled man announced with obvious irritation. "We don't carry cots, baby food or diapers on board. This is an airline, not a nursery."

The very idea of such a suggestion had aggravated the nervous twitch at the corner of his mouth, making his moustache vibrate in a fascinating manner.

"But the Saudia booking office assured me – several times I might add – that this wouldn't be a problem. Why are you acting like I'm making an outrageous request? Surely you must have lots of babies that fly on your airline?"

"First of all, Madam, our booking office ignores company policy," he said. His bushy moustache now took on a life of its own. "Their exaggerated efforts to please customers frequently conflict with the reality of the situation. Secondly, Madam, very few passengers bring babies to Saudi Arabia."

Surprised and somewhat subdued, I requested a bulkhead seat. Surely this nightmare clerk wouldn't find that unreasonable!

"Saudia only has free seating. It's first-come, first-served. No one gets special treatment."

"No family pre-boarding?" I asked incredulously.

"Just be glad you have a seat, Madam."

In accepting my boarding pass, I accepted Saudia's travel conditions – whatever they might be. I prayed the seven-hour flight would be better than the reception at check-in.

We went directly to the gate. I had been forewarned of the airline's notoriety for overbooking and for bumping confirmed passengers if a VIP with his entourage came along at the last minute expecting to get on a flight. This resulted in a panic-inspired dash for seats the instant boarding was announced. I reasoned that if we got there early we could position ourselves at the front of the line.

"Grab a seat, any seat, Missus, and then strap yourself in good and tight. That's wot I do," advised a grizzled old construction worker at the boarding gate. He evidently spoke from long experience. "If any of them bastards, pardon luv, I mean bloody officials, try to get me off the plane they'll 'af to rip the fu..., sorry, they'll 'af to rip the friggin' seat out wif me. Don't let anyone push you around," he warned with gruff concern. To emphasise the point, he shook his stubby, tobacco-stained finger in my face.

Thus, when the call for Riyadh came over the public address system, I found myself rushing forward, babe in arms, ready to fight for the two seats to which we were entitled. I managed to grab an aisle and centre seat near the front of the economy section. Group frenzy invigorated even the most timid souls. Finally, with everyone seated and no one removed, the aircraft doors closed. A collective sigh of relief was breathed as the plane pulled away from its gate.

Reaching altitude signalled a transformation in the majority of passengers as they hastily produced a startling selection of duty-free alcohol. Flight bags, shopping bags and pockets yielded caches of whiskies, gins and vodkas. The excessive weight taxed the pull-down tables.

"No booze allowed in Saudi," explained my seat companion, a red-faced American with an ill-fitting toupée. "Against the religion. Or at least, it's against *their* interpretation of the religion," he added with a smirk. "Saudia doesn't serve the hard stuff but they're happy to provide ice, glasses and mixers." He opened a bottle of scotch and poured himself a lethal measure. "This is the last opportunity for a legal binge. Best to take full advantage. The homemade rotgut can make you blind and the black market booze costs a fortune. Besides, a little insobriety takes the edge off getting through Saudi immigration and customs. Care for a drink, lady?"

I declined. Few of the plane's male passengers showed such restraint. The fact that all alcohol had to be consumed before touching down in Riyadh suggested unpleasant flying conditions for those who chose to remain sober. The American quietly slipped into a drunken stupor before dinner. As the flight progressed, empty bottles and slouched bodies cluttered the aisles, making visits to the toilets hazardous.

Throughout all this, Tara remained unconcerned with her inebriated fellow travellers and enjoyed her bare-bottom freedom. Now that I knew to expect the unexpected, I wanted to save the two diapers I had brought on the flight for as long as possible. To mitigate a crisis, I piled cocktail napkins under Tara and hoped she would keep dry or at least control her aim. I was learning the invaluable skills of improvisation and adaptation.

Although the Saudi construction boom was under way, the migration of Western families was still a trickle. Only two other females travelled with me on the flight. A British lady with the I-can-cope-with-anything look of a seasoned expatriate approached and asked if this was my first trip to Riyadh.

"Yes," I answered, "does it show?"

First Tara received her searching glance, then I.

"I guess you'll survive," she replied pensively. "Some babies do quite well."

Then she abruptly returned to her seat, leaving me to my misgivings.

As we flew into Egyptian airspace, the captain made an announcement.

"Good evening, ladies and gentlemen. Due to a shortage of fuel, we will have to land in Jeddah. During this brief stop everyone must remain on board the aircraft."

How strange, then, that a small group of Saudis from the first-class section was allowed to ignore this instruction. Presumably the fuel story served as a plausible excuse to divert from the scheduled route and disembark some prominent Jeddah passengers who wished to avoid the inconvenience of having to fly all the way to Riyadh.

"So much for the check-in clerk's line about no passengers getting special treatment," I muttered to sleeping Tara.

Moments later we resumed our journey to Riyadh without further change of course.

* * * *

Riyadh introduced itself with a force. A wall of heat hit us as we disembarked from the plane and stepped into the stifling night. Each inhalation of dry air seared my nostrils and throat on its way to my lungs. While my body struggled to adjust to the sudden change in temperature, my mind absorbed a myriad of first impressions – and a growing realisation that the familiarity of the West was a world away.

Armed soldiers lolled about the tarmac, some of them resting on the upward-pointing barrels of their rifles. Casual was obviously the operative word but I nevertheless found it unnerving that passengers from a routine commercial flight should be subjected to military scrutiny – no matter how lax. Suddenly the historical instability of the Middle East jumped out of books and newspapers and into my personal life.

An invisible energy herded us into the arrivals terminal. The structure looked like a poorly constructed tin warehouse. In the large hall, the unruly mass grappled for spots at immigration desks. The notion of orderly queuing had not yet reached Riyadh.

"Go ahead, Madam. You can push forward."

I turned my head toward the source of this strange instruction. A chunky, toothy man with a swarthy Mediterranean complexion flicked the back of his hand at me, urging me to react.

"I'll follow you to make sure you get through," he offered.

Tara and I had blonde hair and blue eyes – the only individuals fitting that description in the whole airport. This irksome little man evidently thought he could make faster progress if he hooked up with us.

"I'd rather just wait my turn, thank you," I said with reserve. "We'll all get through eventually."

I used the excuse of adjusting the straps on the carry pouch that held Tara to try to avoid further contact with this unsavoury character.

"'Eventually' is relative, Madam," he persisted. "Chances are, when it's finally your turn, the immigration officer will decide to go for tea – and there won't be anyone to replace him. When they grow tired of stamping passports they simply walk away. That baby of yours might be fine now but all this pushing and shoving will 'eventually' distress her."

He had a good point. This theoretically straightforward procedure had already disintegrated into a prolonged ordeal for all concerned. Of the few officials on duty, only some bothered to work. The rest preferred to enjoy a relaxed smoke and a chat with colleagues. The unruly passengers recognised a desperate situation when they saw it. Casting aside polite patience, I elbowed my way through the crowd, meeting no resistance. Evidently everyone expected this behaviour. They probably wondered what had taken me so long.

Although not a pessimist by nature, I fully expected that my efforts would be rewarded with the official going off duty. Sure enough, the pencil-thin youth looked me up and down and decided that the lure of a prolonged break held more appeal than a brief encounter with a weary woman and child. Fortunately, the more mature man at the next kiosk took pity on me. He ignored the passenger already at his desk and signalled for me to step forward. He spent more time examining me than my passport but at least he didn't reject me. After I had answered a number of questions seemingly unrelated to the immigration procedure ("Are you happily married?"), he gave me a parting wink and then waved us through.

My relief at getting past immigration was short-lived. Baggage collection, I observed in a stunned stupor, was an almost comic free-for-all. As each piece of luggage furtively appeared on a rickety conveyor belt, an overworked baggage handler unceremoniously hurled the case towards any bit of floor space that could possibly accommodate it. Passengers clambered over the strewn suitcases and each other in an effort to retrieve their belongings.

Adding to the noise and confusion, an onslaught of baggage boys fought for the chance to earn a few riyals. Wiry but strong Yemenis monopolised this position. Their national costume, a long, straight, plaid cotton skirt, a clashing plaid shirt and a colourful head covering tied casually in turban style, markedly distinguished them from other Arabs.

Competition was stiff as they shouted at the passengers in an effort to attract attention. Exhausted and grateful for an extra pair of hands, I gave in to the overtures of a particularly eager and persistent young man.

"How much do you charge?" I asked.

"Fifteen riyals, Sir."

I searched his face to see if he was mocking me. Couldn't he see I was a woman? Why did he call me 'Sir'? Maybe, because there are so few foreign women here, he doesn't know the correct term in English? The question intrigued me; he began to get impatient.

"OK, Sir, ten riyals since you have baby. Where bag?"

I no longer had the mental agility to calculate how much 10 riyals was worth in dollars but the price had just dropped by a third without any effort on my part.

"All right," I agreed. "Let's just hope we can find the bags in this mess," I added… to no one. Like a trained retriever, the man had already shot through the crowd and waited for hand signals from me to indicate which bags were mine. After more pushing and narrowly escaping being clipped on the ear by a projectile backpack, he eventually got all my bags in one spot. A surge of luggage-laden bodies pushed us towards yet another endurance test: customs.

Saudi Arabia imposed no restrictions on quantity or value of incoming items. Because of a chronic shortage of consumer goods in the Kingdom, the government had only five categories of contraband: alcohol, pornography (a category that often encompassed fashion magazines), pork products, drugs and non-Islamic religious objects, especially Bibles and Christmas-related items. Customs officers' individual interpretations of what to include within these classifications sometimes resulted in questionable seizures.

So far, no one had mentioned procedures for making a customs declaration. This small pleasure at the thought of having circumvented bureaucracy proved premature. Although no forms had to be filled out, every piece of baggage, including handbags and briefcases, underwent a thorough search for forbidden items.

The trusty baggage boy swung my suitcases onto the long, metallic customs table. The officer focused his attention on Tara and me, his next victims.

"Show passport, unlock," he ordered, pointing to the bags.

"I've already been through immigration," I said.

My barely concealed impatience cooled when his piercing stare made me understand the irrelevance of any previous checks. This was the Man of the Moment and I had better respond in the proper way. I obeyed his instruction.

"First time Riyadh?" he asked, lazily checking the passport.

"Yes."

The inspector ignored my simmering agitation as he flipped through the pages of my books, sniffed the shampoo which, I realised, was the same colour as whiskey, and delicately avoided touching my underwear. His careless probing had made an unholy mess of a once neat packing job. The thoroughness of the search unnerved me. My concentration on trying to close the crammed cases just one more time distracted me enough that I didn't dwell on what I believed was an unnecessary invasion of privacy.

Then the official languidly chalked an indecipherable mark on the outside of the luggage and hand-carry items, including my expensive leather handbag. His I-dare-you look instantly dispelled my inclination to reprimand him. The marks indicated to the staff at the hall exit that we had passed scrutiny. At last we could move beyond the prying clutches of officialdom.

Outside the restricted area, in the main hall of the terminal, the pandemonium was even greater. Tara and I were adrift in a sea of bearded humanity, all in various states of unwash. The baggage boy expertly manoeuvred the trolley past shoving bodies. He waited for me to indicate which man would lay claim to us – and pay him.

Most of the men wore some sort of head covering: either the white *ghutra* or the red-and-white check *sham'agh* of Saudi Arabia or the turbans or scarf-type coverings of other countries in the region. Sean, with the only tall, balding pate in the unrelenting crowd, stood out like a welcoming beacon.

"Sweetheart, you made it," he said with relief as we finally reached each other. He gave me a warm hug and then eagerly removed Tara from her pouch. She rewarded him with one of her beautiful smiles.

"I'm so relieved that we're finally together," I said, holding Sean's hand possessively. "Let's get out of this bedlam."

The baggage boy cleared his throat politely, interrupting our reunion. The Yemeni's happy salute a moment later indicated that Sean had given him a generous tip.

Then I noticed a towering, solidly built Saudi gentleman standing beside us. Sean introduced his companion.

"Kathy, I'd like you to meet Sami Arab. He works in our office."

Did Saudis really have names like 'Sami Arab'? This sounded like the Saudi equivalent of the American slang 'Joe Cool'. I had to bite my tongue not to blurt out, "Come on, what's his real name?" Tact prevailed.

Sean explained that Sami (this really was his name) was Bechtel's government relations man, or Mr. Fix-It as the position was popularly referred to. Like his counterparts in every foreign company in Saudi Arabia, Sami smoothed the way between Arabs and expatriates, and between the company and government bodies.

"Sami's worth his weight in gold," Sean said. Sami seemed to appreciate the compliment but reacted by modestly lowering his eyes. "Among other things, he makes sure the right visas get into the right passports – on time. Believe me, this is a good man to know."

Sami had accompanied Sean to ensure I had no difficulties with immigration or customs. As it turned out, he had not been required to do anything more than to get us safely through the pressing mob.

Sean guided us towards the relative calm of the airport parking lot and to his new Bechtel-supplied vehicle: a red and white, 4-wheel drive Suburban, a bulky forerunner of the SUV.

"The advantages of height and brawn often prove invaluable in Riyadh's erratic traffic," Sean explained when he saw the unimpressed look on my face. "And, of course, the 4-wheel drive is vital for desert trips."

"Well, I guess this will be my first living-in-Riyadh challenge," I responded, measuring my five-foot two-inch frame against the high step to get into the vehicle.

Looking up at a sky brightly illuminated with millions of stars, I deeply inhaled the unpolluted desert air. The place felt more foreign than any I had been to; instead of apprehension I felt a pleasant tingle of anticipation. I decided then and there I was going to love Saudi Arabia and would allow nothing to change my mind.

And then we went home....

Chapter Four

"Well, this is it," Sean announced after a ten-minute drive from the airport. He parked in front of an eight-foot-high wall the length of half a city block on one side and a full block on the other. "Bechtel has several compounds around town. This one's called 'the fourteen-villa'... for obvious reasons."

I pushed open the creaky sheet-metal gate with a spirit of cautious optimism. After all, this mini-neighbourhood was going to be our home for the next two years. We walked across dusty ground and passed two darkened houses. Ours was the third in a quartet of structurally bland, semi-detached villas.

"No one locks doors here," Sean said, turning the handle of a cheap aluminium and frosted glass front door.

We stepped into a small, rectangular living room that unfolded onto a mirror-image dining room.

"Well," I said with a sinking feeling, "the archway between the rooms might be considered a concession to architectural imagination, and the Danish teak dining room suite is OK."

I searched for something agreeable to say about the rest of the absolutely repulsive furniture. No preconceived notions or expectations about local conditions had prepared me for this dismal set-up.

"Just give me some time." My voice faltered. "I'm trying hard to find redeeming qualities."

Impractical glass-topped tables that showed every mote of dust flanked a sofa and chairs that looked like selections from a 1950s catalogue. Bleak, speckled brown upholstery hid the dirt but crushed the spirit. Indescribably ugly, fuzzy, orange curtains hung over wall-size windows. The dreadful combination made me long for the tasteful furnishings we had consigned to storage in San Francisco.

Sean briefed me on a few facts of Riyadh life.

"In most other societies, a person's choice of housing reflects his social position. Here, the employer provides the accommodation. Nearly everyone lives in less-than-ideal, poorly constructed villas or apartments. We're lucky to have a house that is influenced by American design." He smiled and shrugged at my look of astonishment. "Seriously, this place is great compared to some. The European-style houses have small rooms and no storage space and the Saudi-style houses have hole-in-the-floor toilets with a wall hose instead of toilet paper. I was in a Saudi house that had padded velveteen walls and a TV aerial in the shape of the Eiffel Tower! Trust me, we're not doing too badly. All the Bechtel families have the same vintage furniture. I know it's not much consolation but at least you know that no one will think you're a bad decorator."

"Well that's a relief," I said with a pinch of sarcasm. "Of course, since I can't work, introducing comfort and style will provide a creative challenge to what otherwise might be an empty day."

"Please don't start complaining about not working. You knew the terms before you came and you agreed to 'retire' for the two years we're here."

"You're right. I'm sorry. I just find this space so... so depressing. It's an affront to every artistic bone in my body." I didn't know whether to laugh or cry.

"We'll make it a home, sweetheart. A happy home." Sean, bless him, could find something positive in even the most hopeless of situations.

Tara, whose big blue eyes had been devouring her new surroundings, suddenly announced with a whimper that the excitement of all the unusual activity had caught up with her.

"I'll take her upstairs," Sean volunteered. "You just relax here. It'll only take me a few minutes to put her to bed."

With a tired smile, I gratefully handed Tara to him and then collapsed onto the nasty, soft-cushioned couch. Taking advantage of this momentary solitude, I closed my eyes, willing the nightmare décor to vanish. Instead, more revelations awaited my discovery.

"What on earth is that sticking out of the wall?" I asked when Sean returned. He looked in the direction of my pointing finger. A noisy machine protruded just below ceiling level.

"That's a desert cooler. It circulates water and blows a gentle mist into the room." Seeing my involuntary shudder at yet another unattractive aspect of the house, Sean quickly added, "They're quite good, really, because they add humidity to the dry air."

We walked through the dining room, past a compact guest bathroom with an disproportionately high ceiling, and into the kitchen.

"My God, I thought kitchens like this had died at the turn of the century. No dishwasher?" I remarked, adding this shortfall to the quickly growing list.

"Dishwashers are manual," Sean explained. "Most people have household help."

"Well, the help must be midgets, judging by the height of the sink! And apparently they don't feel the heat, because there's no cooling unit in here. It's uncomfortably hot even now at 2 a.m. Can you imagine what it's like with an oven on during the day?"

My eyes scanned the poorly ventilated room and then focused on metal cupboards and counters with dangerously sharp edges.

"Don't worry, we'll get someone to round off the corners," Sean quickly assured me.

"They're deadly. How on earth can anyone install units like this? We're living in a design disaster."

The tiny laundry room beyond the kitchen displayed a vital concession to modern convenience: a small, front-loading washing machine. I wondered how I could possibly fit a full load of laundry into this junior version of the American models I was used to.

"Where have they hidden the clothes dryer?" I asked.

"With temperatures around 125ºF, you don't need an electric dryer. Nature does the work for you!" Sean smiled. He opened the back door to show me the clothesline.

As it turned out, my clothes hanging days were limited. The city's massive fly population took uninhibited delight in any moisture opportunity. The frenzied creatures fought furiously for a space on the clothesline the instant a piece of laundry appeared. They left behind enough flyspecks to warrant a rewash – and ongoing repeats of the situation. Faced with a barrage of complaints from wives, Bechtel provided all the villas with dryers.

We continued our tour and explored upstairs. In stark contrast to the ground floor, this was a spacious three-bedroom, two-bathroom retreat. We peeked in on Tara sleeping peacefully in her cot. Sean prevented me from opening the door to the second bedroom.

"This is a double of Tara's room. I've been using it for storage," he explained vaguely. "You can check it out when you feel more settled."

I followed Sean into the master bedroom.

"I like the large windows. This must give the room plenty of natural light during the day."

"Yes," Sean agreed. "But because they don't fit properly, it also means an unending battle with sand and dust."

The sub-standard finishes extended to the walls and floors.

"Is it part of a plasterer's job qualification that he has to be able to splatter his work in a broad radius?" I asked sarcastically. The tiles and drains were marred with blobs that had fallen within the wet plaster's flight path.

Although the house left much to be desired, it was rent free. The financial benefit helped negate many of the physical imperfections. More importantly, Sean, Tara and I were together again. This outweighed any disadvantages. How could I possibly complain?

* * * *

As I unpacked, it became horribly apparent that there was more to the house than initially met the eye. Throwing some clothes into the laundry basket, I thought I detected movement. Yes, that shirt definitely redistributed itself. Doubting my notoriously faulty vision, I waited, unblinkingly keeping my eyes on the dirty clothes. Sean began to show mild concern. Then I let out an unholy scream while simultaneously propelling my petite body through the air to the safety of the bed.

"There's a thing in the laundry basket," I announced in a shaky falsetto voice.

Sean cautiously prodded and poked, not knowing what to expect. It didn't take him long to find the cause of the disturbance.

"Relax, Kathy, it's just a cockroach."

"*Just a cockroach*? You're telling me that an insect with the power to vibrate a three-foot basket full of clothes is *just a cockroach*?"

"You'll have to get used to them," Sean announced, ignoring my exaggeration and showing no hint of concern. "The city's crawling with them because there's no garbage collection."

"You've brought our baby and me to a cockroach-infested home? Why didn't you warn me?"

"I never even thought about it," he replied, mystified by my reaction. "Besides, what good would it have done?"

Before the night was over, I encountered other life forms that shared our happy home: there was the lizard whose tail looked deadly enough to crush bones. He was minding his own business on the ceiling at the top of the stairs until I scared him into the next kingdom with another one of my operatic screeches. Then there was the rather personable mouse I discovered snoozing on a box of plastic wrap under the kitchen sink. He disappeared just as I broke the sound barrier. Despite our introductory clash, he braved several return visits during the succeeding months and came to be known as 'the occasional mouse'. The geckos, camel spiders and scorpions that later crossed my path seemed tame in comparison to my baptism of fire. I'd heard about culture shock but no one told me the shock would have such a physical impact.

This wasn't just a holiday-gone-wrong from which we could escape after a couple of weeks. This was going to be our reality for the next two years. Rapidly accumulating evidence indicated that living in Saudi Arabia would require more than a sentimental approach.

Sean watched with amusement as I gingerly opened a dresser drawer, afraid of what surprise might be lurking in the dark corners.

"You must be exhausted," he said after a scream-free moment. "It's been quite a trip for you."

"I am. But if you're not too tired, I'd love to have a coffee and talk for a while. We have so much to catch up on. I can do the rest of the unpacking tomorrow."

As we sat in the harsh light of the dining room's bare-bulbed ceiling fixtures, Sean brought me up to date on his recent experiences and impressions. The most welcome news was that our shipment had arrived. We had squandered some of our precious weight allowance on family silver, Waterford crystal, and artwork in the hope that these few elegant accoutrements would help us forget that we were far from the sophistication of the life we had known.

"I've unpacked all of the boxes and put a lot of the stuff away but I thought you'd like to have a say about where to hang the paintings."

"Great!" I enthused with a new surge of energy. "We can get started tomorrow. Everything got through customs safe and sound?" I carried our cups into the kitchen for refills.

"Well, everything is safe but not exactly sound." Sean's voice wafted from the dining room. For some reason, he hadn't adjusted his volume to account for the distance. I returned to the table in time to hear him say, "All the dishes except a plate, two bowls, four cups, and eight saucers got broken. And you won't believe it but the movers put some of our storage items into the Saudi shipment and a lot of our Saudi shipment into storage." Sean spilled these facts out quickly, hoping perhaps that speed would reduce the negative impact.

"No dishes? How will we manage?" I asked anxiously. "You said there were hardly any Western-style household items here. And how on earth could the movers manage such a feat of packing stupidity? Everything was clearly marked and stored in different rooms!"

"Calm down, Kathy. Look at this as one of those challenges you love so much. We're resourceful; we'll survive with what we have and get what we need as we go along. Bechtel has given us a comprehensive starter kit until we can replace what's missing. A colleague has offered to use his US commissary connection to get whatever we need for Tara."

"Well," I said, allowing Sean's confidence to calm me, "this is definitely going to be one of those assignments that makes us or breaks us, isn't it."

"I know everything's unfamiliar at the moment, sweetheart. Try to think 'exotic' rather than 'strange'. It'll get better. You'll see."

Naively, I believed him. But my initiation was not yet over.

Chapter Five

Too soon after going to sleep, my eyes flew open in shock. My heart pounded, alerted to the possibility of danger. Still drugged with fatigue, I felt disoriented.

"Sean, Sean, wake up. I think I hear lions roaring."

"You do," he mumbled before dozing off again.

"What the hell are lions doing in the middle of the bloody desert," I cried, shaking him and remembering all too clearly my experiences only a few hours previously. Giant cockroaches were one thing; how could I also be expected to cope with the threat of wild beasts?

"The zoo's down the road. It's feeding time. You'll soon learn to sleep through the racket." He rolled over and nodded off.

Then another unfamiliar sound broke the temporary silence. Good grief, could it really be a nasally man singing badly through a megaphone?

"Sean, what's that? Where's it coming from?"

"That's a *muezzin* making the day's first prayer call. We're lucky there's no mosque near the compound or you would have got a real scare."

A *real* scare? *And precisely how,* I wondered, *did that differ from the scare I was presently suffering?*

By now we were more awake than asleep so we got up to witness our first Riyadh sunrise together and to view the neighbourhood from the tiny bedroom balcony.

Our new home was in Malaaz, one of two residential areas preferred by expatriates in those days. The desert, only four blocks away, reminded us that our adopted suburb bore no resemblance to those in which we had grown up. The strange, box houses accentuated the foreignness of the place.

"Water tanks are stored on the flat roofs," Sean explained. "The space is also handy for sleeping under the stars on warm evenings. People who don't have separate servants' quarters will often build a room on the roof for their staff."

After treating ourselves to a quiet cup of coffee, we got Tara up, had an early breakfast and then explored the compound. High concrete walls isolated 14 identical, two-storey villas, a swimming pool and a play area from the rest of the city.

"Behind these walls we can live more or less as we please," Sean said as we stood beside the large, inviting pool. "As soon as we abandon this seclusion, however, we're subject to the mores of the surrounding Arab community. That translates as discretion in both behaviour and attire." He gave me a look that I interpreted as a reminder to curb my spirited personality.

"Speaking of circumspection," he added, "there was an article in the paper the other day quoting King Khaled as saying that "… bare arms and ankles are an abomination to God." I think you'd better get yourself something that does a good cover-up job."

To me, this translated as a sanctioned shopping trip. Every female gene in my body twittered merrily as I anticipated a stylish new wardrobe. Sean's genes must have twittered, too, because he quickly dispelled my fanciful notions.

"Most women wear caftans or have copies of *thobes* made in colourful printed fabrics."

"What exactly are *thobes*?" I asked, unsure whether or not to be pleased. Hopefully they wouldn't be the fashion equivalent of our home décor.

"They're the white, long-sleeved, ankle-length shifts that Saudi men wear. Women like them because they allow air to circulate and they meet the criteria of loose-fitting clothes that cover arms and legs."

"I won't have to wear a veil, will I? My distance vision is bad enough without adding a layer of cloth over my eyes."

"No. Western women aren't expected to veil. There are sporadic suggestions from Saudi officials that they should refrain from wearing *abayas*, the full-length black cloaks. Some Saudis find the way foreigners wear the *abayas* disrespectful of tradition. They'd prefer non-Saudis simply to be conservative in their public dress. This means necklines up to the collarbone, sleeves at least to the elbows and at least calf-length hems. "

It wouldn't be the shopping expedition I'd anticipated but I welcomed the excuse to see what the local market had to offer. I got ready for my first foray into the heart of Riyadh.

* * * *

Moonlight had added mystique to the surroundings. The harsh light of day offered no such mask. In the mid 1970s, Riyadh was an architectural nonentity. Only a few of the picturesque mud houses and palaces still existed in the old part of the city. Their wooden doors, shutters and ceilings painted in vibrant colours and geometric patterns brought the monotone mud to life. In those years of rapid transition, Saudis wanted to distance themselves from anything that emphasised a past they considered obsolete. Bulldozers destroyed premises that had stood for generations to make way for modern structures. By the time nostalgia entered Saudi vocabulary the damage had been done.

We drove past numerous tower cranes and other heavy equipment. They dispelled any romantic notions of Riyadh being the capital of a storybook kingdom. With a speed that only enormous wealth could support, this sleepy oasis had transformed into a giant construction site that would one day be the fastest growing metropolis in the world. In the meantime, few structures over two or three storeys broke the skyline.

Even relatively new construction had a dilapidated appearance as a result of shoddy workmanship, cheap materials and harsh climate. Almost everything was a repetition of dull, square shapes with dirty beige, rough concrete finishes. Every building had the ubiquitous flat roof. Intriguingly, some of the street-side walls had taps.

"Many Saudis grew up with an ongoing threat of thirst," Sean explained. "Providing the luxury of water on demand for workers and passers-by is an act of charity."

There were no landmarks to point out as we drove along but that didn't inhibit Sean's inclination to pass on information he'd acquired.

"This road is called Sitteen."

"What does that mean?" I asked.

"Sixty."

"Sixty what?"

"It refers to the width of the street: sixty metres," Sean elaborated. "There's also Arbaeen, which is forty metres wide and Thalateen, which is thirty metres wide."

"They're not terribly original when it comes to names, are they?" I mused.

"It's not a big deal here." Sean said. "Only the few main streets have official names. A European company has been hired to do a master plan but it will be years before that's complete. In the meantime, the expats just give the most popular streets names that best describe what goes on. Watch Street downtown has lots of watch stores. Chop Square is where the beheadings take place on Fridays. Chicken Street, famous for all its roasted and live chicken shops, is just a few blocks from the compound."

I shook my head, not sure whether or not to believe him but guessing, correctly I later found out, that it was ludicrous enough to be true.

* * * *

As we approached Batha, one of the city's oldest areas, I detected a rank odour.

"Oh, great, I think Tara has a dirty diaper," I said, wrinkling my nose.

"I don't think so," Sean replied with a grin. "You're about to experience, both visually and aromatically, the infamous Batha canal. The art of sewage treatment is still in its infancy here. Hold your breath if you want to avoid the stink... and pray someone doesn't knock us over the edge."

The deep, wide, open channel ran along the centre of Batha Street, one of Riyadh's principal thoroughfares.

"Periodically someone has the misfortune to end up in the canal due to a combination of bad drivers and a lack of protective barriers," Sean said. He was particularly alert on this stretch of road.

Thankfully, we made it to our destination without incident.

"Today's port of call is the Dirah *suq*," Sean announced after he parked the car near the old Masmak Fort. This impressive mud-brick structure had been the centre of the famous battle that won Riyadh for the Al-Sauds from the rival Al-Rashid clan in 1902. "Prepare to step back in time."

We entered an archaic, covered market place. Dirah's dirt floors, with their rises and depressions and ruts and bumps, imitated many of the country's roads in those early days. Rusted tin roofs freckled with holes and gaps offered shelter from the glaring sun but became irrelevant when the weather brought rain or sandstorms. The sloping pathway took us deep into a fascinating warren cluttered with merchandise. Unfamiliar sights, sounds and smells bombarded our senses. Countless little shops, selling everything from enormous cooking pots to incense to curved daggers, nested like cavities in dimly lit jaws. Most of the cupboard-like spaces were of similar size and shared a penchant for disarray. Vendors didn't care about presentation; they piled stock higgly-piggly, knowing that sooner or later buyers would come along, delighted to have found either exactly what they needed or an acceptable alternative.

"I haven't seen kitchen equipment like this since the days of my grandmother," I said, marvelling at the assortment of gadgets that long ago had become defunct in my world. "Maybe I'll do my shopping here instead of in regular stores. This is so much more fun."

"Kathy, there are *no* regular stores like you're imagining. No wholesale outlets, no department stores. People shop in the *suqs* or the supermarkets. Period."

"Oh. That puts a whole new spin on the *suq* if it's going to be my main supply source."

How on earth would we get by? As we continued our journey through the alleyways, I paid greater attention to the items on display. The extensive stock appeared to offer little that could be useful to our daily lives.

"In San Francisco when I fancifully enthused about us being pioneers, I didn't think Fate would take me quite so literally," I said reflectively. "I guess it's time to put on my inventive hat. Maybe this is just the challenge I need to keep my days interesting."

Sean looked relieved at my positive reaction.

Finally we came to the section of the *suq* that specialised in fabrics. The city's limited selection of ready-to-wear clothes made tailoring big business in Riyadh. The spectacular range of textiles included everything from rolls of the latest designer cloths from Paris and Italy to outrageously gaudy or unbelievably tasteless materials from less hallowed sources. I chose three different lengths of cotton fabric. Knowing Sean's aversion to shopping, I assumed that we would now head back to the compound.

"The best is yet to come," Sean said cryptically, leading me deeper into the *suq*.

We turned a few more corners and came upon an almost blinding sight: the flashy gleam of gold. Dozens of hole-in-the-wall shops displayed millions of bangles, ankle bracelets, heavy necklaces, large earrings, pendants and chains. They were casually hung from, draped over or laid across every surface. The riotous profusion looked like garments drying on a clothesline.

"Oh My God," I gasped. "I've never seen so much gold. I need sun glasses to protect my eyes from the glare!"

We wandered up and down the narrow lanes in a state of continual wonder. Everything was at least 18 carat and, more often than not, 21 or 22 carat.

"Look at the size of those necklaces," I observed in awe. 'Saudi women must have pretty impressive chests to support that mass."

"Those ornate necklace-earring-bracelet sets are usually bought as wedding gifts from the groom," Sean said. " Gold jewellery is less fashion accessory and more wearable savings against future financial needs. The women buy bangles or other items whenever they have extra cash. When times get tough, they sell the jewellery back to the *suq* by weight according to the international price of gold. The current rate is 15 riyals, or about $4 a gram."

I was already anticipating starting a little savings plan of my own but, on closer examination, most of the items lacked the fine craftsmanship I was used to. Except for the simpler chains and bangles, I couldn't immediately see anything that I would want to wear. With time – and little effort – I overcame this bias.

A row of elaborate solid gold belts hanging at ceiling height caught my eye.

"Look." I tugged at Sean's arm. He was busy studying a profusion of bangle bracelets in a vast mélange of widths and diameters, from infant size to ones that would fit a XXXL forearm. "Who on earth would wear such a thing?" I asked, pointing to a particularly bulky belt.

At the time, I was more into Gucci than gold but we couldn't resist asking the price. The merchant's long, gnarled fingers tipped with nicotine-stained nails deftly lifted the belt of linked gold squares off its high hook and balanced it on the electronic scale. He stroked his meringue beard as he read the display of numbers that revealed the considerable weight. Then he picked up a calculator and rapidly did a series of multiplications.

"Seven hundred riyals," he pronounced, squinting at us through his one good eye. He probably made more astute judgements with one eye than most of us do with our full sight. His mild disinterest told us he already knew we weren't going to buy the belt. We thanked him for his help and walked on.

"Two hundred dollars for a belt," I gasped when we were out of hearing of the old man. "Can you imagine? It's interesting in an artsy-fartsy way but you can get the finest Italian leather for less than forty dollars. It doesn't make sense to pay five times that amount for something that looks gaudy and is probably uncomfortable to wear!"

Sometimes practicality is such a stupid thing. I always regretted that I hadn't been smart enough to snap up one or two of those rare pieces that are now worth a small fortune. A few years later, Sean bought me a beautiful Bedouin silver belt.

"I don't want to listen to you complaining that you missed yet another belt opportunity!" he explained with a smile as he handed me the treasure.

* * * *

The following afternoon we took my fabrics to a tailor in Malaaz, not far from the compound.

"I'd like to have three *thobes* made, please," I said to the hefty Pakistani behind the counter. He looked like he should have been lifting weights instead of sitting behind a sewing machine.

"Two days come back," he announced as he took the bag of material from my hands and dismissed me by returning to a sewing machine that Singer had probably discontinued long ago.

"Excuse me," I said to his bulky back, "don't you want to take measurements?"

"No need. I see you."

"Please," I insisted, "I'd feel more comfortable knowing that you know exactly what size I am."

Grudgingly, he got up from his machine, unwrapped a frayed tape measure from around his thick, short neck, looked around to make sure no one was watching him, and asked me to put the soiled tape around my chest. He then took the two ends, stood a respectful distance from me and made a note on a dirty scrap of paper: 54 inches.

"Fifty-four inches!" I sputtered. "Not in your wildest dreams am I that size. Here, let me take the measurements and write them down just to make sure there's no mistake."

I hadn't understood the man's concern about being observed by a particularly difficult *mutawwa*, aka religious police. According to strict interpretations of the *Qur'an*, the Muslim holy book, the tailor could have been jailed or at least severely harassed for having such close contact with a woman who didn't belong to his family.

Despite my efforts, the tailor made the *thobes* to his own dimensions, a compromise between my 36 inches and his claim of 54 inches. I was now the owner of three colourful sacks. Because he had correctly eyeballed the neck size and arm length, however, these cool and comfortable garments fit better than I would have imagined possible.

* * * *

Prayer call forced us to cut short our excursion.

"Muslims pray five times a day: at dawn, midday, mid afternoon, sunset and nightfall," Sean explained. "They call the ritual *salah*. The dawn prayer is the only one that doesn't bring commerce to a grinding halt for half an hour."

The *maghrib* prayer at sunset inspired an intriguing form of camaraderie along Sitteen Street. In the relative coolness of the evening, cars would pull over to the sides of the road. The faithful would get out, unfurl their prayer rugs, bow towards Makkah and say the fourth of the day's five prayers. Then they would squat on their haunches or sit cross-legged on the wide sidewalk and enjoy a relaxing cup of cardamom coffee or mint tea.

"It looks so incongruous to see people sitting in the middle of a city sidewalk and socialising. Somehow, though, it's restful. Or perhaps it's the unconventional aspect that appeals to me." Seeing a fleeting look of concern in Sean's eyes, I reassured him. "Don't worry, I'm not suggesting that we adopt this custom. But I won't say 'no' if one of these families invites us to join them," I teased.

* * * *

As Sean parked the Suburban in front of the compound, I thought I saw a large bag flying over the compound wall. Sean noticed it, too.

"That's the local version of waste disposal," Sean commented. "Mohammed, our compound guard, collects all the garbage we so conscientiously put into bins at the back of the house and then he heaves it into the empty lot. It's eaten by the herds of goats and sheep that belong to passing Bedouin tribes. They must think Riyadh is gourmet heaven."

The lack of sanitation measures and lax discipline concerning litter explained why most streets and sidewalks were cluttered with everything from building rubble to orange peels. A Saudi neighbour must have had some influence with local authorities because one evening we went out the compound gate to find neatly swept sidewalks. Then we saw that the pedestrian peril had become a traffic hazard: the work crew had placed the mess in a tidy row along the middle of the road.

* * * *

The plan for Tara and me to arrive after the summer and ease into Riyadh's desert climate had been wise. Even so, temperatures at the end of September hovered in the 115ºF/46ºC range.

No one except new arrivals commented on the weather. Why bother when it remained virtually unchanged? Only the sudden sand storms, which turned the clear sky dusty orange or brown in a matter of minutes, digressed from the endless days of bright sunshine on a rich, blue canvas. The dry heat was entirely bearable from the comfort of a cooled indoor environment or when doing nothing more strenuous outdoors than swimming, enjoying a cold drink and socialising with friends.

"This reminds me of a harem in the Topkapi Palace in Istanbul that I visited years ago," I remarked to Sean as we enjoyed a Friday afternoon by the pool. "Looking at the pleasant living quarters and the beautiful pool,

I thought that it might not be such a bad life. The women weren't exactly prisoners: they could go into town if they had a eunuch with them. Little did I realise I would one day be living a similar kind of life. The only thing missing," I sighed, "is a good-looking eunuch."

I dived into the refreshing water to avoid Sean's playful attack.

"It's amazing, isn't it," I mumbled to Sean. I had resettled on my towel and was baking contentedly in the oven atmosphere. "Some people pay a great deal of money each year for a holiday of sun, sand and pool. Here we are in a situation where someone's actually giving us a great deal of money to endure exactly the same thing!"

"Take off your rose-tinted glasses," Sean replied as he slathered more sun protection onto his fair Irish skin and relocated to some nearby shade. "We're being paid generously because this is a hardship posting. If you don't notice the constraints now, you'll feel them soon enough."

"Ssh. Don't spoil the moment. We'll cross those bridges when we come to them."

Chapter Six

One afternoon, less than a week after arriving in Riyadh, Jackie, the wife of Sean's boss Mike O'Dwyer, sent her young son to invite me to her house. I had a baby to feed and get ready for bed and dinner to prepare but I thought it politic to accept.

Jackie poured two mugs of steaming coffee. She chatted amiably as she took a jug of milk from the refrigerator and gave each coffee a white splash. We brought the mugs into the living room. Abruptly, her demeanour changed.

"There's no need for concern," she said matter-of-factly. "A search party has been out for a couple of hours and the Governor has offered to send a helicopter. The only problem is that it will be dark soon."

"What's everyone searching for?" I asked.

"Why, Sean and Ollie, of course. They drove to the airport site to gather soil samples and didn't return when they should have. Don't worry," Jackie said hastily. "They have emergency supplies and plenty of water. They know they have to stay with the vehicle and the search party knows their general location. They'll probably be home in time for dinner."

Dinner came and went – without Sean's company. Then, at 9:30 p.m., he appeared at the door with a sheepish grin. I was weak with relief.

"We went over a dune and got stuck in the sand," he explained, with growing enthusiasm for the story. "We could see the headlights of the rescue vehicles but they didn't see our signals. We'd just settled down for the night when someone found us."

"Well, Dorothy," I remarked, "I guess we're not in Kansas anymore. Adjusting to life here certainly has some novel twists, doesn't it?"

Although our adaptation process was never again so dramatic, the exercise was constant and involved the most basic aspects of daily existence, not least of which was the supply of water.

'Riyadh' derives from *rowdah*, the Arabic word for 'gardens'. Located in the middle of a vast desert, Riyadh's precious water wells gave it the status of oasis. The growing city supplemented its finite reserves with desalinated water piped in from the Arabian Gulf. The water was supposed to trickle into each villa's tank twice a week. When this didn't happen, everyone had to further budget the already tight ration.

One evening I heard a discreet tap at the back door. The short, wiry shape fidgeting on the other side of the frosted glass could only belong to Mohammed. The compound's wizened gate guard was of seemingly antique age and Yemeni nationality. I opened the door. Mohammed waved a hose toward our large water storage tank. The ugly necessity took up nearly a quarter of the space in the cemented area that passed for our back yard.

"Who's away this time, Mohammed?"

"O'Neill go now," Mohammed replied in his raspy voice.

"OK, fill 'er up."

Mohammed and I had formed a bond that I regularly reinforced with donations of food and clothing. In gratitude, as soon as anyone in the compound went on holiday, Mohammed would siphon water from their tank into ours. This kept water shortages in the Cuddihy household to a minimum. When we did run out, the timing was never convenient.

"Help," I shouted to Sean from the shower. "I've got a head full of lather and there's suddenly no bloody water. Can you pour me a jug of cooking water, please?"

"Sorry, no can do," Sean responded from the bedroom. "You left the jerry can sitting outside in the heat all day. There's a thick layer of green slime on the top. It'll take me a while to siphon it off."

"Well bring me bottled water," I yelled. My voice clearly conveyed impatience.

Meanwhile, I kept massaging my hair so the shampoo wouldn't crust in the furnace-like air. Stubbornly I maintained my position under the showerhead, praying for a miraculous surge of water.

"We used the last bottle at lunch and I forgot to get more. The only thing we have is Perrier. That should give you a bit of a buzz," Sean said playfully.

His amused face appeared around the edge of the shower curtain but disappeared just in time to avoid a large dollop of suds aimed at it.

"OK, OK, just hurry or I'll never get this stuff off," I called after him.

Cleopatra bathed in milk, I recalled. Maybe it wasn't a beauty regimen but a necessity!

* * * *

I had never fully appreciated the blessing of unlimited, potable supplies of this crucial commodity. I could still hear my mother pontificating: "Water and air are the only things that are free." She hadn't taken a desert economy into account!

"Can you believe that a litre of water costs twice as much as a litre of gasoline?" I exclaimed the first time Sean and I pulled into one of Riyadh's deplorably grimy gas stations. The readout on the pumps advertised that a litre of fuel cost the equivalent of about 9 cents US.

Water restrictions explained Riyadh's dearth of vegetation. There were no manicured lawns, no pretty gardens of flowers, no neatly trimmed hedges. Except for vital and versatile date palms, little else grew in the arid, sandy ground. Occasionally an airborne seed took root in the dirt patch between the front of our house and the compound wall a few yards away.

"Leave me to my delusions," I warned Sean as I marched out of the house with a bottle of water.

Starved of greenery, I valiantly persisted in pampering stray seedlings.

"You do realise that you're probably cultivating nothing more exciting than a solitary shaft of wheat," Sean remarked, not unkindly.

He kicked on a pair of sandals and followed me outside to the site of our latest bud.

"I know, but maybe if it's happy here, it'll encourage others and we can have a bunch of shafts of wheat. I just need to see a bit of colour and to know that Mother Nature is propagating herself!"

And so we shared our water with anything that took refuge in our plot of sand, despite fleeting success and disappointing progeny.

One day, Sean came home with a large rubber plant.

"It's beautiful," I cried with delight.

Sean struggled to get it through the front door. I couldn't imagine what such a rarity must have cost him.

"This plant is not only going to survive, it's going to thrive," I announced with determination.

What I couldn't provide through gardening knowledge, I could make up for in love and attention. Experienced gardeners advised of the importance of compost. Riyadh had no commercial horticultural supplies but it had plenty of fertilizer – the fresh, natural variety, courtesy of the city's itinerant goat, sheep and camel herds.

"Sweetheart, I think that in order to give our plant the best possible environment, we should pay a visit to the camel *suq*," I suggested early one Friday morning.

"What on earth does the camel *suq* have to do with environmental conditions for a rubber plant," Sean asked, rather naively.

"We're not going to take the plant to the *suq*, silly. We're going to bring a little bit of *suq* to the plant," I explained patiently. Hopefully my melodious and soothing voice would lull him into acquiescence.

"And just what does this involve?" he asked, nasty suspicion clouding his features.

"A large plastic garbage bag and a shovel." A tilt of my head, a raised brow, and a quick shrug of my shoulders implied that this was nothing to get excited about.

"You can't be serious. Are you actually suggesting that I go to a public *suq* and shovel SHIT?" He, too, raised his brow but the message was one of incredulity.

"Well… yes. I really don't see any reason to get upset. It's for a good cause," I mumbled. My faith in the expedition faltered.

I finally convinced Sean that he would not endanger his standing in the community by collecting a bit of manure.

The camel *suq*'s large, open holding pens made stealth difficult. From the security of the Suburban, I kept guard while Sean crawled through the rough-hewn wood fence.

"It's OK," I assured him in a stage whisper, "no one's looking. Start shovelling."

Sean follows the if-you're-going-to-do-it-do-it-right approach to life. He immediately headed for the largest, freshest pile of poops that he could find. Diligently, if not enthusiastically, my one-of-a-kind man amassed a steaming stash.

By now the camels weren't the only creatures eyeing this bizarre foreigner. A small group of squatting Bedouin curiously observed the activity in the camel pen but respectfully made no comments – at least none we could hear. Rolling the eyeballs probably means the same in any language but they took the sting out of the action by smiling as they did it.

Meanwhile, Sean struggled with his bulging bag.

"I don't think these bags were designed for this type of garbage," he grumbled, keeping a cautious eye on the straining plastic.

"Maybe you should leave some poops behind?" I suggested.

"No, Kathy," Sean replied, panting, "I'm taking a full load because, believe me, I'm not coming back."

More pants and grunts. This wasn't the time to argue the point.

With only minor difficulties, we got the haul through the fence, into the Suburban and back to the house where I dropped generous droppings onto the rubber plant. In no time at all, our house smelled like the camel *suq*, a fact that no doubt accounted for the influx of flies. Worse, the rubber plant showed signs of terminal illness. Too late, I learned I was supposed to dry the fertilizer beforehand.

Intense remedial measures saved the plant; fast-action dung disposal got rid of the unwanted life forms. Sean decided that letting me water stray seedlings outside might not be such a bad idea after all.

* * * *

If water rationing wasn't testing enough, we also had to cope with frequent power outages and irregular supply that could range from 95 to 140 volts in a home wired for 110 volts. Cumbersome voltage regulators augmented messy wires and cords. Both 110- and 220-volt connections prevailed in the city. To add to the confusion, some homes had both.

Power cuts were as tiresome as the water shortages but usually less inconvenient. It was no hardship to temporarily do without the use of the iron or vacuum cleaner, although it could be a nuisance when the washing machine stopped in mid-cycle. Having a gas stove meant outages wouldn't interrupt cooking – unless we forgot to replace an empty gas cylinder. When the power was off for more than a few hours, we stuffed the freezer with newspapers to insulate the thawing food. Admittedly, it was less easy to be blasé in the summer when overworked transformers regularly collapsed under the increased load of air-conditioners and desert coolers.

Annoyingly, almost every time the electricity failed, the phone went on sympathy strike. This meant we couldn't alert anyone to the problem unless we drove to another telephone. It took months for Sean to convince me that the phones didn't run on electricity. Although power failures gradually became rare, I never lost the habit of running to the phone at the first sign of an outage, not to call an electrician but to check for a dial tone.

* * * *

Our compound had only one telephone line. In Canada, at this late stage of the 20th century, it would be unthinkable for 14 houses to share the same line. In this developing oasis we were grateful for a link to the outside world, despite the temperamental nature of the technology and its operators. It wasn't unusual to spend more time trying to get the initial connection than on the actual call. Too often the line suddenly went dead, either because of faulty equipment or deliberate mischief.

All long distance calls had to be placed through an operator. It didn't take us long to figure out that a female voice more readily assured success. I therefore had the task of placing the calls and suffering the tedium of continually dialling for up to 30 minutes before getting a response. This was sometimes a more welcome prospect than subjecting myself to long minutes of idle chatter with a young man who wanted to practise his English. The bored *"Ah-lo"* was my cue to say a cheery *"Sabah al-khair"*.

"Yes, lady, how I can help you?" This was the hopeful query of a man roused from lethargy by the promise of feminine companionship, no matter how brief or disembodied.

"I'd like to call my mother and father in Canada, please." Gratuitous information about the call destination was a critical ingredient in this strange ritual. By appealing to the importance that Arabs place on family, perhaps he would be less likely to cut me off.

"You from Canada, lady?" This translated as the gateway to personal questions.

"Yes, I am," I would respond with false enthusiasm. Slamming the door shut at this point would inspire 'technical' difficulties.

"Canada wonderful country. I have cousin study there. People very friendly. You from Canada so you friendly, no?"

The opening gambit needed polish but in a culture that discouraged non-family male-female interaction, I indulged in tolerance. Besides, I wanted to make my phone call.

Only by subtly introducing details about my happy marriage, my child and the respect and honour of Saudis could I break the cycle.

The benefits far outweighed the disadvantages: we enjoyed long, uninterrupted calls to our families – and seldom received an invoice. The billing procedure was even less developed than the phone system.

Not everyone was so lucky. A colleague of Sean's was devastated when two years of lengthy phone calls to his stateside girlfriend caught up with him. Bechtel deducted the $15,000 bill in monthly instalments from his pay cheque.

Eavesdropping was an inevitable side effect of the Saudi telephone system. Idle curiosity no doubt contributed to the practice but everyone assumed that the government sanctioned the activity. Sometimes a discreet listener almost made you forget about the third party; more often, the telltale breathing, coughing or slurping of tea gave the game away. A Dutch friend even got reprimanded by her listener: "Speak in English. I no understand you langidge."

* * * *

Although television and radio had been introduced by the time we arrived, acceptance of these potentially corrupting devices was not universal. To minimise dissent, content was religious or paralysingly innocuous. All programmes were interrupted for the duration of prayer time, approximately 20 minutes.

The blatant lack of production professionalism provided moments of comic relief. Local TV news broadcasts fascinated us in a hypnotic sort of way. The foreign newspapers hadn't arrived so Sean and I decided to catch the headlines on TV.

"Didn't we see this same news a couple of nights ago?" I asked. " I definitely recognise the rousing background music."

"No," Sean assured me, "that one showed the King saying goodbye to everyone at the airport, getting on the plane in Riyadh, then getting off the plane in Jeddah and greeting everyone. This is the return trip. Saudi TV news always feels like one big rerun."

Until video shops came on the scene, most expats chose not to own a television. With no spoon-fed entertainment – in the home or in public – people had to rely on each other for amusement. This created a unique cohesion of the expat community. On evenings when we weren't with friends, Sean and I developed a comfortable routine of playing games, reading or having stimulating discussions, using our trusty encyclopaedia as arbitrator when necessary. In an environment rife with restrictions, we sustained a richness in our lives that exceeded expectations

* * * *

The easy availability of free repairmen provided another surprise benefit of our new lifestyle. It was shamefully effortless to adapt to this handy perk.

"Sean," I shouted from the top of the stairs one evening, "the hall light has just burned out. Can you please change the bulb?"

"I'll put in a request tomorrow," came a distracted voice from the living room. Sean was happily reading his way through an impressive stack of 3-day-old British newspapers and week-old American news magazines. Foreign publications couldn't appear on the newsstands until they had been screened by the diligent censors in the Ministry of Information.

"A request for what?" I asked, making my way down the darkened stairs. Oscar, who recently had arrived from Canada, greeted me from the shadows. "I'm asking you to change a bulb."

"We don't have any light bulbs in the house. We don't need any," he added, as though this closed the subject. "Don't worry, I'll make sure it gets changed tomorrow, first thing." He reverted to reading about all the sports matches he had missed watching on the weekend.

"Sweetheart, listen up. We *do* need a light bulb. Now. What's the story here?"

With an exaggerated ruffle of pages, Sean put down the newspaper, shrugged his shoulders and explained, "Workers change bulbs."

The matter-of-fact statement astounded me.

"Are you telling me that, in the course of transferring to Saudi Arabia, you have somehow lost the ability to change a light bulb?"

"Of course not," he said testily. "It's just that we work long hours six days a week. The company has maintenance crews on staff to do various repairs during the day. Replacing light bulbs is one of those chores. Besides," he added defensively, "changing that bulb requires a step ladder and we don't have one."

The light bulb was replaced the next morning, as promised, but we also got our own stock of bulbs. Except for the hard-to-reach places, I insisted that we retain this basic skill.

* * * *

I had grown up in the confidence that the constant supply of utilities was my unalienable right. Saudi Arabia taught me that these advantages should never be wasted or taken for granted.

Suffering shortages of water, electricity and other services and adjusting to new routines were, to me, all part of a Great Adventure. Not having access to a talented hairdresser, however, was an affront to my personal well-being.

"I'm dying for a decent haircut," I remarked to my neighbour Jackie. She had dropped in to sample my latest batch of chocolate brownies. "Got any good recommendations?"

"You're in luck," she replied. "The only legal salon in the city is just up the street."

"What do you mean, 'the only legal salon in the city'?" I enquired suspiciously.

Jackie looked surprised that I was ignorant of such important information. "According to Riyadh's right-wing thinkers, hairdressing salons are potential sources of evil," she explained. "There used to be a good salon for women at the InterContinental Hotel but the government closed it because the privilege was abused."

"'Privilege'? Since when is getting a haircut a privilege? And how can that possibly be abused?"

This was beyond my comprehension and the boundaries of my imagination. Were customers doing naughty things with shampoo?

Before moving to Saudi Arabia, I knew women weren't allowed to drive and that they weren't encouraged to work. Nobody thought to mention that beauty salons were taboo! This might have been a deciding factor in whether or not we accepted the transfer!

"Apparently some of the Saudi customers make fake appointments," Jackie said as she ran her fingers through her uneven strands of short brown hair. "They go into the salon through the front door and then immediately exit through the back door for secret rendezvous with their lovers."

"It all sounds very exciting but I'm not sure I'd want to give up a hairdressing appointment, even for a lover!"

"Ain't that the truth," Jackie agreed, helping herself to another brownie.

The local salon, staffed exclusively by young Lebanese women, didn't meet my high standards but it was certainly better than nothing – which is what I faced a couple of months later. When a Saudi client's son became ill during her 'appointment', her husband rushed to the salon to give his wife the news and bring her home. She wasn't there. That marked the end of Riyadh's only surviving salon and the immediate deportation of all the staff.

Needless to say, this sort of reaction didn't stop the subterfuge. Trained expat women opened 'salons' in their homes. Some were more qualified than others. By keeping low-key, hairdressers generally stayed out of trouble. This wasn't always the case with the clientele. Some women suffered butchered cuts and botched colour treatments.

On my next trip to a trendy London salon, my hairdresser gave an involuntary shudder when he saw me.

"'Allo, 'allo. Wot 'av you done wif your 'air?"

"Please, Miko, no judgments," I said, staring at my bedraggled image in the mirror. "Just work a miracle." At the prices he charged, that was the least I could expect.

"That'll be 'ard, wonnit? This, luv, is a comb, not a bleedin' magic wand!"

No one escaped the possibility of misfortune, not even the great Iron Lady herself. On a visit to Jeddah, Maggie Thatcher requested the services of a local hairdresser. The poor girl, in a state of nerves, neglected to check that she had set her equipment for the correct voltage. The hair dryer blew a fuse and Maggie had to go to her engagement with damp locks – no doubt with her own fuse blown.

Understandably, the topic of hairdressing frequently crept into conversations. Jackie and I, sitting together on the shopping bus one morning, ruminated over local solutions to the ongoing problem.

"So what do Saudi women do about getting their hair done?" I asked.

"Ah, now that is particularly interesting," she replied. "Apparently there are legions of Lebanese men who, for exorbitant fees, go to the homes of wealthy women to do the necessary." She gave a wicked smile, implying that they might 'do' more than hair.

"That's a bit silly, isn't it? Why on earth would inviting a foreign man into the home be preferable to having the woman go to an all-women, public salon? Besides, if someone wants to have an affair, blocking off one avenue simply encourages the parties to seek other means."

Jackie just shrugged her shoulders. No one could offer rational answers to a situation beyond logic. Sometimes, though, a haircut is just a haircut.

* * * *

"S.H.I.T."

It was Thursday noon, the start of the Saudi weekend. Sean had just arrived home. He made this pronouncement as he walked into the kitchen.

"What's that supposed to mean?" I asked, giving him a kiss on the cheek.

"Sure Happy It's Thursday," Sean laughed. "It's what they say here instead of T.G.I.F. Different work weeks, different expressions."

"I still can't get used to these Saudi weeks."

"I know," Sean agreed. "The good news, though, is that with Saturday being the first day of the work week, I don't hate Mondays anymore."

Adapting to local concepts of time involved several levels.

"Do you realise that, according to the *hijri* calendar, it's only 1397?" I asked as I carried our plates of salad into the dining room. "I have to admit, sometimes there's a 14th century atmosphere about this place. And God knows there are a few perspectives that belong in the Middle Ages."

Sean grunted his agreement as he sat at the table.

In Saudi Arabia, the *hijri* or Islamic calendar operates concurrently with the Gregorian calendar. Muslims refer to the time after Christ as 'CE' (Christian Era) rather than 'AD' (Anno Domini).

The *hijri* calendar began in the year 622 AD/CE when the Prophet Mohammed emigrated from Makkah to Medina. Muslims everywhere commemorate this event, the *haj*, annually.

As well as different weeks, months and years, we had to get used to local attitudes towards hours of the day. We came to realise that Islam contributes to the somewhat fluid approach. The constantly used phrase *insha'allah*, if God wills, expresses a resignation to accept life as it comes. This covers all situations, from the punctuality of a driver to the start of an official event.

It could be hard to pin Saudis down when it came to exact times. Nevertheless, watches captivated them. Saudis loved giving watches as gifts as much as collecting them for themselves. One friend gave us four watches – in one year.

As the pace of life quickened, Saudis slowly started to recognise that punctuality has its advantages. Yet they retained the inherent attitude that time is something to share rather than something to steal and refused to let it rule their lives.

* * * *

The mystique of Saudi fascinated us. The social restrictions did not.

"I know how you prefer the company of men, Kathy. Please do not, I repeat Do Not, indulge yourself in this innocent pleasure in public when I'm not with you. If you're caught by one of the zealot types, the consequences could be… terminal."

Sean's concern was justified. Everyone had heard stories of women having the misfortune to get caught by the *mutawwa* with a 'non-relative' man. The women were automatically sent to Shemasi Hospital for an internal exam. If doctors found traces of semen, the woman went to jail and was then deported. If no semen was found, she was simply deported.

Nurses in this situation sometimes had 'adulteress' stamped across their passport picture as a final farewell. In rare worst-case scenarios, the woman risked being convicted of adultery, a stoning offense. The biblical scenery came with biblical solutions.

Chapter Seven

By the time Tara and I arrived in Riyadh, Sean already had batches of homemade beer and wine bubbling away in the spare bedroom. This was the 'storage area' from which he had diverted me during my initial house tour. The room had the look and smell of a tavern at the end of a busy Saturday night. It definitely wasn't my decorating scheme of choice but, showing uncharacteristic restraint, I didn't spoil his obvious pleasure.

"It takes three weeks before the wine is ready for bottling and five weeks for the beer," Sean explained. "I wanted to get started as soon as possible."

With a hint of pride, Sean demonstrated his new set of skills. He lifted the lid from the 75-litre red plastic garbage bin and masterfully floated a recently-acquired hydrometer in the yeasty fermentation.

"This measures the specific gravity," he announced.

I gave him a blank stare. My knowledge of a beer's gravity consisted of removing a cap from the bottle and pouring the liquid into a glass.

"I know it feels a bit Arctic in here but don't turn off the air conditioner," Sean instructed. "And be sure to keep the door closed. This keeps the room at optimal temperature for the beer."

He then guided me to the area of the room designated as a winery. Containers of red and white grape juice gurgled contentedly as they underwent the fermentation process. In the corner, dozens of neatly stacked, cleaned grape juice bottles waited to be filled with the new vintages.

"Are these what I think they are?" I asked.

My eyes focused on impressively bulged rubber appendages attached to the spouts of the 20-litre jerry cans.

"Yes," Sean laughed. "Condoms are perfect gauges. They're strong enough to withstand the expansion caused by the gases. When they deflate, you know the wine is ready."

"Isn't all this illegal?" I asked anxiously – and rhetorically.

Up to this point in our lives we had been law-abiding citizens. Now we were choosing to inhabit the ominous grey zone populated by most Saudi expats. Even those who refrained from buying or brewing booze were usually guilty of drinking it when the opportunity presented itself. These 'criminal' activities were punishable by prison, floggings and/or deportation. Despite the substantial risks, few foreigners refused to give up what they considered their right and, in this often stressful environment, their need to enjoy a drink. Nevertheless it made me uneasy to expose ourselves to the possibility of Saudi Arabia's harsh legal recriminations.

"Don't worry," Sean said. "It's one of those contradictions about living here. Saudis usually turn a blind eye and the *mutawwa* can't interfere if people drink in their homes, don't appear drunk in public and, most importantly, don't supply Saudis. Most foreigners make their own booze. I was even given a copy of the Aramco Bible when I arrived. Aramco's the big oil conglomerate that's been in the Eastern Province for years. They're well known for the high quality of their homemade brews. I guess the company doesn't want any unnecessary health mishaps so they've developed safe practices and good recipes for just about every alcohol you can think of. A German construction company here has a professional *Brewmeister* on their local payroll. He's in the Kingdom as a technician or some such thing but his *raison d'etre* is creating excellent ale for his colleagues."

"There certainly are some strange corporate policies in this place," I said, making a move to leave Sean's refrigerated laboratory.

"Yes," Sean agreed as we headed downstairs, "and they're matched by paranoid attitudes. I was warned to be careful about using words like alcohol, gin or Johnny Walker. I was also told to use code words on the phone. It seems a bit drastic but better safe than sorry.

"One code word that's easy to slip in is *sadiki*. That's Arabic for 'my friend'. It's the local, economical alternative to imported spirits."

"Is that what we'd call 'bathtub gin'?" I asked.

"Yes, or 'moonshine'. People make it in home stills using white sugar, water, yeast and a 'fertilizer' such as Calgon. At 190° proof, even the purest runs can be toxic. Production is mainly the domain of the Brits. If they don't get caught, they can clear £50,000 a year – in addition to their regular tax-free salary."

"The stuff sounds deadly," I said. "I don't think I'll be imbibing."

"There are plenty of stories of misuse and abuse," Sean admitted. "I heard a good one about a seriously inebriated fellow who was trying to find his way home. Fortunately he was driving on the quiet, unpoliced streets of his compound. *Un*fortunately he drove into the bedroom wall of one of the houses. Somehow he extricated the car and continued his journey with no further mishaps. The identity of the culprit was a mystery – until the startled bedroom residents discovered a license plate embedded in the wall."

We laughed at this extreme example of drunk driving. Sean offered another amusing encounter.

"I cautioned one of the guys at work to be careful about his *sadiki* intake and reminded him that a bad batch or excess could make him blind. His response was, "Don't worry, I'll only drink it until I need glasses.""

The funny-sad story brought a weak smile to my face.

"Ironically," Sean continued, "the word alcohol comes from the Arabic *al-kuhl*. It was the Arabs who perfected its distillation and who introduced to mankind the pleasure of wine."

"Saudi Arabia's ultra-conservatives certainly ignore these historic contributions, don't they?"

"More than you realise," Sean said. "Alcohol is prohibited in all consumable forms, including everyday products like pure vanilla extract."

"Gosh, I have to admit that I didn't even think about vanilla having alcohol in it. It's such a basic ingredient for baking. What do people use instead?"

"The artificial stuff's available but most people buy things they need and can't get here when they travel outside the Kingdom. The mention of alcohol isn't even allowed in cookbooks. Ads for spirits are blacked out in papers and magazines. For some reason, perfumes and after shaves escape the veto, although I've seen men guzzling the scents in deserted city lots. Interestingly, the *Qur'an* promises rivers of wine in Paradise for all those who have abstained in this life."

"Since intoxication is alcohol's evil, this seems to indicate that Paradise is a befuddle-free zone. Unless, heaven forbid, it's non-alcoholic wine...," I added with a giggle.

I poured us fresh cups of coffee.

"What about getting all the brewing supplies?" I asked. "Isn't that difficult?"

"Not at all," Sean replied. "If you keep the baker's yeast after each batch, it gets better and better as it changes into brewer's yeast. Amazingly, the supermarkets carry tins of Blue Ribbon malt extract. And the grape juice comes in bottles with handy spring-loaded rubber-sealed stoppers. Perfect for bottling wine. It's hard to conceal what you're up to when you have a shopping cart full of cases of grape juice and kilos of sugar."

Sean sipped his coffee as he concluded his update on the ins and outs of this illicit pursuit that would become part of our lives.

"Just like remembering to fill the car with gas or replace used food items, we'll have to keep track of when to bottle and brew. A lapse will mean an empty 'cellar' until the next batch is ready."

"I'm guessing that some people's efforts are better than others?"

"Absolutely," Sean confirmed. "And it's competitive. Reputations are built or busted on good or bad brews. Sam Lackey, one of the guys at work, produces consistently excellent wines, partly because he lets them ferment for longer than most of us. He keeps a log and labels every bottle with its batch and bottle number. Most people, though, aren't looking for perfection. They're simply grateful when they have drinkable bottles to get them through the next few weeks."

* * * *

The civil police were generally pretty decent when handling alcohol-related incidents. The *mutawwa*, however, displayed exaggerated zero tolerance. The morning after one of Sean's colleagues returned to Riyadh from home leave he had to go to the hospital because of an ongoing kidney problem. Tests showed alcohol in the blood, despite the fact that he hadn't had a drink since arriving in the Kingdom. As soon as he was fit to travel, pressure from hospital-based *mutawwa* forced the authorities to deport him for the importation of a banned substance.

Although foreigners were cautioned against giving alcohol to locals, it was a few high-ranked Saudis who tightly controlled the traffic in spirits.

Scotch, gin and vodka sold locally at more than five times the going rate in the rest of the world. Commercial beers and wines were less readily available. The high risks of transport outweighed the comparatively small returns. It was necessary to sell far more bottles of these items to begin to approach the huge profits made from liquor.

The story we heard was that many years ago alcohol had been allowed. Then, at an embassy party in Jeddah, a Saudi prince shot dead the British Consul – something to do with the Consul's wife. Booze was banned and the royal family exiled the guilty prince to Cyprus with a lavish sum of compensation cash. From his new base he started a lucrative black market trade in alcohol. Apparently more Johnny Walker Black Label is sold in Saudi Arabia than anywhere else.

One of the few warnings we had before going to Saudi was, 'If you're an alcoholic, stay away from the Kingdom.' We thought that meant alcoholics wouldn't be able to feed their habit. Now we knew differently.

* * * *

One afternoon Sean arrived home with a case of Black Label.

"Where on earth did that come from?" I asked with disapproval in my voice.

Sean laughed. "A wizened Bedu suddenly appeared in the office saying he had some cases of scotch to sell at a good price. Everyone was wary at first but he proved to be the real deal. In broken English and with lots of hand gestures, he regaled us with stories of being chased through the desert by the border patrol. He pulled up his *thobe* to reveal several old bullet wounds in his legs. Then he invited us outside to show us the goods. His car had as many battle scars as he did. What choice did we have but to relieve him of all those heavy boxes? What a character!"

And what a salesman. Sean and others in the office became regular customers. I saw the extravagant expenditure as money figuratively and literally going down the toilet.

Chapter Eight

After only a few weeks, Sean and I had adapted ourselves to Riyadh's relaxed rhythm. We welcomed a return to routine – relatively speaking. Life in Riyadh for us would never be completely routine because there was always a different facet of the culture to discover.

We began to hear the word *haj* with increasing frequency. This, we learned, was the annual pilgrimage to Makkah, the birthplace of the Prophet Mohammed and where he first received God's revelations. This fifth pillar in the Islamic faith stipulates that *haj* need be made only once in a lifetime and only if the pilgrim (*haji*) is physically and financially able. Because Saudi months follow the lunar calendar, *haj* moves forward 11-12 days each year. In 1976 it fell in late November.

During *haj* season, Saudi Arabia is inundated with Muslims from all over the world who come to fulfill this part of their religious duty. Before cheap flights became predominant, many pilgrims made the arduous trek overland. The trip often took months and could cost *hajis* their life savings. For some, it was their final journey: they came to Makkah to die and attain special glory in heaven.

As newly arrived expats we hadn't had time to absorb and appreciate the deep religious meanings of the Saudi culture. In fact, this significant event might have passed us by except that everyone was excitedly planning short-haul get-aways for *'eid al adha*, the second most important holiday in the Saudi calendar. This three-day celebration at the end of the *haj* was an ideal opportunity for resident foreigners to explore the region.

"A few people in the office are talking about going to Iran for the *'eid*. Would you like to go?" Sean asked when he came home from work.

"Wow. That sounds exotically tempting," I said. "We could go wild shopping for hand-woven carpets, Persian miniatures and other arty treasures. My aunt and uncle were posted there years ago. The place has always fascinated me."

"Why do women wangle shopping into every excursion?" Sean asked, shaking his head in dismay.

"Don't worry," I assured him. "As much as I love to travel and have new experiences, I'm actually going to vote that we stay home. For one thing, I'm not sure I'm ready to face the Riyadh airport ordeal again so soon. And secondly, it's probably better for us to focus on saving before we indulge in more spending."

"I agree," Sean said, looking relieved at my uncharacteristic retail restraint. "There'll be other trips. Christmas is just around the corner. Let's concentrate on that holiday for now. In this restrictive environment, it could well provide you with one of those 'new experiences' you crave."

* * * *

The onset of our first Riyadh Christmas awakened in me a primal stirring. The time of 'peace on earth, good will to men' was upon us. Except it wasn't. We were hunkered down in a desert. And in a country that didn't permit any religious observances other than those of Islam – a faith that is supposed to embrace 'people of the book'. Yet, no churches or synagogues dotted the landscape. Non-Muslims practised their religions in secrecy and at the risk of being deported. Lumping together location and attitude, the prospects didn't look good for a joyous holiday season.

"How can people who live in places without snow possibly know the excitement of Christmas?" I asked Sean as he dressed for work. "This time of year needs runny noses that come from dashing into warm stores from cold streets. It needs sidewalks crowded with last-minute shoppers. And, apart from weather issues, it needs that special holiday spirit. It's Christmas, for goodness sake. What can Muslims possibly fear from Christians celebrating this time of togetherness? I thought they were big on the family thing."

"Well, think about it," Sean replied in his usual rational manner. He straightened his tie in the bathroom mirror. "Christmas began in this part of the world. This climate's as authentic as it gets. And true Christmas spirit has nothing to do with the commercialism that runs rampant in the West."

There certainly was no fear of Christmas commercialism in Riyadh. Religious conservatives made sure that stores did not display anything that might be associated with this ostentatious infidel practice. The Western world's most celebrated holy day was Saudi Arabia's most forbidden celebration.

Due to customs restrictions, we couldn't bring a Christmas tree with us to Riyadh but we did smuggle in a few ornaments. Sean had dared to query the inclusion of a tree stand in our limited shipping allowance.

"We're going to a country that has hardly any trees, let alone Christmas trees. Do you think we'll have a lot of use for this?" he had asked.

My don't-mess-with-me-on-this-issue glare immediately closed the subject.

In mid December, we received a pleasant surprise.

"Bechtel has flown in three Christmas trees from Germany," Sean announced at lunch one day. He gave Oscar a playful pat on the back and took six-month-old Tara from my arms, treating her to kisses and a toss in the air. "They've offered one to us because it's Tara's first Christmas."

Tara laughed, seemingly thrilled with the news.

"That's incredible," I responded with a mix of awe and excitement. "I thought Christmas trees weren't allowed! How did they do it?"

"I think they've come in under the guise of a corporate planting programme or some such thing," Sean replied, putting Tara into her playpen. She stuffed a teething ring into her mouth and drooled contentedly as we sat down to eat. "Anyway, it doesn't matter how they got through customs; let's just be grateful that we have a real tree for our first family Christmas."

I managed to bite back "I told you so" and restricted my victory to "I'll look for the tree stand".

* * * *

A real tree wasn't my only surprise that first Christmas. I had brought a few gifts with me but Sean had to forage locally. Judging from the number of presents waiting to be opened, it looked like he had succeeded in his quest.

The three of us gathered around the tree early on Christmas morning. Excitedly, I ferreted out a small box from under a thick branch. I could hear something jiggling inside. Diamond earrings, perhaps? I forced myself to remove the wrapping in a ladylike manner. Pure astonishment registered on my face.

"Th-thumb tacks?" I stuttered.

"Yes," Sean smiled. "Coloured ones! I know how you like desky things."

"Thank you, sweetheart. That's… so… thoughtful of you."

My pretended gratitude took immense effort. We opened more presents. Tara, too young to appreciate the event, took pleasure in playing with ribbons and wrappings. Finally, only one box remained, another gift for me from Sean. I prayed he'd redeem himself with this one. Cautiously I peeled off the paper.

"Oh My God. Why… it's just what I need." Adequate words failed me.

"You've had such a bad cold for the last few days," Sean enthused. "I thought you'd like to have your own box of Kleenex."

Had the man lost his mind? Doesn't he know that women don't want PRACTICAL gifts? I opened the box to pull out a tissue. I couldn't decide whether to blow my nose or wipe my tearing eyes.

"These bloody tissues don't even pop up properly," I complained.

Then I gasped.

"What on earth? This is like a Cracker Jack box. I think I've just got a prize!"

My fingers had latched onto something heavy and metallic. I pulled gently. Out came a solid gold necklace.

"The gold *suq* takes all the worry out of Christmas shopping," Sean said.

"It's beautiful," I said sincerely. "Thank you so much."

Then a sudden thought struck. I retrieved the packet of coloured thumb tacks. It *looked* normal. But then, so had the Kleenex. I carefully peeled off the cardboard backing and made a happy discovery.

"Earrings! How on earth did you get them into the box without any sign of tampering?"

"It was fiddly work," Sean admitted. "But well worth the look on your face."

"I wasn't very good at hiding my disappointment, was I?" I asked shamefully.

"No, but your pleasure was equally real. That's what I wanted to see."

"I'll never doubt you again," I promised. "From now on I'll always expect awesome gifts."

I laughed at the flash of worry on Sean's face. To my delight, he never dropped the high standards he set that first Christmas.

Chapter Nine

Our first Riyadh dinner invitation was distinctive – in the extreme. I had sent some meals to a Lebanese colleague of Sean's who was temporarily on single status. Now that his wife and children had returned to Riyadh, he wanted to repay us with the hospitality of his home – a traditional mud house.

"I appreciate Abed's kindness but do you think it's safe?" I anxiously asked Sean when he phoned to convey the news. "I mean, how could it be anything but dirty inside? What if Tara becomes ill? Maybe we should just make polite excuses."

"I think it would cause offence if we refused," Sean said. "People have lived in mud houses for thousands of years. It can't be that bad, especially when we're only being asked to endure it for a few hours. Think it over. I'll give Abed an answer tomorrow."

Eventually, my inquisitiveness and good manners overcame frets about hygiene.

Just before sunset on the appointed evening, we parked on the narrow street in front of Abed's house. The large Suburban occupied more than its fair share of space. An old man leading a donkey cart stared at us, no doubt curious to know what brought Western strangers into the heart of the old city's humble residential area.

The fascination of stepping back in time temporarily distracted me from the concerns I had about this outing. We knocked on a heavy, weather-worn wooden door and waited expectantly. Even Tara, only eight months old, sensed the adventure and cooed happily in my arms. Suddenly she gave a delighted squeak and pointed towards a mud-coloured gecko whose suction-cup feet secured it to the side of the dusty wall. The reminder of a creature-infested house jarred me back to modern reality. Sean gave me one of his there's-no-going-back-now looks nanoseconds before Abed answered the door and welcomed us. His sturdy wife and two small children crowded behind him, eager to have a look at their foreign guests. Apparently, no such people had crossed their threshold. Our fair skin and hair provided a sharp contrast to their sun-kissed complexions and curly, blue-black locks.

The house's comfortable temperature struck me immediately.

"The thick walls keep the heat out in summer and retain the warmth inside in winter," Abed explained. "As an added bonus, we don't have to suffer the noise of air conditioners or desert coolers."

We moved past the entrance and an interior reception room to a pleasant atrium. The rustic backdrop made the simple, sparse furnishings and lack of décor look artistically minimalist rather than modest. To my relief – and surprise – the house was spotlessly clean. I had no hesitation about indulging in yet another new experience: sitting on the earthen floor to eat from a cloth laden with a feast.

"My goodness, you must have been cooking for a week to prepare all this food," Sean said with admiration. He certainly had no exposure to such spousal diligence.

Abed's wife laughed. "My mother and her mother taught me cooking since I was small. We spend much of our lives in the kitchen and take pride in preparing good food. I hope you like it."

"I don't think you have to worry about that," I said, already salivating from the bombardment of heady odours. "Please, tell us what all these dishes are."

Abed and his wife then proceeded to take us on a gastronomic tour of more than a dozen platters that tasted as delicious as they looked and smelled: *hommos, baba ghannouj, kebbe, tabouleh* and *fattouch* were only a few of the dishes in a remarkable spread. This introduction to Lebanese food was the start of our long romance with a richly varied cuisine.

Small cups of sweet coffee brought our visit to an end.

"Thank you so much for a wonderful evening," Sean and I said with much feeling.

"It has been an honour to have you in our home," Abed replied.

"No," we quickly responded with sincerity, "the honour has been ours. Thank you for showing us such generous hospitality."

"Well, I've learned something from this visit," I said to Sean as we drove back to the compound. "I shouldn't be too quick to judge what I don't know.

That was an interesting evening that we all too easily could have missed out on because of my baseless fears and preconceived notions."

* * * *

Mud houses aside, Saudi Arabia challenged our adaptation process in different ways on a regular basis.

Sean's work on the construction management of Riyadh's new airport entailed 10-hour workdays and five-and-a-half-day weeks. He drove to the office in a 4-wheel drive vehicle that carried a shovel, blankets and a supply of bottled water in case he got stuck in the desert on a site visit. My workday, on the other hand, disappeared altogether. Unwillingly unemployed for the first time in my life, I had to figure out how to fill my time in a worthwhile manner. A steady dose of women from my own culture tested me more than coping with the idiosyncrasies of Saudi culture.

"I swear I'll scream if I get one more invitation to a mind-numbing coffee morning, ladies' lunch or afternoon tea," I fumed at Sean. He had come home for what he thought would be a peaceful lunch. "I feel like I'm being sucked into a vortex of small talk and gossip. The politics drives me crazy, too. There's a pecking order among the women that reflects the husband's seniority, for goodness sake. It's all too much. I'm resigning; I've decided to become a recluse."

"Your personality won't allow it," Sean responded calmly, taking a large bite of his grilled cheese sandwich. "Besides," he said, trying to speak and chew at the same time, "if you adopt such obvious isolationist behaviour, you'll be the victim of the back stabbing."

"Now I'm *really* worried."

I slammed my napkin on the table and got up abruptly. Oscar hastily retreated to another room. Tara, who had been amusing herself in her playpen in a corner of the dining room, reacted to my raised voice and began to cry. Calming myself, I then concentrated on calming Tara, feeling guilty at my loss of self-control.

"Give yourself time, sweetheart," Sean said, gently trying to bring the situation into perspective. "You'll meet women you have a lot in common with and then there'll be no looking back."

"But that's the problem! I don't know how to act with women, especially large groups. I've never had to be around swarms of them before. I was a tomboy as a child and most of my friends ever since have been men. Enforced female companionship is alien territory."

"You can't say you weren't warned," Sean said. I could tell he was losing patience with my moaning. "If most of the women can't work and all of the men can, it stands to reason you'll be in the stay-at-home crowd. The reality of the situation is that this is Saudi Arabia, the land that knows how to keep their women in line." He smiled to show that the last comment was a fun jab but then became serious again. "You can suffer through this two-year assignment or you can learn how to like women and get on with your life."

Sean was right… as usual. Instead of trying to overcome my apprehensions, I was making a mountain out of a mole hill. Perhaps the adjustment might not have appeared so monumental if I wasn't also trying to come to terms with motherhood. The first four months of Tara's life had been ones of general disruption in which I had no fixed mother-baby routine for any length of time. Three months after Tara's birth, we had relocated ourselves halfway across the world, spending a month hopping from one destination to another along the route. Being housebound most of the time and reliant on someone else if I decided to leave the compound exaggerated the difficulties of my initiation into this new environment and my new role in life.

To complicate matters further, I was unfamiliar with the prescribed conventions of suburban living, particularly when applied to the confined space of a walled compound. We should have had privacy within our homes but sometimes bored neighbours intruded unexpectedly. An overly friendly Indonesian woman brought the situation to a head. She suddenly appeared beside me in the kitchen one morning while her undisciplined toddler scrambled up the stairs in search of Tara.

"Good grief, Yonti, you scared the wits out of me. How did you get in the house?"

"I walk in! Door not lock, you home, we friend, no need invitation."

Yonti's soft brown eyes looked confused. Why, she must have wondered, would I ask such a silly question? And why wasn't I more enthusiastic about her visit?

"I'm sure that in Jakarta people walk into the homes of friends all the time without knocking," I said, struggling to express myself without offending this well-meaning soul. "I'm just not used to it."

"That OK. You get use," Yonti bubbled, not taking the hint.

"Actually, Yonti, I don't want to get used to it right now, if you don't mind."

She nervously twirled a long a strand of her thick, black hair around her finger and stared at the floor. This wasn't going well. I tried to explain my reasons as considerately as possible.

"I've never been a housewife or a mother," I began. "I feel as though my independence is being eroded in uncontrollable chunks. I need time to feel comfortable in this situation. While I'm doing that, I have to ask you to respect my privacy. I need a bit of space, for now at least."

Yonti nodded in mute agreement, although she obviously couldn't understand my attitude. Her innocent goodwill crumbled my resolve.

"C'mon, Yonti," I said, feeling slightly better for having expressed myself. "Let's bring the kids downstairs so we can keep an eye on them. Then we'll sit and have a nice cup of coffee. I can always go into seclusion tomorrow."

* * * *

A note on a supermarket bulletin board caught my attention. I stared at it like a startled rabbit caught in the glare of oncoming headlights: *New playgroup opening in October. Children from 12 months welcome.*

Could it be true? Could someone actually want to take on such a job? Guilt washed over me when I realised how excited the news made me. Motherhood was unrelenting in this environment: the city had no playgrounds and I didn't have a personal driver to take me whenever I felt like it to the homes of friends with similarly-aged children – if I had known any such people. Tara needed stimulation. And I needed a break.

As soon as I got home, I phoned Jean Robinson, the British woman who ran the group, for details. Satisfied with the information she gave me, I pledged 16-month-old Tara to a new learning experience. The move was good for both of us. Tara had the benefit of social interaction with her peer group three mornings a week and I had freedom.

But what was I going to do with my new liberty? I chatted with Stephanie Gliebe, another Bechtel wife and compound neighbour. Stephanie didn't have time for boredom in her busy schedule. She had done what no one else in the compound had dared to do: she had made friends beyond the walls and outside the company. I liked her style. Stephanie was my light in the tunnel.

"Do you play tennis?" Stephanie asked as we toasted our bodies beside the pool one afternoon. Her fit, suntanned body and her shoulder-length blond hair defined her as a perfect specimen of a California Girl even before she verbally confirmed my assumption.

"No," I replied languidly, blindly feeling for the bottle of cold water beside me. I took a generous swig and, on impulse, poured the rest on my head. Refreshed, I turned over to give my back a chance to cook.

"If you'd like to learn, I could see if my teacher can fit you into one of her classes," she offered, massaging another layer of lotion on her long, mahogany-coloured legs.

Here was an opportunity to escape from the compound. Nevertheless, I hesitated, unsure whether I wanted to commit to lessons in anything at this stage, let alone a sport. Short on options, I forced myself to appear enthusiastic.

"Sure. Why not give it a try?" I smiled, wondering what I was getting myself into.

By noon the next day, Stephanie had made all the arrangements.

"You start at 8 a.m. on Sunday. Don't be late," she warned.

"Will I be in your class?" I asked. I felt I needed the crutch of Stephanie's moral support.

"No, I go on Tuesdays. You'll be fine."

And I was. Suddenly I had a tennis coach – and a new passion. I was hooked. The hard, fast game fed my competitive nature, allowed me to release my frustrations and gave me some much-needed exercise. Equally important, I met genuinely nice people. New friendships were formed. It wasn't unusual for Sean to be wakened in the early hours of the morning by the sound of a gently closing drawer.

"Let me guess," he said sleepily, "you're off to the tennis courts again."

I groped for my tennis socks in the darkened room, found the familiar lump of thick, nubby cotton and went over to Sean's side of the bed for a quick snuggle.

"I never thought I'd say this but women can be just as entertaining as men."

Sean gave me a gentle pat on the back as he hugged me, a gesture that implied his satisfaction that I had at last overcome a major hurdle.

* * * *

"It's not natural. OK, it's not *un*natural, but it's definitely not healthy."

I had been curled up on a chair in the living room, brooding quietly and scratching Oscar's ears on the ticklish spot that made his leg jerk reflexively. Now, in concert with my sudden outburst, I jumped up, startling Sean and Oscar. I began pacing the room like a caged tiger.

"What on earth are you talking about? What's not healthy?" Sean allowed himself to be distracted from his newspapers. It was a lazy Friday afternoon, the end of the Saudi weekend.

"Our life," I said in frustration. "We're cloistered behind walls where our neighbours are your work colleagues and our social circle doesn't extend beyond the borders of Bechtel. It's… I don't know… it's incestuous. I feel trapped. I feel like I have to be a good little company wife or it will hinder your chances for promotion. I need space to be me, not Sean's wife. My independent, unconventional nature feels stifled."

"And just how do you propose to unstifle it?" Sean asked with growing interest. He purposefully laid down the newspapers, refilled his glass with homemade *grande reserve* red wine and gave me his full attention.

"Well, what about having a dinner party? We'll invite people who have nothing to do with Bechtel."

"It's a nice idea but where are you going to find these people? We don't know anyone else."

"True, but I've seen people who look interesting. I bet I could just stand in the middle of an aisle in the supermarket and spot dozens of people who might be good dinner party material."

At this suggestion, Sean's eyes hooded almost imperceptibly. I could imagine him praying for divine intervention to restrict yet another of my wild impulses. Wisely, he didn't voice any objection.

"Do what you have to do. Just try to act... responsibly." He returned to the predictable security of his reading material, undoubtedly hoping I'd find something else to occupy my imagination before this offbeat plan had a chance to brew.

The vigilant *mutawwa* were forbidden to enter homes or compounds unless they had convincing proof that immoral acts were being committed. This constraint allowed foreigners to get together in mixed company, drink alcohol and dress as they pleased, activities the *mutawwa* perceived as beyond the boundaries of decency and against the dictates of Islam. If we hoped to expand our social contacts in Riyadh's strict environment, private dinner parties were the safest option.

"It's all set," I announced two days later when Sean arrived home for lunch. I gave him a quick welcome kiss and then happily shared the news of my accomplishment. "I've invited three couples for dinner next Thursday."

"Great," he responded cautiously. "Who are they?"

"There's Carolyn Wilkinson. She's in my tennis class. She seems to be sophisticated but fun. She's very attractive: slim, jet black hair and an easy laugh; I think you'll like her. Then there's Jean Robinson. She's the woman who runs Tara's playgroup. She's not exactly vivacious but she's definitely pleasant. Caroline Pye is one of the mothers I've seen when I leave Tara at Jean's. She's got a spirited personality. They're all British, so there won't be any language difficulties. With luck, it'll be a good group."

"What about the husbands?" Sean asked, valiantly trying to recover his composure.

"Ah, that's the mystery ingredient. Exciting, isn't it?" I rubbed my palms together and shot my eyebrows up and down theatrically.

Sean didn't look excited but he good-naturedly gave his blessing to my attempt to break free of suffocating company ties.

Thursday evening arrived and so did our gaggle of guests. Although none of the couples had met socially, everyone bonded immediately. The husbands were as congenial as the wives. Like Sean, they worked in the construction industry.

That evening marked the beginning of an incredibly active social life. Each of the three couples invited us to their homes where we met more people and exchanged phone numbers. We soon had impressively diverse circles of friends and acquaintances. The next time I suggested we have a dinner party, Sean at least knew the guests before they arrived.

* * * *

Betty de Lurie, the wife of one of Bechtel's senior managers, voiced what many of us didn't realise about our Riyadh experience: "Everyone at home tells me how interesting my letters are. I started thinking about it. Maybe I *am* having a good time!"

Buoyed by my positive encounters, I decided to be more proactive and discover my own 'good time'. The logical place to start seemed to be the International Women's Club. The group held monthly gatherings at the InterContinental Hotel. I was surprised at how many women attended the meeting and impressed with the group's businesslike organisation.

"Welcome, honey," greeted the cheery, plump Southern Belle who manned the newcomer's table. "You jes put yo name on this li'l piece o' paper, gimme 50 riyals, and then I can congratulate you on membership in the IWC."

The members I met were so friendly that I didn't need convincing. I paid my dues, accepted the offer of a pre-meeting cup of coffee and a donut, and researched the many information tables. The IWC newsletter advertised a comprehensive selection of club-sponsored courses and events. Through its auspices, women could meet other women and become involved in a variety of activities. Maybe I could have a life in Riyadh after all.

One of the club's projects that immediately appealed to me was updating the IWC Welcome to Riyadh handbook. Because I had been an editor and technical writer before relocating to Riyadh, this task suited my experience. The initial 12 volunteers eventually dwindled to three as the scope of the job became apparent. Liz Beckford, an energetic English woman who had lived in Africa, Sue Thomas, a statuesque Australian who was also my next-door neighbour, and I formed a small but efficient committee. We worked well together, made time for fun and discovered we had a lot in common, not least of which was an aversion to coffee mornings. Without this camaraderie we couldn't have succeeded in our task. Difficulties and disappointments were inevitable: few streets had names and no buildings had numbers. Changes occurred rapidly in Riyadh. Too often, no sooner had we gathered pertinent information, quite a feat in itself, than it was out of date. The embryonic telephone system and the absence of telephone books meant that everything needed a visit for verification. Still, the demands of the undertaking kept us occupied, made us familiar with the community at large and, more importantly, injected us into a wider network.

Just as Sean predicted, I became more at ease with other women. Through my chosen friends I met other interesting women. I attended obligatory lunches and coffee mornings once in a while but instead of regarding these occasions as tests of endurance, I now used them to greater advantage: as opportunities to build meaningful relationships and extend my growing web of contacts.

When I was able to look at the picture from a different perspective, I was astonished to find how much the picture changed for the better. I finally learned that what women have to say was something I wanted and needed to hear.

Chapter Ten

Language barriers and the fact that Saudi men seldom socialise with their wives in public meant that activities shared by Saudi and Western families were rare. Furthermore, high concrete walls around the city's villas and compounds discourage contact with outsiders. Yet, our Arabian experience surely couldn't be complete unless Sean and I got to know Saudis on a personal level. We remained determined. Eventually an opportunity presented itself. Saleh, one of Sean's Saudi colleagues approached him with a request.

"A friend of mine has asked me to help him find an English teacher. He's a businessman from a good family who's willing to pay whatever you ask. Would Kathy be interested in the job?"

Sean broached the subject with me at dinner that night.

"Did you tell him I don't have any qualifications?" I asked, helping myself to another portion of honeyed carrots.

"I mentioned it but I'll remind him if you like. More importantly," Sean pointed out with justifiable concern, "we have to consider that it might be a cultural blunder for a Western woman to teach English to a Saudi man in private."

Saleh eased our minds on the first stumbling block and laid the ground rules on the second.

"My friend already speaks a bit of English. He just wants to practise conversation. Sean's presence during the visits will make the situation perfectly acceptable."

Sean had no objection. After all, this was so far the only opportunity we had had to meet a Saudi socially.

One evening soon afterwards, Saleh brought Yousef to the house and introduced us.

"Good evening," Yousef said shyly as he extended his hand in greeting. We liked Yousef right away. There was kindness and honesty in his face; his thickset body radiated jolliness. Unfortunately, linguistic limitations hindered Yousef's eagerness. His frequently ill-chosen words and sometimes impossible pronunciation tested our comprehension skills to the limit that first evening.

As Yousef's vocabulary improved, the weekly visits became increasingly satisfying for everyone. Each of us was curious to know about the other's culture. One week, in response to our many questions about the Kingdom and its people, Yousef proposed a special outing.

"Why not my family and your family we go Eastern Province? We stay hotel, we go beach, we have fun. You be my guests," he offered, more than a little pleased at his perceived fluency.

"What a great idea," I responded enthusiastically. We hadn't been anywhere in the Kingdom yet. "It would be an honour to have you show us part of your country. But we shouldn't go as your guests."

We still weren't used to Saudi generosity and found it difficult to be willing recipients of unearned rewards. Yousef, however, would not be swayed on this matter.

According to the itinerary, we would spend the night in Hofuf, a lush oasis between Riyadh in the centre of the country and Al-Khobar on the Arabian Gulf coast. Travelling through the desert, albeit on a paved road, to an oasis had the makings of an odyssey. Of course, I imagined a positive odyssey.

On Thursday afternoon, Yousef arrived at our compound with his wife Hayat and infant daughter Ahlam. Hayat mirrored Yousef in stocky stature and apparent shyness. I suspected her timidity stemmed only from the fact that she spoke no English. Her curt commands to Yousef in Arabic indicated that she wore the pants in the family.

As we finished loading our 4-wheel drive, Yousef came to the back of the vehicle and forced a large cardboard box into a small clearing on the floor.

"What's this?" Sean asked

"These are emergency rations," Yousef replied with a broad grin.

Something about Yousef's tone of voice and twinkling eyes made Sean hesitate and then press for a better explanation.

"What kind of emergency rations, Yousef?"

Now it was Sean's tone of voice that made Yousef pause. Still smiling, Yousef carefully opened the lid of the box. Our stomachs did a small somersault when we saw the contents: 12 bottles of Johnny Walker Black Label.

"Oh, Yousef," Sean said quietly, "there's no way I'm going to carry a case of scotch in my car. We have to pass through roadblocks after we leave the city. If the police find this, the very least that will happen is that I'll be deported. This is not a good idea, my friend."

"No, no, *mafi mushkila*, no problem, Sean. I drive before you and tell guards you friend. Police maybe wanna check my car, not yours. You visitor. Really, no worry. I know my country."

Against his better judgment, Sean agreed. I'm not sure how the police didn't hear our hearts pounding but, with bored disinterest, they waved us through the checkpoints, exactly as Yousef had predicted.

By the time we arrived in Hofuf it was dark. Yousef had told us we would be staying at the town's best hotel. He didn't tell us he hadn't made a reservation.

"No worry. We go second-best hotel," Yousef assured us after being turned away from the fully-booked first choice.

As we approached a building that looked like it belonged on the set of a biblical movie, I assured myself that second best in an oasis was probably fine. Wrong. In the lobby, Tara became fascinated with a large cockroach edging its way across the reception counter. The desk clerk, clad in a grubby *thobe*, eyed us suspiciously. An overpowering inclination made me want to exit with all haste but we couldn't embarrass Yousef by refusing to stay, especially since the standards didn't seem to cause unease to him or his wife. Besides, where would we go?

"I'm not sure I can do this," I said to Sean in a shocked voice as we entered our room. "It's bad enough there's no carpet but it doesn't even look like the floor has been finished. What are all these gouges and holes in the concrete? And what are those blood-like stains?" I held Tara closer to me, instinctively trying to protect her from some invisible threat.

"Come on, Kathy, it's just for one night. Once we're asleep we won't be aware of the surroundings. It'll be morning in no time and we'll be on our way."

Rusted, popping bed springs forced us to put our mattress on the floor – in cockroach country. The nasty critters were big enough and the mattress shallow enough that they were almost at eye level.

"So close your eyes," was Sean's drowsy solution to the problem.

The next morning, after an uncomfortable night of frequently broken sleep, I wearily and cautiously made my way to the bathroom down the hall. There was no hot water, so I hastily splashed cold water on my face, getting the rest of me wet in the process. But why were my feet also sodden? Fascinated by this seemingly impossible occurrence, I looked under the sink – and discovered that the water ran directly from the basin onto the floor. The prospect of an imminent departure made me generous in my observation of the situation: in an oasis, I should be grateful for water, no matter where it comes from – or where it goes.

After a Spartan breakfast of fruit and bitter coffee, we left Hofuf, mentally promising ourselves that a return journey wouldn't be on the cards in the near future. We survived yet more police checks and arrived safely at the modern Al-Gosaibi hotel in Al-Khobar. Properly plumbed water in an ensuite bathroom, comfortable beds and clean rooms made us think we'd checked into heaven.

Yousef revealed his plans for dinner and a show in the hotel that evening. The invitation pleased – and confused – us.

"Do you mean 'show' as in 'entertainment'?" Sean queried. "Isn't that sort of thing illegal?"

Yousef laughed, happy he could reveal a different, more relaxed side of Saudi culture.

"Al-Khobar no like Riyadh. Here life easier. People live normal."

As though to emphasise this point, Yousef asked Sean to bring a bottle of scotch with him to dinner.

"I can't walk into the dining room with a bottle of scotch, Yousef. I'll be arrested right away. I definitely have to draw the line here."

"*Mafi mushkila.* Everyone bring own drink. You see. I come your room and collect bottle. No worry for you. No worry."

Yousef's confidence didn't reduce our anxiety, of course, but at least the evidence would be in his hands, not ours.

What a surprise to arrive in the hotel's packed dining room to a scene of quality entertainment openly enjoyed by an ebullient mix of Saudis and Westerners. The contrast between accepted practice in the Eastern Province and the ultra-conservative norms of Riyadh astounded us. As a nod to cultural courtesy, guests usually kept the alcohol under the tables, sometimes camouflaged in brown paper bags. Conversely, there was no subterfuge when glasses needed replenishing.

The depleted scotch bottle signalled the end of the evening. I worried that leaving with an empty bottle would be no less incriminating than arriving with a full one.

"No worry," came Yousef's clichéd reply, this time punctuated with a slur. "Just leave bottle under table. Waiters clean. *Mafi mushkila, insha'allah.*"

"But, Yousef, the hotel staff know we booked this table. They can trace the bottle back to us," I argued.

Yousef gave me a sloppy smile and limply waved his arm around the emptying room. Sure enough, bottles littered the floor. Nevertheless, Sean took the probably unnecessary precaution of depositing our bottle onto a pile under an adjacent table.

The weekend jaunt had shown us contradictory examples of Saudi life. Once again, it was clear that we could never become complacent about this mysterious land; it would always have a new surprise for us.

* * * *

Not all excursions with Yousef were fun. One Friday, Sean and Yousef went to Dirah *suq*.

"Oh-oh. Not so good," Yousef said, seeing unusually large crowds.

"What's wrong?" Sean asked.

"Today cut head in square."

"Really?"

Despite Sean's anti-death penalty stance, the grisly statement whetted his morbid curiosity. Yousef enquired from a man in the crowd the nature of the crime and passed on the information to Sean.

"Bad man. Take boy in desert, rape, kill. No good. I no like see this killing."

"I'm going to stay to have a look," Sean called to Yousef's retreating back. "We'll catch up later."

Sean edged forward. A wall of soldiers kept the crowd away from the centre of the large square. Men stood on the tops of cars and trucks in order to have a better view of the spectacle. Two police vans pulled up. A guard led the blindfolded prisoner to an appointed spot, made him kneel on the ground and pulled the neck of the young man's *thobe* down over his shoulders. The oversized swordsman raised the long, curved, silver blade. Despite the executioner's height and strength, it took him three swipes to sever the head. Blood gushed onto the pavement. Then, to Sean's surprise, a second prisoner appeared. Three swipes and he, too, had been despatched. The crowd, including women and children, cheered and spat in contempt. The vans removed the heads and bodies and everyone dispersed, satisfied that justice had been done.

"You like?" Yousef asked when Sean and he met up.

"Like? Of course not. Something made me watch but I would never want to repeat the experience. I know those men committed terrible crimes but I can't pretend to enjoy the punishment."

"I feel same way," Yousef agreed sombrely.

Sean had witnessed the graphic reality of 'eye-for-an-eye' retribution.

"There has to be a better way, Yousef."

"You probable right," Yousef said with resignation. "Someday maybe we learn to fix problem instead of punish symptom. For now, though, old ways still too strong.

* * * *

Although we looked upon our weekly get-togethers as a social encounter, Yousef saw them as a business deal and wanted to compensate us for our time and effort.

"Please, you must let me pay you. I am student, you are teacher. I must pay."

"That's rather difficult, Yousef," I tried to explain. "We aren't proper teachers and we have no idea what the going rate is for this sort of thing."

Yousef remained unconvinced until I finally promised to come up with a fee. I stalled for as long as possible. By the time he brought up the subject once again, this time with some urgency, we had established a comfortable relationship.

"Yousef," I explained gently, "if you are going to make such an effort to learn English, you should also learn something about our culture. You wouldn't want to accidentally offend anyone, would you?"

"Of course not," he replied with fervour. He could easily relate to this line of thought.

"Well, Yousef, in our society, friends don't accept money from one another just for being friends. It would hurt us if you insisted on paying for what we feel has become a friendship. Can you understand that?"

This was something that Yousef could understand very well; he accepted the situation without another word. In his own way, Yousef repaid us generously with his many kindnesses over the years. The subject of money never came up again and all of us were richer for it.

* * * *

Our Saudi circle unexpectedly expanded as a result of my walks with Oscar. Women were advised not to walk alone on Riyadh's streets but Oscar needed exercise; I counted on his black bulk to protect me from unwelcome approaches.

Oscar's early morning constitutional coincided with a Saudi man escorting his young brothers to school. His tall, good looks caught my attention. Cappuccino, I mused impertinently, as I observed his pleasant, mocha-tone face topped with a flowing white *ghutra*.

I responded politely to his daily greetings but, in the interests of propriety, didn't encourage conversation. Despite my aloofness, he introduced himself as 'Fahad' and persisted with his genial banter. Gradually I succumbed to his friendly nature and began to look forward to our brief chats. One morning he announced that he'd like to come to my house to meet my family.

Fahad's boldness surprised me. I had thought that Saudis would never be so forward, especially with a Western woman, unless they had ulterior motives. Yet, his unthreatening attitude made him seem harmless enough. I didn't want to offend Fahad or appear inhospitable but I also wouldn't extend such an invitation without consulting Sean.

"What's he like?" Sean enquired cautiously when I reported this development.

"He's friendly… obviously. It's hard to tell his age. He could be 18 or 28. His skin looks young but he has old eyes. I haven't got into any deep conversations with him, so I don't know much about who he is or what he does. He doesn't give off any bad vibes, though."

"Go ahead, then, invite him to come over tomorrow evening if he's free."

Fahad arrived in the company of his cousin Majed. Their command of English and the entertaining conversation inspired us to extend a further invitation. Fahad and Majed became regular visitors.

A few months into the relationship, Fahad introduced new faces: a police captain who sat inside with us or a bodyguard who stood watch outside.

"My father holds an important position in the National Guard," Fahad explained. "He likes me to always have someone with me."

Everyone seemed at ease with the arrangement, so we didn't question it.

When asked about his line of work, Fahad had always remained vague. Then, unexpectedly one evening, he revealed that he was in police intelligence. He glanced quickly at the police captain who had accompanied him on this visit and added, "We're not supposed to discuss what we do."

One day Fahad invited us to the Malaaz police station for afternoon tea. The 'station' was actually a large villa that had seen better days. Now it was dilapidated on the outside and shabby on the inside. The policemen's lethargic lack of urgency didn't inspire us with confidence in their crime prevention/solving abilities. We could find no fault, however, with their hospitality. After a courteous welcome an officer escorted us to Fahad.

We hid our astonishment only with great effort. Fahad sat on a rusty metal chair, staring blindly at the threadbare carpet. A solitary light bulb hanging from the ceiling on a twisted wire and a dirty telephone were the only other items in the dreary, square room. Fahad jumped up when he saw us, covering his embarrassment with unfailing charm.

"Excuse the room. I use it as a temporary office when I'm between assignments. Let's go into the garden. It's more pleasant out there. We can drink our tea to the music of the birds."

Several tall trees in the otherwise barren area provided welcome shade and a leafy home for flocks of noisy birds. I hadn't realised how much I had missed their song. A barefoot Pakistani man brought us small glasses of sweet mint tea as we relaxed on woven carpets that covered the ground. During the course of the conversation, I mentioned that I was going to go shopping at the gold *suq* for gifts for my family.

"One of my men has to go the Saudi Embassy in Ottawa next week. If you can get a package to me by then, I'll make sure it gets to wherever it needs to go."

"That's kind of you, Fahad," I said, "but it's too much of an imposition."

"Don't be silly. You've given me a second home. It would be an honour to do this small favour for you," he insisted.

Sean and I exchanged glances. We sometimes found it difficult to tread the fine line between refusing an offer and causing offence.

"Thank you," Sean responded. "If you're sure that it won't be a problem, we'd appreciate it."

A few days later we were back at the police station with a thick, padded envelope laden with gold jewellery. When my parents didn't receive anything after a couple of weeks, we mentioned our concern to Fahad.

"Don't worry," he assured us. "The fellow had his trip postponed. He's leaving next week."

The excuses continued. Then Fahad could no longer be contacted. Majed came alone to visit us one day.

"I tried to retrieve your package for you," Majed announced, obviously suffering acute discomfort to be the bearer of such news. "Fahad told me he had sold the gold to meet some of his expenses. I'm so terribly sorry. What Fahad has done is wrong and it casts shame on our family. You have to forget about it, though. His father is powerful. If you pursue the matter, there could be problems for you. Please just let it rest."

"I can't believe he would be so dishonourable," I said, refusing to immediately accept what had long been suspected.

"In the circumstances, I feel I should tell you about Fahad. You've both been so kind to us. It's not fair to deceive you any longer. Fahad is not a good person. He doesn't work for the police. He's a prisoner."

"What?" Sean and I exclaimed.

"How on earth could he be a prisoner when he visited us all the time?" Sean asked in a shocked voice.

"In recent months he never came to your house by himself, did he?"

"That's true," Sean admitted. "But in the Arab culture uninvited guests are a common, almost expected, occurrence. His various companions never made us suspicious. What crime did he commit?"

"He killed his mother-in-law," Majed answered bluntly. His announcement met stunned silence. Neither of us could digest the fact that we had been entertaining a murderer in our home.

"My God!" I said, feeling numb.

"If he committed a murder," Sean said, taking a more practical approach, "how is he allowed out of jail? I thought murderers were beheaded here."

"I told you," Majed repeated patiently, "his father's influential. Besides, his mother-in-law was German. That puts a different slant on things."

"How?" I asked, my curiosity piqued.

Majed shrugged his shoulders. "Well, she wasn't a Saudi, so that can change the situation."

My instinct told me that an accurate explanation might embarrass Majed further so I didn't pursue the matter. We had enough to absorb without delving into the quirks of Saudi law, the xenophobic attitude of some Saudis and the convolutions of international diplomacy.

We never heard from Fahad again. When we repeated the story to a friend, he told us we were lucky to lose only gold. We felt we had lost more.

* * * *

It seemed incongruous to live in Saudi Arabia and help Saudis with their English when we should be learning Arabic. The Berlitz course we had taken in San Francisco proved woefully inadequate outside the classroom. The different accent and impractical vocabulary of our Egyptian instructor didn't transfer well to the streets of Riyadh.

Sean's long work hours made it difficult for him to devote the necessary time to language study. I had no such excuse. When Vicki Callen, a favourite tennis buddy, heard that I was looking for a good Arabic teacher, she suggested Margot Daher.

"She's Syrian," Vicki said as we relaxed after a game of tennis. "Everyone at the bank uses her. She's not cheap but her success rate justifies the cost. I'll give you her number if you like."

Vicki's husband Mike was the head of Saudi-American Bank. Their upscale compound had the tennis courts where I took my lessons. Tennis had brought Vicki and me together but Vicki's mildly eccentric, humorously non-conformist character bonded us. I valued Vicki's recommendation.

Margot had an easy and logical system. I made rapid progress. It wasn't long before I wanted to supplement the theory with practical experience. But how? The few Saudis we knew spoke good English; it would have been difficult to discipline myself to speak Arabic with them.

Ironically, the solution appeared at one of those women's coffee mornings that I usually tried to avoid. One of the guests was the wife of Sami Arab, Bechtel's government relations man. Samira didn't speak a word of English, yet she didn't look awkward or uncomfortable in this *mêlée* of foreign ladies. Her large, intelligent, black eyes continually scanned the room, trying to absorb everything the novel environment had to offer. She was probably only in her early 20s but she seemed older and wiser. Her serene nature attracted me. The coffee morning had nearly ended before I found the courage to approach her.

"*Sabah al-khair,*" I said self-consciously. Some of the other women discreetly peered at me over the rims of their coffee cups, wondering what I could possibly have to say to this quiet Saudi. I introduced myself and, in simplistic Arabic, told her about meeting her husband at the airport when I first arrived in Riyadh. A perfect Colgate smile acknowledged my effort.

"*Sabah al-noor,*" Samira responded pleasantly, as though it were the most natural thing in the world that I would cross the room to talk to her – in Arabic. Her melodious voice perfectly complemented her beautiful face. "Please, sit beside me. Tell me about yourself."

Our few minutes of conversation convinced me that I had found someone who could be a friend – if only we could talk to each other without a language barrier! I was determined to overcome this inconvenience. Samira was a perfect candidate for my Daring Plan.

Sean acted as a go-between and asked Sami if Samira would be willing to visit me one morning a week so I could speak Arabic with her. Based on the laboured conversation that paraded my inadequacies, Samira knew it would be slow going. Nevertheless, she agreed to participate. She offered to begin immediately.

That first morning was an ordeal of the highest order. More than ever, I could sympathise with Yousef's emotions during his initial visits to our place. With pained perseverance, relieved with frequent bouts of laughter, we spent three long hours trying to communicate. To add to my difficulties of a limited vocabulary, I had to attune my ear to Samira's local pronunciation. Amazingly, Samira offered to renew our efforts the following week. She invited me to her house.

Not wanting to have to suffer another morning of mental exhaustion, I studied even harder than usual. This time I had the new vocabulary learned from Samira, which Margot clarified and expanded upon during my next lessons. That, plus the novelty of visiting a Saudi home, made a striking difference.

Samira and her husband and son lived in a two-bedroom apartment. She didn't have to contend with decorating disasters because there was almost no furniture. We sat cross-legged on the floor, drank cardamom coffee from tiny cups and ate a tasty selection of savouries and sweets with our fingers.

As the relationship developed, Samira and I eagerly anticipated our weekly visits, one time at Samira's place and then at mine. I planned conversation scripts and made sure I knew enough vocabulary to keep the pace going. Samira introduced me to some of her friends and to many of her customs. Eventually I felt comfortable enough to broach intimate subjects.

"What do you people do about hair removal," I asked Samira one day. Razor blades surely aren't part of a Bedouin's baggage. "Arab women have hairless skin. What's the secret?"

"We use sugar water," Samira explained. "If you like, I'll remove your hair for you."

This offer took me off guard. It was fine collecting information. It was also fine, up to a point, having first-hand experiences. But did I want this one?

"On what part of my body are you planning to remove hair?" I asked hesitantly.

Samira laughed and pointed to my clean-shaven legs. "First you'll have to let the hair grow. Maybe a couple of weeks."

"Samira," I gasped, "I'm at the pool or on the tennis court every day with bare legs. If I don't shave, they'll be HAIRY." The thought appalled me.

"It's up to you," she shrugged. Then she smiled teasingly. "I thought you welcomed the unknown."

Right. Dammit.

I gave up swimming and tennis as soon as my legs became noticeably hirsute.

"How much longer do we have to wait, Samira? I'm going to have to start braiding the hair on my legs if you don't hurry up."

Finally Samira gave the procedure the green light.

"First we melt the sugar in the water," Samira instructed as she stirred the mixture on the stove.

"You're not going to put that boiling liquid on my legs are you?" I asked, justifiably concerned.

"No, we let it cool a little first. As it cools it becomes syrupy," came the ever-patient reply.

"Cool a little? Let's let it cool a lot." I was becoming less enthusiastic about this experience the closer we got to it. Samira said nothing but her glance told me to get a grip on myself.

"OK", she said at last, "lift your leg onto the edge of the table. And keep still. I'm going to spread the mixture with this spatula and then quickly rip off the paste."

Up went my leg and bang, bang pounded my heart. This experiment looked less and less appealing but pride made me go through with it. I couldn't let her think Canadian women were a bunch of sissies. I said little except "Jeez, Samira, that syrup is bloody hot!"

Samira persevered with compassion if not finesse. After mild agony and no small amount of gooey mess, I had hairless legs – which had lots of red blotches and were also missing small patches of skin here and there. This was a tradition best left to the natives.

In addition to the harsh lesson in local depilatory techniques, Samira gave me valuable insights into Saudi culture and how Saudi women view life. I questioned some of the conventions, most notably concerning the *abaya* and veil.

"Would you walk naked in the streets?" Samira asked with a hint of annoyance in her voice.

"Of course not," I said, surprised at her reaction.

"If I appeared in public without my *abaya* and *tarha* I would feel naked. I couldn't bear to have men degrade me with their stares. I've seen the way some women dress in the West, the way they demean themselves. This is not the Saudi way."

"Women can dress modestly without wearing an *abaya*, Samira. And it wouldn't take men and women long to get used to unveiled faces. Most other Muslim countries don't have this restriction. There are even parts of Saudi where it's not required. Shouldn't people have choices?"

"There may be Saudi women who think like you do but I think most women here believe it is not yet time to cast aside the traditions which have evolved over many generations. I know our ways are different and sometimes imperfect," she added more kindly, "but that doesn't make them wrong. Does it not occur to you that we Saudis find many of *your* customs strange and unacceptable?"

The question made me stop and think – and reminded me to view situations from other perspectives before jumping to conclusions. It humbled me that this woman with no formal education had to prompt me about such basic concepts as understanding and tolerance.

* * * *

Our first invitation as a couple to a Saudi home came from Rashid Al-Rayyan, one of the contractors Sean oversaw on the airport project.

"Do you think we'll have to sit on the floor?" I quizzed Sean when he told me about the invitation. "Will we eat with our hands?"

Samira's apartment could best be described as warm Spartan. Rashid lived on a different social scale. Would that make a difference, I wondered?

"I don't know. I've never been to his house. Rashid's pretty sophisticated, though. I'm guessing he's probably got plenty of furniture." Sean loosened and removed his tie and tried to ignore Oscar's nudges and whines. It was time for his evening desert run and Oscar didn't like to be kept waiting.

"Will I be able to eat with you and Rashid or will I be relegated to some sectioned-off area with the women?" I asked with sudden concern. My temperament wouldn't take kindly to being 'relegated' anywhere I didn't want to go!

"Kathy, I don't know the answers to these questions any better than you do." Oscar was doing his best to distract Sean from my petty concerns. "It's not like we can consult the neighbours about this. Not many foreigners get invited into Saudi homes."

Probably to bring a halt to my inane questions, Sean gave Oscar the welcome departure signal, leaving me to devote my imaginative energy to the upcoming lunch.

Rashid's home, as it turned out, was perfectly normal. It was almost disappointing to find that they lived much the same way as we did – but with nicer furniture. I suppose I yearned for something utterly exotic, like Nubian slaves serving us bowls of fresh camel milk, or some such thing.

When lunch was announced, we were led to a long dining room table with places set for only three people.

"Won't your wife be joining us?" I asked. We had met Mrs Al-Rayyan when we arrived but hadn't seen her since.

"No," Rashid replied, "she's supervising the food preparation in the kitchen."

When there are guests, it is the custom in Arab families for the men to eat separately from the women. My inclusion at the men's table was obviously a concession.

Suddenly the kitchen door swung open. A large, black, buxom servant appeared with a tray of steaks. Multiple plates of salads and other savouries followed, carried by more female servants. They didn't resemble the tall, handsome Nubians of my imagination but their number and the sheer quantity of food astonished me. We ate until we thought we'd burst – and then a towering platter of roasted chickens appeared.

"Rashid," I gasped, abandoning any pretence of tact and seriously disturbed by what appeared to be blatant excess, "how can anyone possibly eat this much?"

"Don't worry," he laughed, "nothing gets thrown away. We have a large household and the staff enjoys all the leftovers." Still seeing concern on my face, he explained further. "It would be a grave dishonour to me if I felt that any of my guests had not had enough to eat. It is more important for an Arab host to know there was no want rather than to worry about the unlikely possibility of waste."

We forced ourselves to sample some of the delicious chicken and then deliberately left food on the plate. We had surpassed our comfortable limit but we wanted Rashid to know that we had absorbed the subtle lesson he had taught us about Saudi etiquette.

* * * *

Cross-cultural friendships in 1970s Riyadh were few and far between. Our determination to know Saudis was regarded sceptically by most of our Western friends. No doubt their fear of being reported to the police for having alcohol in the house nurtured much of the mistrust. Unwittingly, Yousef caused a surge in this reticence within our social circle.

"*Ilhamdullilah* you safe, Kathy," Yousef said fervently when he came to our house shortly after I returned from having had an operation in Montreal. "Thanks God you home. I so happy, I have desert party for you. You invite 100 best friends."

"Thank you so much, Yousef, but good grief, I'd be hard pressed to find 100 individuals, let alone 'best friends'."

I passed Yousef a plate of homemade mini quiches as I marshalled my thoughts. I knew I'd never be able to get so many people together for a Saudi-hosted event. How on earth could I get out of this without appearing ungrateful?

"Actually, Yousef," I improvised, "many of our friends are out of the country at the moment. It would be a shame for you to go to so much trouble for only a few people, wouldn't it?'

Yousef helped himself to several quiches at the same time. He loved the many Western foods to which we introduced him. After an unnerving pause, he announced, "Pick day, please. Invite people who here. Party be for everyone. Bring kids." I gave a weak smile and nodded.

Going through my contact list, I noted there were about 12 families who might be suitable invitees. I began making my calls. Almost everyone came up with a reason, veiled or otherwise, why they couldn't attend. In the end, only four couples agreed to accompany us. This just wasn't good enough. Yousef would surely lose face with such a low turnout.

I started redialling numbers. This time, I vowed, there would be no asking; anyone who wanted to remain on our dinner list was going to show up unless they had an ironclad excuse. This method, thankfully, got a higher success rate: nine families. It was a far cry from '100 best friends', but at least there was now a respectable number of warm bodies.

We met at our compound and then travelled in convoy to Yousef's desert camp. Everyone poured out of their 4-wheel drives wondering what to expect. The older kids soon lost their inhibitions when they saw the Saudis youths kicking a soccer ball. The younger children revelled in the freedom of the open desert, to them a giant sand box. Sean and I introduced Yousef to his guests. His offer of scotch impressed the men. The picnic was underway.

An important distinction of Saudi picnics is that there are no sandwiches. It's meat on the hoof – until the throat is slit and it's immediately prepared for cooking over a large fire.

"*Mafi mushkila*, Kathy," Yousef assured me, "no kill here. I know you no like. I get special lamb cooked in King's ovens. Very delicious. Very, very special for you." Dear Yousef beamed with pride.

When it was finally time to eat, everyone hungrily gathered around the huge trays piled high with rice and an aromatic whole lamb. Plates and cutlery were noticeably absent.

As the guest of honour, I suddenly had a terrible thought.

"Yousef, I wouldn't want to offend you in any way, but before you present me with an eyeball, I have to ask you to consider that this might result in an involuntary and embarrassing physical response on my part." I paled at the thought of trying to ingest this prized morsel.

"No worry, Kathy," Yousef laughed heartily. "I know you too well. No killing, no eyeballs."

"Or any other balls, please, Yousef," I added as a precaution, in case I had overlooked an obscure tribal tradition.

Everyone agreed that the delicious lunch was truly fit for a king. The charm and generous hospitality of Yousef and his friends had successfully bridged the cultural chasm. Never again did I have to twist arms to mix Western and Saudi friends.

* * * *

My excursions into town exposed me to the olde worlde atmosphere of cultural costumes. The spectrum went from Saudi women enveloped in black cloth from head to toe to colourful turbans and rich flowing robes. Jeans and t-shirts were definitely out of place in this antique land.

One evening as I picked up toys in the living room, I shared with Sean a thought that had been on my mind.

"I've never taken any special interest in men's hair – unless it looks particularly weird or wonderful."

Sean glanced up from his newspaper, suspicious about where my musing might lead. I ignored the look and babbled on while reaching under the couch to retrieve a stuffed animal.

"Saudi men, though, arouse in me a distracting curiosity. I've never seen one without his head covering. What goes on under that piece of cloth? Are they bald? Do they have comb-overs? Ponytails? It's a delicious enigma."

Slowly but firmly Sean lowered his newspaper.

"Never, I repeat *never*, ask a Saudi to remove his *ghutra*. It's not like a hat. It's part and parcel of their cultural garb."

"But surely they must take off the *ghutra* at some point during the day," I responded. This new dictum fanned the fire of my interest.

"Of course. In the privacy of their homes or when they're in a relaxed environment with friends. They do not, however, remove it to indulge the inquisitiveness of foreign women."

Subject closed. I had been warned. Over the years various Saudi friends satisfied this quirky fascination. Alas, each and every one of them had perfectly normal hair.

Chapter Eleven

Tara was sick. Nothing serious, we believed, but enough to warrant confirmation by a professional. A work colleague recommended a Lebanese general practitioner.

"A couple of people in the office have used him. No one's died so far." He was only half joking. In the late 1970s in Saudi Arabia, hospitalisation usually meant exposure to unsanitary conditions and well-intentioned but substandard care. Relatively minor illnesses or injuries could result in death due to negligent or incorrect treatment.

The doctor's office was located in a tumbledown building overlooking Riyadh's infamous Chop Square, where the condemned lose their heads to the swordsman on Fridays.

We climbed three flights of chipped and cracking concrete stairs, fumbling all the while up the darkened stairwell. Provision for lighting existed, but no one had replaced the burned out bulbs.

"Are we sure we want to go through with this?" I whispered to Sean.

I positioned myself firmly in the middle of the stairs, avoiding the grime-caked walls.

"We're absolutely sure," Sean replied with conviction. "Tara's not well and she needs medical attention. The doctor's probably fine. He can't control building maintenance."

But he can control conditions in his own office, I thought. He didn't bother. We stared incredulously at the dirty and disintegrating state of the ceiling, walls, floor and furniture.

"At the moment, only Tara is sick," I said in a low voice. "Can you guarantee we'll walk out of here in the same state of health we were in before we arrived?"

"One thing's certain," Sean muttered in response, "Never again will I complain about the sterile atmosphere of doctors' waiting rooms at home."

Just as we came to a mutual, silent agreement about the folly of this visit, the doctor emerged from his consulting room. Sensing our discomfort, his short, round figure immediately duckwalked toward us. He extended his chubby hand in greeting and ushered us into his cluttered office ahead of the multitude of hacking and rheumy patients who seemed unconcerned about their surroundings. After a brief and admittedly satisfactory consultation he diagnosed a common virus, scribbled a prescription and dismissed us, reaching up to give Sean a friendly pat on the back. Tara made a full and speedy recovery; we prayed for continued good health so we wouldn't have to repeat this exercise.

Although we never returned to his office, we did have further contact when I became ill with a stomach malady. The severe pain precluded me from going to the doctor, so he kindly volunteered to come to me.

"Where does it hurt, my dear?" the doctor enquired with sincere consideration and a consoling bedside manner.

With an agony of movement, I placed my hands across my abdomen.

"Are you on any form of contraceptive?" he asked

"Yes," I gasped, "the Pill."

Having taken the Pill on and off for several years, I couldn't imagine that it would suddenly give me such violent side effects. But he was the doctor; perhaps there were new developments in this field?

"Are you not aware that God has put women on earth in order to have children?"

Now he had my attention. Surely it was impossible that this gentle man was giving me a religious reprimand! Not even our fervent Muslim hosts had tried to impose religion like this Lebanese Christian was trying to do.

"It is wrong to inhibit His will in any way. Perhaps He has meted out this punishment to you for not allowing many babies to come. In the Holy Scriptures it says...".

He exposed me to endless biblical quotations but no medical diagnosis.

The intense pain became of secondary importance when I realised that getting well would depend primarily on sheer willpower! Fortunately my mystery ailment disappeared – in spite of 'medical' attention.

* * * *

Riyadh's few good hospitals restricted admission to individuals qualified to use the facilities. For instance, the Military Hospital accepted only armed forces personnel, employees from certain companies working on military contracts and life-or-death emergency situations. In most hospitals, administrative staff had the discretion to admit non-eligible patients but too often they followed a policy of 'wealth before health': rich and influential patients with minor ailments got admitted more readily than ordinary but seriously ill people.

Medical evacuation was standard procedure for emergencies or complicated cases. Even something as routine as pregnancy could become a matter of planning and coordination. When expat women wondered where they were going to have their babies, the question didn't just refer to what hospital but to which country: stay in Saudi or go home.

In 1977, I became pregnant with our second child. My decision to remain in Riyadh for the delivery was made partly for logistical reasons: it would have been too disruptive to our family life to camp out in Canada or Ireland for a couple of months waiting for the birth. More telling, however, was the fact I now felt Riyadh was home. This was where I wanted to be; I didn't need to go elsewhere.

Despite my excellent general health and normal pregnancy, my considerate gynaecologist referred me to the quintessential comfort and care of the King Faisal Specialist Hospital and Research Centre. At that time and for several years afterwards, KFSH gloried in its status as one of the most advanced hospitals in the world. Originally built for the Saudi royal family, whose members are legion, the late King Faisal donated this venerable facility to the people of Saudi Arabia for the treatment of rare diseases or illnesses not cared for elsewhere in the Kingdom. Since I fell into neither of these categories, I had to get the agreement of the KFSH admissions physician; he might not be so accommodating.

My first visit to the hospital left me in a state of awe. The government had spared no expense on this masterpiece that looked like a luxurious grand hotel. The reception area had magnificent mosaics on the walls and thick carpets on the floor. Richly upholstered furniture graced an impressive lounge. Even the elevators were striking with their plush, carpet-lined walls. Gold leaf ceilings adorned the doctors' research library. Needless to say, all the equipment represented state-of-the-art technology.

I presented myself in front of the tasteful reproduction desk of the admissions doctor, a rotund and self-important Egyptian. He made me feel as though I was being vetted for acceptance into a posh country club. He scrutinised me from under his heavy black eyebrows, reviewed the referral notes from my doctor and asked some token questions. Then, almost grudgingly, he nodded his shiny bald head in approval. I was in.

In such a hallowed environment, you never knew whom you might meet. One afternoon, as Sean and I arrived at the hospital for my monthly pre-natal checkup, we saw a black Rolls Royce parked by the entrance. It flew the Spanish flag,

"The King of Spain is in Riyadh on an official visit," Sean said. "He must be touring the hospital today."

There was no security detail to shoosh us away, so we waited for a while, hoping to see the King as he left. Eventually, worried that I would be late for my appointment, we abandoned our post.

After seeing the doctor, I eagerly checked to see if the Rolls was still there. It was. Noticing a group of women standing in the lobby, I zeroed in on an elegant lady holding a cup of tea.

"Hello," I said cheerfully. "Are you waiting to see the King of Spain?"

She smiled at me and her eyes twinkled. As she opened her mouth to speak, the woman beside her frostily informed me that I was addressing the Queen of Spain.

* * * *

The difference between giving birth to Tara in San Francisco and having a baby in the desert hospital of a developing nation was remarkable. Riyadh came out way ahead. In San Francisco I had shared a room with a woman who, when she didn't have visitors for hours at a time, watched TV with the volume on high. Sean brought me home-cooked meals to replace the dreadful hospital food. In Riyadh, I had a pleasant, private room equipped with high-tech gadgets. Delicious meals arrived with gold-plated cutlery. A host of English, Scottish and Irish nurses, delighted to have an English-speaking patient, pampered me royally. Too soon, I had to relinquish my in-patient status; reluctantly I left this lap of luxury with newborn Kieran and retuned to our comparatively humble home.

Sensing a good investment opportunity, Saudi businessmen soon began to open modern hospitals and clinics. In a country more accustomed to folk therapies, including drastic techniques such as cauterization, this development was the first occasion for many Saudis to experience Western medicine. Acceptance of an onslaught of new-fangled methods and technologies wasn't easy for some patients. One doctor had an elderly woman in his office who didn't want to go for an X-ray.

"Everything will be all right," he reassured her. "I'll take you there myself."

They walked toward the elevator together. Suddenly the old lady stopped in her tracks.

"I'm not going into that thing," she stated adamantly.

"Why not?" the doctor enquired.

"Because I saw another woman get in and when the door opened again, she had disappeared."

* * * *

Although the new hospitals had the best equipment money could buy, work conditions were not always ideal. Patients could be a considerable threat to job security. Many a nurse was summarily dismissed and deported because she unwittingly ruffled the feathers of a difficult VIP patient.

Doctors are even more at risk. No doctor likes to see his patient die but in Saudi Arabia a strong ulterior motive attaches itself to the sentiment: even natural deaths can be imprisonable offenses.

We heard a grim tale about a National Guard soldier who brought his ailing father on a long, bumpy journey across the desert to Riyadh's Military Hospital. By the time they arrived, the father evidently had been dead for some time.

"Please try to do something," the distraught man begged. "I've come so far. You're my only hope. Please give my father a chance."

As a humane gesture rather than medical wisdom, the hospital emergency team made every effort to revive the old man. The soldier finally accepted that his father had died – but he charged the entire team with killing the old man with the cardiac defibrillators.

"I saw with my own eyes the body of my father responding to the equipment. He jumped on the table when you put those things on his chest. He must have been alive then and he is dead now. The only answer is that you killed him with your machines. You have murdered my father and I will see that you suffer just as you made him suffer."

The emergency team was incarcerated until everything could be sorted out. The hospital eventually deported the senior doctor.

Because Islam does not allow post-mortems, there is no way to prove the cause of death. No matter how outrageous they might be, allegations tend to stand, particularly if the accuser is an influential Saudi and the accused is a foreigner.

* * * *

With so many foreign medical staff, translators play a vital role in the diagnosis and treatment of patients. Dr. Derrick Barnes, a dentist friend, always called his interpreter an 'interrupter' because he had a timely habit of interrupting and putting him on the right track. A good example of this was the story Derrick told us about a patient who fainted following a local anaesthetic.

"I revived her, removed her tooth without a problem and then sent her home with routine instructions to have something to eat. On the way, the hot car with no air conditioning brought on another fainting spell. The husband brought her back to the surgery. After reviving her again, I gave her some glucose. I repeated the need for her to eat something."

When the husband and wife showed up a third time, the interpreter asked to let him give his own explanation to the man. With a glow of comprehension, the husband left with his wife and didn't return. Derek asked how he finally get through to the man.

"Very simple, Doctor," explained the translator. "I said that an empty sack always falls down. If the sack is filled with rice, it will stand up all by itself. The man has taken his wife home to fill her with rice."

* * * *

Dental practices, at first, did not keep pace with the burgeoning medical business. Investors reasoned this avenue wouldn't be as lucrative because many Saudis went to a dentist only when they were already in pain, not for regular checkups.

Part of the reason for a studied avoidance of dentists could be attributed to lingering old wives' tales. One superstition concerns a relationship between the removal of teeth from a pregnant woman and the sex of her unborn child. Our dentist friends became justifiably nervous when they heard about the consequences suffered by a colleague who removed the tooth of a pregnant Saudi woman. Eventually the woman gave birth to a healthy baby girl. The angry father pressed charges against the unfortunate dentist, claiming that the child had originally been a boy but the removal of the tooth had altered his sex! The dentist spent three weeks in jail.

As well as myths, dentists often had to cope with the rigours of tradition. Orthodox Muslim women insist on jealously guarding the concealment of all regions above the upper lip. Dentists, hindered by folds of black veil that the woman tightly raises to a position of minimum exposure, require dexterity to complete work successfully.

Additionally, the dentist must cope with a woman's husband or male members of her family who crowd into the surgery to ensure that she, and therefore the family, is not dishonoured.

The population, however, is not without a tradition of dental hygiene. The *miswak*, an ingenious and aromatic 'toothbrush', comes from the roots of certain trees. The most favoured of these is the arak tree. When first purchased, usually from vendors who sit cross-legged on city sidewalks, the *miswak* resembles a small stick about six inches long and the thickness of a woman's finger. After soaking one end of the twig in water for several hours to make it more pliable, about 1/2 inch of the bark is removed from the moistened end. Gentle gnawing on the exposed fibres softens them sufficiently to massage the gums and brush the teeth. Scientific studies confirm that the *miswak*'s antiseptic properties naturally destroy oral bacteria and remove plaque.

Chapter Twelve

Housekeeping in Riyadh's desert environment was an endless battle. The slightest breeze blew thin, beige veils of powder-fine sand under and around the poorly constructed doors and windows. Sudden desert winds known as *shamaals* left more conspicuous deposits. Only a couple of hours after polishing them to perfection, the glass tops of our living room tables would wear a layer of dust thick enough in which to write legible messages. This giant beach was not a housekeeper's friend.

"Why don't you think about getting a houseboy?" Sean suggested.

"It's hard to justify the luxury since I'm at home all day," I answered. *With not much else to do,* I thought.

"The going rate's about ten riyals an hour. That's less than three dollars. It's an affordable luxury, sweetheart. Besides, domestic chores seem to suppress your usual good humour."

And I'm getting tired of coming home to a complaining wife, he might have added.

"I'm not sure I'd feel comfortable alone in the house with a strange man cleaning and ironing."

"You choose, Kathy. Give up a little privacy and get a lot of freedom or resign yourself to housework on a full-time basis. Just don't keep me updated with frivolous statistics on dust build-up or how fast cockroaches appear when food is dropped. Make a decision and live with it."

Now there's an ultimatum. I had to admit Sean was right. What might otherwise seem like an indulgence takes on a dimension of virtual necessity in Riyadh. It was time to call in reinforcements.

William, a young Indian man, worked at Bechtel's bachelor-status compound but he had free time in the afternoons. During the interview, I asked if he could spare two hours three times a week. His head made a curious bobbing motion, like a floater on rough water. Since a smile accompanied the dizzying movement, I took the answer to be 'yes'.

William worked out so well that we readily agreed to William's request to employ a friend of his who wanted some part-time work. Nazeer looked after the downstairs and washed windows and floors. William cleaned upstairs and did the ironing. This minimum interference gave maximum results.

In no time at all we wondered how we could ever have lived without the joy of household help. For a small outlay of cash, Sean enjoyed freshly ironed clothes, a clean house and a spouse who didn't feel and look like a skivvy.

About a year later, a departing Canadian acquaintance was trying to find a replacement family for Maria, her Sudanese maid. She persuaded me that it was time for us to move to the next stage of help: a live-in maid.

Now it was just a matter of bringing Sean on board. I waited until after dinner to give my well-prepared sales pitch that included the lure of a built-in babysitter. We had two young children and an active social life. William frequently babysat but Sean had to pick him up and take him home. A live-in maid would bring a welcome end to these journeys.

Sean glanced at me over the top of his newspaper. "A live-in maid probably won't cost a lot more than two houseboys three times a week. For me, the babysitting advantage is the selling point. Go ahead and hire her if you think she's OK."

Maria had been highly recommended as "a superb housekeeper and great with children." Perfect. Or so I thought. To my dismay, Maria's performance fell far short of her references.

The euphoria of having a live-in maid dissipated when excusable blunders during the adjustment period developed into major and persistent aggravations. Her inventiveness in finding places to misplace items wore me down. I learned to look for tarragon vinegar where the floor cleaners were kept and to find olive oil in the refrigerator. Too often my stomach muscles churned when I opened a cupboard door. What surprise would I find? What wouldn't be there that should be there? Sometimes her foibles were expensive: one day she stacked a dozen Waterford crystal glasses and then couldn't unstack them without breaking or scratching most of them. When an ulcer threatened to become a by-product of Maria's employment, I came to the uncomfortable conclusion that we would have to fire her.

"What will happen to Maria?" I worried. "Will she have to wander the streets, homeless and jobless? The woman is irritating but she doesn't deserve a fate like that."

The prospect of firing Maria had become as unsettling as the unacceptable alternative of keeping her.

We had decided to use the quiet time after dinner to tackle the issue head on. Sean poured himself a glass of wine as he gave the matter some thought.

"Maria's well plugged into the Sudanese network. She'll be fine. I'm more concerned about the possible legal ramifications."

Maria was a local hire. This meant that we paid her substantially more than if we had brought her into the country under our sponsorship but we didn't have the liabilities of a sponsor: we didn't have to buy her a ticket to go home each year and we weren't responsible for any of her expenses except food. If the work of local hires is unsatisfactory, they can be terminated at no cost to the employer other than wages due. The concern was that a disgruntled employee might register a complaint, justified or not, against the employer with the labour office. No one wanted to attract undue official attention.

"I think the best thing to do for all concerned is to give her a month's salary in lieu of notice." Sean had a knack for anticipating problems and taking sensible steps to avoid them.

All that remained was the unpleasant task of letting her go. Fortunately, Maria spared us any awkward conflicts. Her solitary act of 'getting it right' was to resign.

"Madam, although it make me much sad to leave such happy home, my mother badly sick and need me. I must return Sudan by end of week."

"I'm so sorry, Maria. We'll miss you," I lied.

"But, Madam, you no upset having no one clean for you?" she asked.

"Of course it will be an inconvenience. Nevertheless, your first duty must be to your mother. Go with my blessing. We'd like to give you an extra month's salary to help with your expenses." This was a win-win situation!

At the time, I believed Maria's explanation for leaving. Later on, however, I suspected that this may have been a tactful excuse to remove herself from a disintegrating relationship. Saudi Arabia was teaching me that not all cultures believe honesty is always the best policy; avoiding the prospect of offending someone usually validates the necessity of a white lie. Shamefully, it took several years for me to recognise this basic consideration, accept it, and judiciously incorporate the attitude into my own behaviour, albeit in irregular and imperfect fashion.

As liberating as it was to get rid of Maria, her absence left me back at square one as far as household help was concerned. My faithful houseboys returned on a temporary basis. Despite the difficulties with Maria, I had become hooked on the convenience of live-in help. Invisible tom-toms beating out the news of Job Available resulted in a tall, black, scar-faced man appearing at our door.

"My sister can work for you," he solemnly announced.

Not wanting to have another Maria on my hands, I insisted on interviewing the woman. We met the next day. I could find no fault with Letai, a painfully slender Eritrean girl in her early 20s who exuded calm and ability. The sticking point in the negotiations was salary. Her brother stoutly defended a premium rate of 1,300 riyals a month, saying Letai worked hard and was trustworthy. I held my position at 1,100 riyals, arguing that she wouldn't be overburdened with chores. As a concession, I offered to give her a raise after three months if she was as good as advertised. The brother wouldn't compromise – until I got up to walk out. This wasn't a bargaining ploy on my part; I simply refused to repeat my previous mistakes. His sudden agreement to my conditions, however, taught me to keep this trick up my sleeve.

Letai moved in the following afternoon. I introduced her to precocious but manageable 2-year-old Tara and then took her upstairs to meet cute but hyperactive 7-month-old Kieran.

Kieran outdid himself for his first encounter with Letai. I opened the door to the darkened room where he supposedly had been napping. An overpowering odour momentarily immobilised me.

"I. Don't. Believe. It," I breathed, identifying the source of the smell. "Honestly, Letai, Kieran has *never* done anything like this."

And I can't imagine why he would choose this afternoon to take the contents of his dirty diaper and paint his curtains, wall, bed and mattress.

Amazingly, Letai didn't miss a beat. With confident authority, she asked me where to find a bucket, soap and rags so she could clean the crime scene. Kieran had met his match in unflappable Letai; they remained fast friends for the duration of her employment. Letai's salary jumped to the premium rate the following month.

* * * *

Like most villas in Riyadh, ours included a servant's quarters. This small but comfortable accommodation behind the house had a bed-sitting room and bathroom. To Tara and Kieran, the 'little house' was a source of discovery and delight. Here they could evade parental discipline and enter a world where our resident maid and her friends revelled in Kieran's impishness and Tara's enthusiasm for makeup and dressing up. In this happy sanctuary they mastered the arts of eating hot foods with their hands and communicating in Eritrean.

Because the 'little house' had no kitchen, the maids used ours for their personal cooking. For us, this arrangement was an entrée to the culinary pleasures of Eritrean cuisine. Although we couldn't easily remember or pronounce the names of many of the concoctions, we soon developed a taste for most of the dishes we sampled.

Sabah, the Eritrean successor to Letai, used to prepare a superb tomato sauce heavily spiced with a blend of exotic condiments. My nose would hover over the simmering sauce inhaling the intoxicating aroma until I could no longer refuse my palate a share in the pleasure.

"Ma'am," Sabah would laughingly scold, "that's four time I see you take big taste from my pot! Maybe I have no dinner tonight!"

Another maid, Mama Medina, had a weekly ritual that everyone eagerly anticipated: Wednesday mornings she baked two large, round loaves of her native Eritrean raisin bread. The mouth-watering smell wafting through the house brought me back to my childhood when my Scottish grandmother indulged us with delicious scones. With the bread, Medina served hot, pungent cardamom coffee. She brewed it in a fat-bellied clay pot with a tall, narrow neck boldly decorated with colourful African beads on a primitive coal burner in our back garden. Tara and Kieran and their gang of friends thought it very 'adult' to squat on their haunches and sip the yellowish liquid from the special little cups.

Sometimes our maid would have one or two unemployed friends staying with her. They cheerfully helped with the housework, often humming melodic tunes from their native lands. Sabah always sang when she ironed. Back and forth her arm would go to the rhythm of her music. Kieran used to sit happily on the floor nearby and perfectly imitate Sabah's movements and melodies. I came to believe that the creases came out more easily when song accompanied the effort.

Chapter Thirteen

"If you want to leave, I'll understand," Sean said.

Adapting to life in Riyadh had been fascinating and frustrating, probably in equal extremes. Now it was time to choose whether or not to return to a more predictable environment.

In what seemed to be the blink of an eye, Sean's two-year contract was coming to an end. Bechtel offered him an indefinite renewal but the promise I had extracted in San Francisco of "…only for two years. Not a minute longer," hung in the air. Sean wanted clearance before making a new commitment. After putting the kids to bed, we had one of those Discussing Our Future conversations. I sat curled on the couch beside Sean, absorbing the welcome news of an extension, especially one that meant we could stay as long as we wanted.

"This is a bit like two years ago in reverse, isn't it? Then, I didn't want to leave San Francisco to go to Riyadh. Now I can't imagine leaving Riyadh to return to San Francisco."

"We have a good life here," Sean admitted.

"We have a great life here," I corrected. "You have a job you enjoy, I have help with the kids and the house and we have a fantastic social life and unlimited travel opportunities. Most impressive of all, we're decidedly solvent. The decision's a no-brainer, isn't it?"

"The positive aspects definitely outweigh the negatives but you know yourself it's not all smooth sailing," Sean cautioned. "The daily hassles and restrictions won't suddenly disappear."

"Of course they won't. But we've always been pretty resilient. And we've got a wealth of experience under our belts. Surely we can cope with new challenges. How unexpected can unexpected be?"

Sean confirmed to Bechtel our decision to stay. We happily ensconced ourselves into the routines we once considered unconventional but now accepted as normal.

But Riyadh still had some surprises in store for us. I soon found out that 'unexpected' can be unexpected indeed.

* * * *

The urgency of world events touched us late or not at all. We had restricted television reception and no radio. Local newspapers steered clear of anything that might cause a blip on the religious or political radar. Exaggerated censorship plagued foreign publications. Empty city lots populated by grazing goats and sheep underlined the fact that our lives had been simplified.

The region in which we lived was a hotbed of political intrigue but the problems of neighbouring nations seemed distant. Then, events in Iran in January 1979 dramatically blew the lid off the simmering pot of discontent. The overthrow of the Shah by religious clerics fuelled a similar uprising in Saudi Arabia. In November, at the start of the annual *haj*, several hundred armed dissidents did the unthinkable and laid siege to the Grand Mosque in Makkah. They protested against the government's pro-Western attitudes and the growing tendency towards giving women a greater role in society. Western expats became potential peripheral targets.

"Y'all better git yerselves a gun," a Texan colleague warned Sean. "Thar's no tellin' what them crazies'll do. Wouldn't surprise me if they came over the compound walls and killed every man, woman and child they saw. Git a gun. It's th'only safe thing t'do."

Without consulting me, Sean took his advice. I was horrified.

"A gun? Are you crazy? We have children in the house!"

"We'll keep it in the cupboard, away from the kids," Sean said, trying to calm me. "The mood on the street is ugly. It's foolish not to have some sort of protection."

"I've never held a handgun in my life," I argued. "I wouldn't know what to do with it."

"I'll teach you. Then, if you have to, just point and squeeze the trigger."

It sounded far too violent and bloody for my nature. Canadians and handguns don't blend comfortably. I knew, though, that in a worst-case scenario I'd want to be able to defend the children and myself with more than a pair of scissors.

"Fine. But we keep the bullets separate from the gun," I said.

"That kind of defeats the purpose, don't you think?"

Sean could see I wouldn't be moved on this point, so he relented.

The siege lasted for two tense weeks. During this time, foreigners remained unharmed and unthreatened but hundreds of pilgrim hostages, military and dissidents lost their lives. The 70 surviving insurgents were beheaded in four cities around the Kingdom. The Saudi government retreated behind a wall of Islamic rectitude and tabled plans for social reforms.

Sean disposed of the gun when the danger had passed. The high drama made us realise how fleeting peace can be in such an environment. We learned to better appreciate the tranquility of grazing goats.

Chapter Fourteen

In a city with no mixed public entertainment, the unsegregated annual King's Camel Race was a big deal. Started in 1974, the February event attracted entrants from all around the Gulf and allowed expat families to witness a unique snapshot of Saudi tradition. It hadn't taken much to persuade Sean and me to join a group of friends and see for ourselves what all the excitement was about.

We drove to the appointed site north of Riyadh. The race started 50 kilometres out in the desert, so we had only an approximate time when the first riders would reach our location. Punctuality wasn't part of the procedure.

As we stepped out of the Suburban, a low-flying surveillance helicopter created a sea of swirling sand.

"Jeez, Sean, I can hardly breath," I shouted, holding Tara close to me to protect her from the smothering blast.

"It'll pass soon," Sean shouted in reply. I couldn't see his body; it was reassuring to hear his voice. "They're reporting the progress of the riders."

Once the wretched helicopters had disappeared, we explored the area. Large tents provided food, drink and shelter for the milling masses. After a dusty eternity, a large cloud appeared on the horizon.

"They're coming," someone shouted.

"But not anytime soon," I retorted. They were still many kilometres away. My hair, face and clothes were now caked with multiple layers of sand particles. The noise of rotors agitated Tara. This was not the fun outing I had anticipated. Sean, on the other hand, mingled happily. I figured the sport fell into the category of 'man thing'.

Soon the cloud got closer – and bigger. A couple of hundred loping camels and several circling helicopters ensured polluted breathing conditions. When they finally came into focus, each of the small child riders looked like nothing more than a colourful cist on the camel's hump.

The young winner claimed his prize of cash, a Mercedes water truck and thousands of kilos of barley camel feed; the second prize was less cash, a Range Rover and thousands of kilos of barley. The last rider straggled in about half an hour after the others.

"Right," I announced to Sean. "We've seen the famous camel race. Now let's go home and have a shower. And remind me never to repeat this performance."

A few years later, friends once again invited us to the camel races.

"No thanks," I said firmly. "I've had my camel race initiation. Once is enough."

"It's different now," they insisted. "There's a brand new circular track. It's more organised."

Against my better judgment, I let myself be persuaded.

The track had helped to reduce the dust – helicopters didn't need to report on progress – but introduced a new frustration: false starts. Manoeuvring camels back to the starting point after they had got their long necks caught under the railings was complex and time consuming. In lieu of the original 50-kilometre race, the modern version required the riders to do three circuits totalling 22 kilometres. The aspect of endurance remained but in an abbreviated format.

A combination of Riyadh's increased size and the race's renown swelled the crowds to many thousands of onlookers and more than 1,000 camels. Long lines made it impossible to simply wander into a tent for a break.

"Well, I know one thing for sure. I do not enjoy camel races. The first race was supposed to start two hours ago and the jockeys are still trying to unravel necks and get the bloody animals to the starting gate."

My friend Mike, standing beside me, looked astonished that I didn't find all the excitement thrilling. This was definitely a man thing.

* * * *

Weddings were another aspect of Saudi culture that fascinated foreigners. During one of his weekly English sessions, Yousef presented me with an intriguing opportunity.

"You bin to Saudi wedding yet?"

"No, but I've heard a bit about them," I responded with interest. "They sound quite colourful."

"I don't know. I only go to men's party. Men meet for dinner after *isha* prayer, talk, then go home."

This didn't sound like a lot of fun. Yousef explained that there were no exceptions to the strict segregation rules. Women partied in one location, men in another, often not even in the same building.

"My brother will get married next week. Please you go."

"Thank you so much, Yousef. I'd love to go. What should I wear?"

My question was met with a gaze of incomprehension. Yousef, whose major fashion decision each day didn't extend beyond choosing which white *thobe* to wear, could offer no suggestions.

"Long dress. Like always," he suggested.

His vague answer gave no clues. I chose the prettiest caftan in my now extensive collection and hoped it would be appropriate.

Around 9 p.m., Sean dropped me at the Al-Yamama Hotel on Airport Road. The friendly welcome I received from other guests made me forget that I didn't know a single soul there. I was the only *khawaji* (foreigner) in the room.

Saudi weddings bear no resemblance to standard Western operating procedures. First of all – and this is a major point, all things considered – there is no 'wedding' for guests to witness. A religious judge conducts a ceremony in the bride's home where men and women – even the bride- and groom-to-be – are kept separate. Completion of the paperwork isn't necessarily a green light for consummation. Depending on circumstances, this might not occur until days, weeks or months later. The party is the prelude to the start of their lives together.

The second oddity, apart from the fact that there were no men in the room, was the décor. With the exception of two throne-like chairs on an elevated platform, 'décor' was strikingly absent. Metal folding chairs filled much of the space. A few women sat on the chairs but, for the most part, guests stacked their *abaya*s on them and then milled about and caught up with friends.

For me, seeing Saudi women without *abaya*s and veils was the main event. Comprehensive coverings in public gave no hint of what Saudi fashion looked like. An all-female gathering allowed the guests to discard traditional outer garb and reveal personal preferences.

Most of the dowager crowd wore heavy, dark, caftan-like dresses. The younger generation expressed flair – or lack of it – in a range of styles that covered the full spectrum of taste, colour and fabric. Many had replaced modesty with spaghetti straps and *décolletés*.

As additional fashion accessories, intricate patterns of henna covered hands and nails. Shades ranged from reddish-orange to almost black. This was the same paste used to highlight women's hair and to redden the beards of men who had returned from *haj*.

A four-woman Bedouin band sat on the floor. They rhythmically beat small drums and chanted a litany of tunes that inspired the young women to dance, sensually swinging their long black hair and slender hips. I learned that this display was meant to attract the attention of older women on the lookout for suitable brides for their sons or male relatives. In such a segregated society, these important choices were influenced by women observing women. Periodically a servant appeared waving an incense censor. My new friends showed me how to waft the scented smoke into my hair and up the bottom of my dress.

"Perfume stay with you many days. Make good smells in bed for your husband," a black-eyed beauty giggled.

Cups of cardamom coffee and mint tea appeared with regularity. But where was the food? It was nearly midnight. I felt faint with hunger.

"Dinner after bride and groom come," my companion assured me.

So what was taking them so long? Suddenly the music changed to a more rousing drumbeat. An outburst of ululations echoed in the hall. This trick with the tongue and voice sounds like the Arab equivalent of yodelling. The bride and groom had arrived.

As well as welcoming the wedding party, the noise warned women to cover their faces – if they chose to do so. In a unique dispensation, the groom's immediate male relatives accompany him into the gathering of unveiled, unrelated women. I could feel the buzz of testosterone as the unmarried men hastily scanned the room for potential mates.

The bride and groom made their way to the prepared stage. Special guests (including me) paid their respects. Some (not me!) presented gifts of gold. Then, after only about half an hour, the newlyweds and their male entourage left. This signalled the start of the feast.

Judging by the charge of nearly 200 women, it seems I wasn't the only person whose stomach rebelled after hours of deprivation. Like everyone else, I hurried to the well-stocked buffet, greedily piled my plate with enough food to feed a family of four and hastily found a table. My seven dinner companions greeted me politely but, for the most part, they concentrated on nourishment going into their mouths rather than on conversation coming out. After eating, everyone went home, tired and satiated.

A few months after the first brother married, Yousef extended an invitation to the wedding of another brother. I looked forward to once again meeting Saudi women in this otherwise closed and mysterious society.

"Instead of in a hotel, the wedding will be in a garden," Yousef informed me.

Before the advent of hotels with large indoor space for functions, wedding celebrations had been held at home. The tradition was already becoming less common among families whose new financial freedom allowed them to enjoy the latest trends.

"Would you mind if I brought the children?" I asked Yousef. "I saw lots of kids at the last wedding. Tara and Kieran might enjoy the experience."

"*Itfaddal*, please do," Yousef replied with pleasure.

I made sure all of us were well fed and well rested before our nocturnal outing.

This wedding had less than 60 guests. Like the previous wedding, there were no other foreigners. Again, I received a warm welcome and was made to feel like part of the family. Two-year-old Kieran and four-year-old Tara, both with white-blond hair, attracted unrestrained attention.

A couple of hours into the evening, before the arrival of the bride and groom, the lights went out. Another Riyadh power failure. For some reason, the hostess brought us into the house and up the darkened stairs to the rooftop. Everyone sat in rows on the ever-present metal folding chairs, as though we were waiting for a performance to begin. I noticed quite a few pregnant women. To stave off boredom, I took a gold chain from around my neck, attached a key to it and offered to do 'the old key trick'.

"When I hang this over your abdomen," I explained to my first 'subject', "the key will start to move in a circle. If it goes in a clockwise direction it means you'll have a boy; a counter clockwise direction indicates it's a girl."

The woman was thrilled to have news of a boy. Soon every swollen belly in the room had gone under the key. Then a slender, much older woman appeared. She insisted she was pregnant and demanded I use this magic on her as well. Nothing. Not even a shiver of movement from the key. I tried several times but the result was always the same. The woman was not amused. I felt my little party trick had run its course. At that point, thank goodness, the lights came on. We all went downstairs. The 'non-pregnant' woman avoided me for the rest of the evening.

Although the walled garden had little vegetation, the delightful ambiance made it more pleasant than an impersonal hotel. Perhaps it was the heady smell of jasmine in the warm night air or the informality of sitting on the ground to eat dinner. Whatever it was, the overall effect was enchanting.

A long, narrow oilcloth served as the base for the huge trays of mutton-topped rice and the many platters of fruit. Fortunately, our maids had schooled Tara and Kieran well in the art of local eating techniques. Without waiting for the senior guests to be seated, Kieran moseyed along the centre of the 'table' and examined the eye-level animal carcass. With professional ease, he used his right hand to ball the hot rice and tear off a piece of meat. I was mortified at this apparent breach of etiquette but everyone else laughed and gave Kieran a mighty applause, impressed by his unexpected prowess.

I attended a number of Saudi weddings over the years, some of them elaborate royal affairs that went on for three or four days. Stunning dresses often took second place to magnificent jewels. Even in museums, I had seldom seen the quantity or quality of those on display at top tier events: a sapphire the size of a robin's egg, flawless emeralds to complement flawless beauty, large diamonds that dripped from ears and covered necks. Décor, too, improved. The most extravagant weddings had exotic themes, such as an African safari with real animals. The simple garden celebration, however, was for me the most memorable.

Chapter Fifteen

When we moved to Riyadh in 1976, I reluctantly accepted Saudi Arabia's restrictions on the employment of women. By 1979, I had adjusted to filling my time with looking after our two children and managing a busy social life. Still, I suffered an occasional yearning to get back into the working world. Not at the expense of hands-on motherhood but, ideally, in conjunction with it. Such a goal seemed unattainable. Then, as Carolyn Wilkinson and I chatted after a tough game of tennis, she floated an unexpected possibility.

"A friend of mine is having visa problems," Carolyn said as she placed her racquet back in its case. "She's going to be delayed getting back to her administrative job at a local Saudi company. Would you be interested in stepping in?"

"You're suggesting that I not only work illegally but that I do so in a Saudi company?" I said in astonishment. "Isn't that pushing the envelope a bit?"

"Officially women are allowed to work only in places like hospitals or schools or all-female environments," Carolyn confirmed. "Unofficially, everyone turns a blind eye. Lots of women work in other fields. There's a big demand for good secretaries. Saudis need efficient staff as much as anyone – and maybe more so! Look, it's just temporary. Besides, it would give you a break from Kieran."

Now, that was definitely an incentive. Hyperactive Kieran was not yet two years old and he had already exhausted me. I loved his mischievous spirit but sanctioned breathing space might help restore my sanity.

"OK," I agreed. "What's the harm? If Sean doesn't have any objections, I'll go for the interview."

The next day I sat in front of Kamal Aboukhater, the genial Lebanese manager of Al-Sharif Trading. The company sold construction equipment and other products that fuelled Riyadh's boom. Like most companies in those days, Al-Sharif was located in an old villa that had been reconfigured to make offices.

"I have to stress that this would only be for two weeks," Kamal reminded me during the interview. "Is that acceptable?"

"That's fine but I have tennis lessons on Sunday mornings. Since I'll be working here for such a short time, I'd hate to lose my place in the class."

"Not a problem," came Kamal's quick reply. "Presumably you won't miss more than a couple of hours of work?"

Boy, was this a great example of flexi-time.

The big hiccup was my lack of a driver. Bechtel definitely wouldn't provide transportation for this 'illegal' activity.

"Don't worry," Kamal assured me again. "Our driver will pick you up and take you home." He smiled, anticipating the next stumbling block. "And we'll make sure you finish work in time to pick your kids up from playgroup at 1 p.m."

Half days, tennis class tolerated and transport – how could I refuse? The real clincher, though, was a generous salary. At 16 dollars an hour tax free and without deductions, I would be taking home more than I'd earned in San Francisco – for half the work hours. We sealed the deal with a firm handshake. I was a working woman once again.

The office had only a few employees. The most vital member of staff, as far as I was concerned, was a delightful young man whose sole job it was to make a range of coffees – American, Lebanese, cardamom – and teas – English or mint – for everyone all day. Pacing himself perfectly, Salim always instinctively knew when anyone needed a caffeine jolt or a sugar fix.

The special treat each morning was delicious, hot-from-the-bakery *zaatar*: a large round of unleavened pita bread topped with various herbs and oil and baked in a clay oven. This traditional Lebanese breakfast was comfort food. I gave silent thanks that tennis prevented any permanent lips-to-hips damage that over-indulgence in *zaatar* might incur. Employment in a Saudi company definitely had some unexpected perks.

At the end of two weeks, Kamal called me into his office.

"Would you be interested in staying on for another week or two? Our regular secretary still hasn't got her visa issues sorted out."

Eureka! My good fortune would continue for a while longer. Although the work wasn't exciting, it was invigorating to meet new people and to be back in a male domain.

After nearly a month of uncertainty, Kamal made my temporary position permanent. I never knew if the original secretary made it back into the Kingdom. I was just grateful to be a full-fledged member in the ranks of the employed, especially since I didn't have to compromise my motherhood role.

* * * *

I had been working at the company for several months when the Saudi owner, Kamal Al-Sharif, arrived at the office in a state of agitation.

"It's a disaster," he said to no one in particular as he clenched and unclenched his fists. "They gave me their word."

The tea boy and I exchanged anxious glances.

"Kamal, is there anything I can do to help?" I offered.

"I don't think anyone can help. I'm stuck with a container of sheets. A retailer in the *suq* agreed to the purchase but he's backed out. I can't find a replacement buyer."

"That's all?" I said with relief. "For goodness sake, I'll get rid of your sheets for you if that's what's worrying you."

Kamal stared at me in astonishment. Could his dilemma be resolved so easily?

"Really? I'd certainly appreciate it. In fact, I'll pay you a commission of five percent of the profit."

I hadn't thought about the monetary side but I'd been in the Kingdom long enough to know that bargaining was a necessary feature of any deal.

"Five percent of the selling price," I countered. I figured that on so few sheets, the difference would be negligible.

Kamal's bottom jaw dropped but desperation forced him to acquiesce.

"OK, so tell me," I said, eager to get the stock moved, "how many sheets are in the box?"

"Container, Kathy, not box." he corrected.

"Well, Kamal, a box *is* a container." I enjoyed helping people improve their English.

"True," he said, starting to look worried again, "but this container definitely isn't a box. I'm talking about a 20-foot-long shipping container. There are 20,000 sheets and pillowcases. And very few of them match each other. I bought a job lot of seconds out of New York."

Now it was my turn to look concerned. The hovering tea boy ran off to get me a restorative cup of coffee.

"I don't have that many friends," I said faintly. Then, warming to the challenge, I reassured him. "Give me a car and a driver and I'll get rid of every last one of these sheets… somehow."

Everyone I knew soon owned some of my job-lot linens but these sales barely made a dent in the supply. I had to go further afield. Who could use or sell thousands of mismatched sheets and pillowcases? Then, in a flash of brilliance, I saw the solution: supermarkets. Everyone went to the few supermarkets in the city. Their customers could be my customers!

Of the three supermarkets I decided to target, Al-Johar had the largest housewares section. This would be my first stop.

Barely able to hide his curiosity, a clerk led me to the manager's office where Muteb, a son of the store's owner, greeted me. His roly-poly body gave him a falsely jolly appearance. Dark eyes reflected a crafty business mind that wasn't interested in a win-win deal. He definitely belonged to the take-no-prisoners school. I would have to keep on my toes.

We sized each other up during the various Arab courtesies of tea, coffee and light conversation. It would be a gruelling negotiating session if I hoped to succeed with this important order.

Muteb probably thought the game was over before it began. What could this perky foreign woman know about business? My secret weapon, though, was my understanding of Arabic, an ability I chose not to reveal. All those private lessons and my practice sessions with Samira were finally paying off. No doubt it surprised him when I consistently anticipated the moves he plotted with his assistant in numerous Arabic asides. Eventually, after two long hours, we had a deal. And what a deal. Al-Johar Supermarket had agreed to take 10,000 sheets and pillowcases.

"I did it, I did it!" These simple words were accompanied by exaggerated hand gestures, little jumps and excited shouting at the two Kamals and everyone else within a 30-metre radius. The staff, unused to such emotional outbursts in the office, nevertheless smiled and congratulated me on my unexpected and seriously substantial success.

The next day I went to the warehouse and helped Hassan, Al-Sharif's Egyptian delivery man, to sort the cartons, count the stock and load everything onto the truck. Hassan must have found it strange to have a woman assisting him but an extra pair of hands meant we could both get out of the hot sun sooner. Besides, this was the only possible scenario for my perfectionist nature. I needed to know that every item was in good condition and had been counted correctly. Muteb would have no excuse for dissatisfaction.

The following morning I waited impatiently at the office for Hassan's arrival. What was taking him so long, for goodness sake? Finally he made an appearance.

"So, Hassan, everything went all right?" I enquired rhetorically.

"No, not so good," came his mumbled reply.

Hassan shuffled his dusty, sandaled feet. He kept his head of curly black hair tilted downward, studiously avoiding eye contact.

"Speak to me, Hassan, and explain 'not so good'."

The coldness in my voice signalled Salim to bring a fresh round of tea for the tense and quiet office.

"Mr Muteb send all things back. No say why. Not accept order."

My brain froze. What on earth could have gone wrong? In a state of numbed shock, I dialled Muteb's number.

"Ah, good morning, Kathy," Muteb said pleasantly.

I listened for any sign of awkwardness in his voice but there was none. In fact, was that a hint of smugness?

"Good morning, Muteb. My deliveryman tells me you've returned the entire order of sheets. What was the problem?" I used every effort to harness my growing irritation.

"Yes, of course. Too many of the boxes were damaged. Some of them were even torn. I was expecting to buy perfect stock."

With a sickening certainty, I realised I'd been had. Muteb obviously didn't like being out-bargained by an annoyingly tenacious female. He never had any intention of taking delivery. Torn boxes were a convenient 'out'.

"Muteb," I said, feeling my control slip away, "every single one of those sheets and pillowcases is perfect. You can blame the damaged boxes on your customs officials who are so rough in their inspections."

I paused. An inner voice unsuccessfully tried to warn my mouth not to say anything that might upset this person who could denounce me to the authorities. Then I exploded; the most unlikely words poured into the telephone.

"What would your mother say, Muteb! We had an agreement and shook hands. Did your mother bring you up to be dishonourable?"

Pregnant seconds passed. I suffered a twinge of regret at my rashness as I pictured myself being dragged away to a Saudi prison. Then Muteb made an abrupt pronouncement.

"Send everything back. Your man won't have any difficulties with the delivery this time."

And he didn't. Neither for that delivery, nor for the many others he made to Muteb, who became my best customer. Muteb continued to be a tough negotiator but, with me at least, he was always the model of a principled man.

Two other supermarkets joined Al-Johar as my core customers. My success impressed Kamal Al-Sharif. He ordered another container. And then another.

I was well into sales on the third container when I noticed a full-page ad in the local English newspaper. Cannon Sheets was offering major discounts. The prices for their first-quality merchandise even undercut the best price I could offer on my seconds stock. My sales performance had evidently been hurting Cannon's business. They were subtly warning this perplexing interloper that enough was enough. Kamal was not a Canon agent and therefore not supposed to be importing and selling this product. That was aside from the fact that I was taking a risk doing business with men! Kamal and I agreed that it was time to pull down the shutters on a profitable sideline.

* * * *

On occasion, some of Al-Sharif's clients provided interesting diversion.

Over the course of several visits to the office, the Iraqi businessman Hadir Farisi and I became friendly. Even though our conversations were relatively brief, Hadir impressed me with his quiet dignity and his kind and amiable nature. It intrigued me that his wife was Saudi. What an impressive source of cultural information this could be.

One day Hadir came to the office, not to see Kamal but to extend an invitation to me.

"I hear Greenhouse Supermarket has just received a shipment of prime Irish beef. Would you and your husband like to come to dinner tomorrow night? I could pick up some nice steaks."

I didn't even consult Sean. This was too good an opportunity to miss.

"We'd love to, Hadir. Thank you," I responded enthusiastically.

Sean was slightly reticent when I gave him the news.

"What is it that attracts you to the idea of dinners where most of the guests don't know each other?" Sean asked. He clearly didn't share this social quirk of mine.

Sean needn't have worried. The four of us were kindred spirits. Firyal was a beautiful, refined woman and a perfect complement to Hadir. Rich displays of art and artefacts made their house a comfortable home. That delightful evening was the first of many we shared with our new friends. Although I worked for Al-Sharif Trading for only a couple of years, our friendship with Hadir and Firyal lasted for all our Saudi days.

Chapter Sixteen

Saudi Arabia's blinkered opposition to allowing females to drive left women at the mercy of hired male drivers who were often undependable and rarely skilled. The situation invited disruption in domestic harmony.

"When I was young, I thought the epitome of luxury would be to have my own chauffer-driven car. This situation is definitely not what I had in mind."

I was on the phone, releasing my anger at my blameless but convenient husband.

"What happened this time?" Sean asked, probably not wanting to know the gory details.

"I'm at the doctor's office... and the driver is not. When he dropped me off – more than an hour ago, I might add – he said he was going to get gas. I haven't seen him since! The bloody gas station is only a couple of blocks away, for goodness sake." I paused briefly to let my blood pressure return to safe levels. "It's bad enough when he's late picking me up at home but it makes me crazy when he leaves me stranded. At least I have access to a phone this time!"

"Relax, Kathy. Give me ten minutes and I'll pick you up. If the driver gets there first, send him back to the office ... without abuse, please."

This scenario wasn't unusual. Not for Sean, not for thousands of husbands just like him. Men frequently had to leave work on family retrieval missions. Unreliability was an on-going side effect of a questionable system. One company got so fed up with a driver's late morning arrivals that it gave him a large alarm clock with a loud bell. This proved to be an exercise in futility: it transpired that the man didn't know how to tell the time.

"I've learned to live with cockroaches, sand storms and bad hairdressers. Delinquent drivers exceed my coping skills," I said on the way home after Sean's rescue. "Punctuality never used to be an issue with me."

"That's because you didn't have to encounter a lack of it on a regular basis." Sean stated the obvious.

"I swear this aspect of life in Riyadh gives me knots in my stomach. I've turned into a time psycho! If the driver's not at the door the minute I need to leave, I automatically assume that he's left the office late – or has forgotten me altogether. Going out should be a pleasure, not a health hazard!"

"You have to admit, even annoying drivers have their uses. You don't have to worry about parking anymore: they drop you off and pick you up at the door." Sean took his eyes of the road for a moment to give me a smile that brought my frustration down a notch.

"If I'm lucky," I retorted.

"And they sometimes run errands for you."

"That's true. But if I had the independence to drive myself, I wouldn't need someone else to run my errands, would I?"

Many companies either hired a driver for the personal use of an executive's wife or had a small pool of drivers for all the wives to share. Too often, bad drivers outnumbered the good, diminishing the benefits.

"What really ticks me off is that this bloody driving ban has nothing to do with religion," I continued. "It's a cultural prohibition. As far as I'm concerned, this is simply another example of a bunch of insecure men wanting to exert control over women."

"I tend to agree with you… but perhaps not to such a choleric degree," Sean admitted. "If Saudis want to protect their women and children, why would they hire strangers? That sounds like a morally riskier option to me."

"I tell you, it won't be high-minded ideals like democracy that eventually make women march in the street," I said angrily. "It will be a demand to do away with this unnecessary expense and inconvenience and give them freedom of movement: a driving license."

Although not permitted to drive in their own country, many Saudi women cheerfully take to the road once they get beyond the Kingdom's borders. Some rebellious females don't even wait until they leave: they either disguise themselves with a *ghutra* or hide behind the anonymity of darkened windows.

Independent-minded Bedouin women have a maverick approach to the impractical driving constraint: they ignore it altogether. Bedu regularly perform their chores with the aid of Toyota or Datsun pick-ups whose sturdy frames cope well with desert dunes and rough tracks. These are the modern-day equivalents of the camel. Bedu men *and* women need to be able to handle the trucks in order to survive in their harsh environment.

One day, police arrested a feisty female Bedu who strayed from her duned domain into the city. She stubbornly refused to sign a paper promising never to drive again. The police hauled her in front of Prince Salman bin Sultan, the Governor of Riyadh. Maybe his authority would intimidate her.

"This ruling is in place in order to protect women from the possible dangers of encountering unknown men," Prince Salman admonished.

· "And yet it's all right for women to drive camels," the woman retorted with spunk. "Don't you realise that on a camel I'm more exposed? Some man could jump me from behind and rape me! At least in my car I can close the windows and lock the doors."

Prince Salman possibly agreed with her but had to tow the party line. He sent her off with a reprimand, telling her not to get caught again.

* * * *

Vehicles often reflect the owner's personality. Some large trucks look like rolling art galleries with colourful paintings of lakes, windmills and houses brightly decorating the side panels. Goodies such as worry beads, baby booties and sponge dice might hang from rear-view mirrors. More demonstrative drivers prefer rambling bouquets of artificial flowers that seek out the furthest reaches of the back window, happily growing on a bed of green, furry nylon pile. In the ultimate attempt at coordination, upholstery of dubious décor appears unreservedly on dashboards, floors and even ceilings.

At the other extreme, cars might have all the back windows draped in tightly pleated curtains. Although maximising privacy, this preference limits rear vision. Evidently, it's not enough to veil the women; it seems they have to veil the cars as well.

* * * *

The sudden wealth of the boom years allowed most families to have cars and many to have drivers. Because of limited demand from the Saudi population, public transport never developed at a satisfactory pace. Unregulated taxis and overcrowded jitney buses prevailed, weaving recklessly in and out of traffic, halting whenever a potential passenger flagged them down. The jitney buses were filled to bursting, partly because of the convenience but especially because of price. At 1 riyal (about 30 cents), they were an affordable way for the many labourers to get around the city. Taxis, too, were relatively inexpensive but customers were expected to negotiate the price before getting into the unmetered vehicles. The timid or uninitiated who accepted the first quote were taken for a ride in more ways than one!

In 1979, the Saudi Arabian Public Transport Company introduced modern city buses with fixed routes. Fare structures depended on destination. This major development became a topic of conversation at a card game one evening at our place.

"Did you hear that the religious authorities want separate buses for men and women?" Steve said as he discarded two cards, picked up two more and checked his hand.

"They were overruled," Warren contributed, "but women have been kept in their place: a partition and separate entrance restrict females to the back of the bus." He chortled. Was he laughing *at* Saudis – or with them?

"Perhaps," I commented, "the symbolism implied in having women to the fore, even in a bus, is a too a much of a threat for some men."

* * * *

Like the Wild West, Riyadh had its share of cowboys. These ones drove brand new Mercedes, Datsuns and Toyotas.

"I notice there are no old cars," I remarked on one of our shopping outings. "Not a single one."

"Well," Sean explained, "as recently as the previous generation, camels or donkeys were the most common form of domestic transportation. Few people could afford cars and the road links were negligible. I read that in 1953 there were only 239 kilometres of roads in the entire country. The increase has been dramatic, probably unheard of in such a short period. The Kingdom can measure its march to modernity in asphalt.

"Of course, the other reason there aren't any old cars, is that they don't survive long enough to age! Despite the fact the roads aren't crowded, you take your life in your hands when you get behind the wheel." His eyes remained fixed on the road ahead. "The government has a lot of priorities at the moment. Driving safety isn't at the top of the list."

"It's like participating in a stockcar race!" I agreed. "And you can't blame this craziness on women drivers because there aren't any – which is a serious oversight. Women, at least, have a regard for the sanctity of life!"

Sean nodded, not rising to the bait, as he expertly manoeuvred the hefty Suburban around a Toyota pickup whose driver studiously kept the dividing line in the middle of his path. The two camels in the back flapped their thick, hairy lips and looked disdainful of wheeled transport.

"In order to survive, you quickly have to learn to be shrewd enough to anticipate other drivers' irrational moves."

As though to emphasise the point, he swerved sharply. An oblivious driver sped toward him on the wrong side of the road. Sean narrowly avoided a collision.

Insane stunts like this made roads the Kingdom's number one killer. Sitting around the compound pool one Friday, a group of us compared traffic horror stories. Our neighbour Jim Gliebe offered a sobering piece of information.

"Did you know that for the past few years there have been more traffic deaths in Saudi Arabia than live births? Half the fatalities involve pedestrians! No one is safe."

As daily witnesses to the chaos, the statistic didn't surprise any of us.

"Well, something's going to have to be done or there won't be anyone left to employ us," observed his cynical wife Stephanie.

"And few motorists have insurance coverage," Jim continued. He was on a roll. "There's virtually no protection, physical or financial."

"It's all happening too quickly," Sean said. "Road systems and cars have multiplied like fruit flies. The real problem, though, is that Saudis consider insurance to be a type of gambling and therefore disapprove of it. It'll get sorted eventually. The best plan of action is to avoid accidents."

Sean's self-evident remark made sense in more ways than one. In fatal accidents, the family of the deceased victim receives blood money. In the case of injury, the guilty party goes to jail until the victim has recovered – however long it may take.

"If you're going to hit someone, make sure you kill them," a colleague warned Sean. "If the person's in a coma for a few years, you'll wish you'd taken the option of blood money."

To further complicate accident situations, no one, not even medical professionals, can offer assistance until the injuries have been identified and a police officer has investigated the cause of the accident. Many victims die needlessly.

A two-year study in the early 1980s revealed that 41 per cent of drivers were unlicensed or underage. When testing became the norm, getting a license wasn't for the faint-hearted. After obtaining the required permission to take the test, the applicant faced hours of queuing, hoping all the while that the instructor would show up. Dubious eye exams did not deem colour vision testing necessary, classroom instruction was in Arabic only and minimal time was given to in-car experience. On top of all this, applicants had to navigate trick questions and commands. The examiners had a notorious reputation for issuing erroneous instructions such as telling the candidate to stop where stopping was prohibited. Needless to say, failures were frequent and frequently for inconsequential faults, although these were never revealed to the people being tested. Such a system encouraged driving without a valid license.

A lot of Saudis drove their new vehicles with the same reckless abandon as they had ridden their camels in the recent past: they watched out for obstacles in front; everyone behind them was supposed to do the same. A policeman pulled an old Bedouin to the side of the road and reprimanded him for committing the common sin of cutting across oncoming lanes of traffic to make a left turn.

"You didn't even bother to signal," he said strictly.

"Signal?" the Bedu responded with exasperation. "If the other drivers can't see my whole car, how do you expect them to be able to see my hand?"

* * * *

To compound the situation, many drivers came from countries with lax road and licensing rules. An Indian who tried to exchange his international driving license for a Saudi license had no knowledge of driving fundamentals. During his test, according to the Saudi Gazette, "he crashed into three cars and almost killed the traffic official who was testing him."

Clearly, something had to be done to stop the disregard for rules of the road and the resulting carnage. The government acted in several ways. First, it tried to make the roads themselves safer. Stop signs bloomed on suburban street corners. These were moderately successful but not in the way authorities had planned.

"Jeez, Saleh, I've told you that those red signs mean STOP, not plough through at an increased speed."

I gripped the back seat door handle, closed my eyes tightly and prayed no one would hit us. Saleh was an unusually good driver – except for this dangerous habit.

"You don't understand, Madam Kathy. Everyone knows bad drivers in Riyadh won't stop at signs. Everyone stops on roads with no sign. But it's best to drive extra fast through roads with stop sign, just in case a bad driver doesn't stop on the road without a sign."

As often as not, the logic worked. And I was learning a whole new way to think outside the box.

The introduction of traffic lights spawned a similar logic: orange meant 'speed up'. Sensible drivers waited a few seconds after the light had turned green. This allowed time for the crazies to drive through the red light. The delay had a downside: instantaneous and intense horn honking. It was ironic that these same people who seldom let time rule their lives were in such a hurry when they got behind the wheel. To minimise crash incidents, at 4-way junctions only one set of lights turned green at a time.

Finally the government used a stick along with the carrots. Fines and jail sentences became more severe and were handed out even for minor offenses. Jumping a red light, for example, could earn the offender 15 days behind bars as well as a substantial fine. The amount of the fine depended on the class of the violation. The published lists included gems such as driving in the opposite direction of traffic, using motor vehicles for 'immoral acts', hanging from moving vehicles and failure to equip an animal-drawn vehicle with speed-reducing and stopping devices.

It wasn't just the public who needed to be educated about the law. Too often the traffic police dispensed on-the-spot justice unfairly, influenced by the offender's nationality or position in the community. Many blameless people went to jail, like the unlucky American who came to an area of extensive roadwork. The diversion signs led him up a one-way street, against the normal flow of traffic. As the driver cautiously proceeded, a traffic policeman stopped him because he was 'driving the wrong way'. Rational arguments had no bearing on the matter. The man, due to leave the country for good in a week, went to the nearby police station to pay the fine. To his surprise, the policeman had written in Arabic on the note to the station officer that in addition to the fine of 300 riyals he had to spend three days in jail!

In accidents, apportioning blame could sometimes be random or illogical, despite damning evidence. On occasion, the innocent party must take the full burden of responsibility. Jeremy, a colleague of Sean's, contributed his latest tale of woe as we relaxed by the pool one Friday.

"I grabbed a taxi to go to a meeting. One minute I had my nose buried in a report, the next minute we had crashed into a wall. I have no idea how it happened. When the police arrived, they gave me 100 per cent of the blame: if I hadn't hired the taxi, the incident wouldn't have occurred!"

Not all traffic problems were due to bad driving. Sometimes they were the result of no driving. One evening in downtown Riyadh, Sean and I encountered a frenzy of horn honking, flag waving and male bodies hanging out of car windows shouting unintelligible words in a state of euphoria.

"Well, at least we know it's not another accident," I remarked to Sean.

"It's probably worse," he grumbled. "I forgot about the big soccer game tonight. Evidently Saudi won. We may be here for a while."

By now our progress had slowed to a crawl. Uninvolved motorists had to carefully make their way around cars that had stopped in the middle of the road for a spontaneous celebration. Excited youths danced in the street, heedless of the miles of stalled traffic their antics created.

"Cars are relatively new," I remarked. "The joy of victory is primal."

Chapter Seventeen

After suffering butter shortages two years in a row, starting in November and lasting as long as January, I became convinced that religious conservatives were scheming to stop Westerners from doing their Christmas baking. I learned to begin my butter search in October. Cramped, dingy but well-stocked Riyadh Supermarket was my first stop. The friendly Palestinian checkout man listened sympathetically to my request for large quantities of salted butter. He furtively looked over his shoulder to make sure no one was watching and then whispered, "Follow me," through well-spaced, brown, crooked teeth which exuded evidence of his last meal.

Up narrow, creaking, cracking, worn, wooden stairs, Sean, Mohammed, and I climbed to the shop's attic storage room. A dilapidated freezer sat in the middle of the sagging floor. Mohammed carefully adjusted the broken hinges and then, with a proud flourish, lifted the lid to reveal a precious cache of Irish Kerrygold butter.

"This all stock," Mohammed said in a conspiratorial voice. ""You take what you need today because probable gone tomorrow."

We loaded our arms with a siege supply of cholesterol and quickly proceeded to the checkout counter. Less favoured customers hovered with covetous looks in their eyes and sinister stirrings in their hearts.

"Don't think about sharing," Sean warned quietly. "Our hoard will be depleted when we discover how much is rancid."

The battered and misshapen packs told us the butter had melted and been refrozen, probably more than once. Still, we managed to salvage enough to cope with that year's Christmas demands.

* * * *

When we arrived in Riyadh in late 1976, the import boom focused on cars and construction equipment. The frustration of not finding favourite brands or recognisable substitutes often overshadowed food shopping but Riyadh residents could never complain about a lack of quantity and variety. No one would starve if compromise was part of the diet.

The available food was not necessarily consistent with the daily needs of Western families. We couldn't buy fresh milk or unfrozen meat except local lamb or camel. Yet it was not unusual to see delicacies from Europe and the Far East on the shelves of the city's three original supermarkets: Spinney's, Riyadh Supermarket and Al-Sadhan.

Spinney's, with decent size aisles and good lighting, was the most pleasant of the grocery stores. Rats sometimes peeked from stock on the lower shelves at Riyadh Supermarket but the shop had no competition when it came to unusual and hard-to-find items. Al-Sadhan, the most convenient to our house, didn't inspire our patronage because of unfriendly personnel and the emphasis on Arab foods.

Shop owners, inexperienced with an exploding population with excess cash, did not possess foresight when placing orders. No matter how much customers complained, managers refused to reorder stocks before they disappeared, or in increased quantities to meet demand. Meanwhile, it could take several months for new supplies to arrive on boats that were further delayed in the Kingdom's crowded ports. It's not hard to understand why everyone became adept at culinary improvisation – and at stockpiling.

Joyce Lovell, a friend, who arrived several years after us, once stared in amazement at my seemingly excessive food reserves.

"But, Kathy," she sighed, "you can get almost everything here now. Why do you still think you have to hoard?"

"Old habits die hard," I replied.

And then I waited. Two weeks later she appeared at my door in a panic. Wide-eyed, she obviously couldn't believe this was happening to her.

"Help! I have people coming for dinner. I've searched every store in the city for cream and tinned tomatoes. You're my last chance."

I calmly retreated to my trusty pantry and produced the missing ingredients. The next time I saw Joyce pushing a shopping cart, she was loading it with backups of each item on her list.

* * * *

The quality of foodstuffs was another problem. Weevils commonly infested dry goods. We threw away most items in this condition as soon as the package contents revealed the busy movements of disturbed colonies of bugs. Flour and rice never fell into the category of instant rejects because they were important staples.

"Insects are inevitable in these products," said my more experienced neighbour Jackie.

She watched me unpack groceries and stare in dismay at movement in the rice I had so carefully selected from an open bin.

"There's no point in hoping you'll get a bug-free bag. It isn't going to happen."

"But where do they come from? Are you telling me that all the rice- and flour-based food I eat here is cooked with bugs? That's disgusting," I moaned heading towards the garbage.

"Don't throw it out," Jackie said as she rushed to stop me from this rash act. "Dealing with the problem is simpler than you think. Just put the required portion of rice in the cooking pot, add enough water to more than cover it and then swish the rice around. All the unwanted life forms will float to the surface, along with sundry other paraphernalia, such as slivers of wood, small scraps of paper and pieces of string. You might want to rinse the rice several times," she added when she saw the expression on my face.

Jackie paused to make sure I was absorbing her instructions and then continued. "For flour, put the unopened bags into the freezer and leave them there for a few days. Once the wildlife has frozen to death, you can sift out the easily recognisable black bodies – and hopefully most of the less visible eggs."

"There doesn't seem to be much of a choice, does there?" I sighed with resignation.

Jackie gave a knowing smile and opened the freezer for me.

* * * *

In addition to freezing flour and swooshing rice, I learned to perform the food-related rituals of soaking fresh vegetables in a sterilising liquid called Milton, washing chicken poop off fresh eggs and spinning eggs on the counter to make sure they hadn't gone bad.

We creatively used whatever was available and didn't particularly miss what we didn't have – except milk. In such a nomadic society, dairy products were not native to the Saudi diet. What little milk the local population drank came from camels or goats. Foreigners had to get used to the taste of powdered milk or go without. Suppliers who eventually imported long-life cream from Europe made small fortunes: a litre cost 35 riyals (10 dollars). People paid the price willingly. Until we could enjoy the luxury of fresh or long-life cream, we made our own, courtesy of a British expat whose plump figure gave credibility to the excellence of her ingenious recipe: for whipping cream, heat 1 pound of unsalted butter with 1 pint of milk until the butter melts. Do not boil. Whip the mixture in a blender for 45 seconds and leave it overnight in the refrigerator. The next day, scrape the bubbly scum off the top and the cream is ready for whipping. Make single cream in a similar way, using 1/2 pound of unsalted butter to 1 pint of milk.

In the late 1970s, the government subsidised, at vast expense, the air freighting of herds of pedigree cows into the country. Dairy farms flourished in the Al-Kharj area just outside Riyadh. The only thing missing from the restful rural scenes and the familiar farm smells was the sight of the cows grazing on acres of grass. The greening of the desert hadn't quite reached that stage yet. Instead, the animals waited patiently in their specially shaded paddocks or their comfortably misted stalls, having their fodder brought to them and producing excellent Saudi milk.

It surprised the fledgling dairies to discover that, despite encouragingly high sales, almost 90 per cent of the population didn't want milk in its natural form. Because their stomachs could not easily digest the enzymes in cow's milk, Saudis used the product as a convenient base to make *laban*, their traditional cultured yoghurt-type drink. Once the dairies figured this out, they grasped the opportunity and produced *laban* in commercial quantities. Like everyone else, businesses had to learn how to adapt in this uncharted environment.

* * * *

Le Gourmet, an elegant little shop in the developing Olaya district, heralded the beginning of a new era. Epicurean delights such as fresh asparagus, mushrooms, strawberries and Belgian chocolates became available to an eager market. Sean and I were regular customers. The pleasant Lebanese clerk knew I loved smoked salmon. He also realised the stock often sold out before I could get to the shop.

"Look," he offered, "if you have a phone number, I could call you as soon as the shipment arrives. You'd have to come here almost immediately, though."

What a wonderful solution. All 14 villas in our compound shared the same line but at least we had a phone, a luxury in those days. A couple of weeks passed and I wondered why there had been no phone call. Using the excuse of getting an update, I indulged myself and went in person to see what was happening.

"But, Madam, we've phoned you on two occasions and someone has come to collect your order," he said, baffled.

My brain quickly ticked through possible explanations. Of course, the party line.

"Did you ask for me specifically?" I asked.

"I said it was Le Gourmet calling and then I asked to speak to Madam Kathy. A pleasant-sounding lady said she would give you a message. Did I do the wrong thing?"

"Not at all," I lied. "It's probably better, though, to speak only to me – and not to identify yourself as Le Gourmet!"

Who, I wondered, would do such a thing? Who on our compound liked smoked salmon as much as I did – and wouldn't hesitate to stoop to deception to get it? My suspicions settled on Wanda, a brassy American dame who, when confronted with her misdemeanour, shrugged her shoulders and showed no remorse.

"Hey, honey, this is a hardship posting. We all gotta do what we gotta do to survive."

Lesson learned. Revised tactics ensured future receipt of smoked salmon stocks.

Over the years, Riyadh became a food shopper's paradise, tempting hardened stockpilers to restrict themselves to realistic quantities. Even the less exotic suppliers began to expand their once narrow product lines.

We heard an exciting rumour that celery had arrived in Riyadh. We never arrived at the vegetable *suq* in time to get the robust, fresh stalks but we considered ourselves fortunate if we found a few stringy strands of the elusive vegetable. These we meted out with culinary imagination to favoured guests. We wasted nothing, even drying the leaves and using them to flavour soups or stews.

When I was visibly ready to produce our second child, a neighbour of American Indian descent, John Youngblood, appeared at our door. His arms were laden with brown paper bags bulging with celery.

"It's an old Indian custom," he said proudly, "that if a woman eats quantities of celery in her ninth month of pregnancy it will bring on labour."

The kind gesture inspired gratitude and a mild celery overdose but no labour.

Sometimes scarce but popular items never made it to the shelves. Spotting a manager checking produce, I asked if he had any idea when Baker's coconut was coming to Riyadh.

"It's been almost two years since I've been able to find any!" I said wistfully.

The manager's face lit up.

"You're in luck," he said, leading me to the huge stockroom at the side of the store. "Six cases. That's all they sent us. And small ones at that," he said with regret. He pointed to some boxes with the familiar Baker's logo.

At this news, my hoarder's instincts surged.

"That's more than enough," I said gratefully. "I only need one case."

What was I saying? How could I possibly get through a case of coconut? Nevertheless I didn't change my order.

Then, with the fervour of a Good Samaritan, I guided my shopping cart towards other Western women in the supermarket who looked as though they might be coconut users. Some thanked me politely; they probably wondered why I was getting so excited about sweetened coconut. Others got a glint in the eye as they received the valuable information and hastily redirected their carts in mid sentence towards the stockroom.

A Greek manager of Greenhouse Supermarket kept quantities of Lyle's Golden Syrup, a much sought-after item in the British community, in his office. For some time, Greenhouse was the only place in town that sold it, albeit clandestinely. Customers had to make discreet enquiries. If they passed scrutiny, they were led upstairs to the office. We suspected that the reason for the secrecy was severely restricted stocks; the manager was simply taking precautions against hoarders. On the other hand, Lyle's might have been on the infamous and capricious boycott list and he was being cautious about selling contraband goods. In any event, Golden Syrup eventually became readily available in Riyadh. Although I seldom used the product, I found myself buying tins in pairs... just in case.

Not all grocery shopping happened in supermarkets. In the old days, the big outing for the week involved going to the fish *suq* on Thursday afternoon, the start of the Saudi weekend. Here we socialised with friends while awaiting the arrival of the refrigerated truck from the Eastern Province. It was a sybaritic adventure choosing from the copious quantities of fresh Gulf seafood whose names and flavours we didn't know.

Fruit and vegetable vendors always provided hard-to-beat shopping entertainment. When a seller showed particular persistence or charm, I would stop to examine his selection. Some had a talent for showmanship.

"How much are these tomatoes?" I asked a vendor, careful not to appear too interested.

"Ten riyals a box, Madam," came his eager reply.

"Are they top quality?" I asked.

"They are the best, Madam. Every one of them is fresh, firm and delicious."

"And these mouldy ones?" I asked, showing him my bottom-of-the-box discoveries.

The weathered little man gave a cry of incredulous dismay. How could this possibly have happened, his gestures imply as his arms fly into the air and his eyes grow large and look to heaven for an answer.

"Perhaps we can still do business," I consoled. "A significant lowering of your price would help me to decide."

"Of course, Madam. Please take them for only eight riyals."

"Actually, I had something like five riyals in mind."

The vendor feigned shock and then gave his counter-offer.

"I am prepared to make a sacrifice and let you have the entire box for seven riyals."

"I'll tell you what. Let me replace some of those furry specimens and I will relieve you of the box for the generous amount of six riyals."

As my little friend reluctantly handed me my box of hard-won tomatoes he stated, "Are you sure you don't have Arab blood in your veins?"

What a lovely compliment. Now, doesn't a little exchange like that make supermarkets seem cold and impersonal? In a store I would have quietly picked my tomatoes, paid for them and left. In the *suq*, I have the satisfaction of thinking I got the tomatoes for a great price, although I know full well that the engaging old man who sold them to me didn't lose out. He probably wishes all his customers afforded him as much profit as I did.

Successful bargaining is a fun aspect of shopping here, equalled perhaps only by the delightful tradition of *baksheesh*. Small gifts of fresh ginger, an extra piece of fruit or a handful of beans added after everything has been weighed and paid for were always given with grace and received with pleasure.

Occasionally, a seller would give me *baksheesh* that had particular pertinence. During negotiations for a box of potatoes, the lively young wag appealed to my emotions.

"I am just a poor man who must look after his very large family. Why do you want to deprive me of a few riyals?"

"My friend, I sympathise. I am a poor woman trying to clear her bank overdraft. I would never consider depriving you, just as I hope you would never think of excessively profiting from me. Therefore I surely must have misheard your last price, since it was higher than anyone else's."

Eventually we came to an agreement.

"Madam, your persistence has won. Take your potatoes."

"Thank you. I would happily have given in to you except that my bank manager is also persistent."

Just as I was about to leave, the good-humoured character handed me a bag of plump, fresh garlic.

"Please accept this gift. I understand that in your culture you have a superstition that says garlic keeps vampires away. Perhaps it might help in the case of your bank manager."

Supermarkets definitely weren't this much fun!

* * * *

The erratic and limited supply of items wasn't just the fault of cautious ordering and slow boats. Politics and religion also had an impact. Cornish hens, for instance, disappeared for many months while officials investigated the importer on suspicion of dealing with Israel. Gelatine was *haram* because of the possibility that it was made with pig products or came from animals slaughtered in an un-Islamic way. Ground nutmeg vanished off the shelves from one day to the next. It came as a surprise to us to learn that when mixed with other ingredients it forms a volatile concoction. Inexplicably, whole nutmeg could still be bought. According to a fast-spreading rumour, officials were threatening to forbid 'dangerous' Perrier: all that gas could make the bottles explode – what nasty effects might it have on the body? For that product at least, common sense prevailed.

* * * *

As well as increases in the availability of food, Riyadh witnessed decreases in its cost. Improved national agricultural yields accounted for some of this, making the country less dependent on imports. Primarily, though, the lower prices were due to the growth of the supermarket business. More stores, alas, didn't mean better stores: the narrow aisles and sometimes unkempt shelves remained unchanged. Then, when I was in Europe, Sean phoned from Riyadh.

"There's a Panda in town!" he exclaimed, excitement resonating in his voice.

"Good grief, what's a panda doing in Riyadh?" I asked incredulously. "Surely it's too hot for the poor creature. Where will they get enough bamboo shoots to feed him?"

"Not that kind of panda," Sean said with a hint of exasperation. "A Panda supermarket."

"What on earth is a panda supermarket? Is it a store specialising in bamboo shoots?"

"It's a supermarket – a REAL AMERICAN SUPERMARKET," Sean said with renewed enthusiasm. "It has wide aisles, properly stocked shelves, freezers that work and decent-size shopping baskets! No more of those

European doll carts. It's fantastic!" Sean proceeded to rattle off various items we hadn't been able to buy for years.

This marked the birth of the supermarket boom; everyone wanted to get in on the act. Competition for customers became fierce – and shoppers loved it. Each new supermarket was bigger and better than the previous one. Each featured something different that hopefully would draw business away from the others: one would specialise in beautiful and varied fresh fruits and vegetables; another's *pièce de résistance* would be meat flown in daily from Europe, Australia, New Zealand or the US; yet another would distinguish itself with bakery items. Some catered to the British community, others to the American sector. Hussam Stores carried a wide range of German products but that wasn't what made the store the talk of the town when it opened. Hussam's had installed the city's first escalator. Many people had never seen such a contraption. Customers flocked to the store to experience the thrill of riding up and down the moving stairs.

One of the few drawbacks of such vast improvements in the range and availability of food supplies was the modernised management style. In these sophisticated new outlets, the man behind the cash register was no longer your friendly neighbourhood grocer who probably owned the shop. Now the clerks were foreigners who took their orders from a command centre invisible to the customer. They had no authority to condone the good-natured bargaining that was a way of life here. The charming tradition of offering *baksheesh* suddenly became unacceptable because it was now considered unprofitable. So, too, did the practice of rounding account totals down to the nearest riyal, the paper currency; often a few riyals got knocked off in this antique form of good public relations.

Returning from a long summer holiday, I visited the new City Supermarket, a forerunner of the super-duper supermarkets. I stood at the checkout counter with fingers clenching a wad of bills, ready to peel off the required number.

"This is 82 riyals and 35 halalas, please Madam," announced the polite Indian cashier.

I handed him 80 riyals and prepared to take my bags.

"Excuse me, Madam, but you still owe two riyals and 35 halalas," he persisted.

I smiled weakly at what I thought was the man's attempt at humour, and then became annoyed to realise he meant what he said! I gave him two more riyals.

"And 35 halalas, please, Madam."

My mouth fell open. What kind of operation was this?

"Sorry, Madam, no *baksheesh* this store. Boss no let. So sorry. Must have all money or boss take from my salary. So sorry."

No one carried coins in those days, so I gave him another riyal, took my change and mentally vowed not to return. It wasn't the 35 halalas – the equivalent of 10 cents – that hurt; it was the loss of a quaint and lovely custom. . . .

Going to the supermarket could be social as well as practical. Initially there were relatively few Westerners in the city. Expats often studied each other surreptitiously in the aisles. Sometimes excuses were found to start conversations: "Excuse me, but I see your child wears disposable diapers. Did you manage to find them in Riyadh?" Occasionally a friendly chat inspired an invitation to dinner. Sometimes we would meet someone new at a social event but be bothered by the vague familiarity of the face. Then recognition would dawn: "Ah, yes, the meat section at Spinney's, about two weeks ago!"

Chapter Eighteen

A conspicuous absence of spacious, orderly, retail outlets left Riyadh consumers with no shopping option other than *suqs*. These cluttered but fascinating markets sold some version – good or bad, real or counterfeit – of a wide range of commodities, from car parts to camels.

It wasn't always clear what a store specialised in. Signage written in Arabic or baffling and often amusing English could hinder the identification process. I tried for years to decipher 'Carpets and Moketts'. The shop window, crowded with machine-made carpets, verified half the description. Eventually I figured out that 'moketts' was an Anglicised French word (*moquette*) meaning thick carpet or upholstery fabric. Once in a while, signs were written in perfect English but had an unintended double meaning. The favourite example of this was the drycleaner who enticed customers with the phrase 'Drop Your Pants Here'.

Communicating with vendors could be just as confusing as signage. Jackie O'Dwyer gave us a chuckle when she dropped by to relate her morning's strange shopping encounter.

"I went to buy film," she said, shaking her head in disbelief. "The man tried to sell me a camera. I finally picked up the film and said, 'How much?' He said, '40 riyals.' I handed him 15 riyals and got seven riyals in change."

Saudi Arabia of the 1970s was a cash economy. No one issued or accepted credit cards. Carrying substantial amounts of bank notes in the purse or pocket – or stashed in a huge pile from the armpit to the tip of the finger – was normal and perfectly safe. Only when stores became more sophisticated and international chains appeared would plastic payments become the norm. Cash, however, never lost its caché.

As it did with all aspects of Saudi life, religion influenced the flow of commerce. Everything closed at the noon prayer and didn't reopen until at least 4 p.m. Businesses shut again at the dusk prayer for half an hour and an hour later for another half hour. It was like running a gauntlet trying to get errands accomplished without hitting *salah* (prayer).

During Ramadan, the Muslim month of physical temperance and spiritual renewal, the rules changed yet again: shops might open late in the morning or not until late afternoon. There was no consistency and a shop could change its opening hours without notification. On the other hand, they stayed open until the small hours of the morning in order to accommodate the late-night clientele.

Exchanging or returning an item for any reason, including faulty merchandise, was usually a losing battle. All sales were final. Even the most prestigious stores followed this practice, as I found out when I took a new Rolex watch into the local dealer.

"A friend has just given me this beautiful watch but it's too big," I explained to the manager. "Since there aren't any links in the strap, I think it might have to be cut. Can you do that?"

"I'm sorry, Madam, but this is a solid gold strap. It can't be adjusted to fit such a small wrist."

"Then can I exchange the watch for another one that would fit me? I'm happy to pay any difference in price."

"No, Madam, we don't do exchanges or returns."

Surely this was carrying the 'no returns' policy a little far? Not willing to let the matter go, I contacted Rolex in Geneva. Their roving representative made an appointment to meet me in the shop the following week.

"You have an especially small wrist. Our agent is correct; this strap can't be adjusted. Is there anything else you see that you like?" asked the more amenable rep.

"Actually, the only watch that interested me has been sold. I'm going to London and Paris next week. May I check out Rolex dealers there?"

"Please do," he replied. "In the meantime I'll give you a credit note for this watch."

To my surprise, the same selection appeared in every Rolex outlet – until I discovered the luxurious Paris jeweller Fred. They had an eye-popping display of exclusive designs. Securing a precious catalogue, I wrote to Rolex, listing several possible alternatives.

"If the first choice exceeds my credit, please keep moving down the list," I instructed.

With true public relations mastery, Rolex custom-made my first option. Sometimes a no-returns policy has its advantages.

* * * *

I loved antique hunting with trendy friends in Europe. In hushed tones we would discuss the merits of this piece of silver or that item of furniture. I told myself that someday I, too, would have a sharp eye for a bargain and finessed negotiating abilities. When we moved to Riyadh I learned that the city boasted a thriving antique *suq*. Here was a chance to come into my own as a connoisseur of *objets d'art*.

Off I traipsed, not knowing quite what to expect but confident that antique shops must look much the same anywhere. I was wrong. Tucked in behind the main Dirah *suq* were funny little hole-in-the-wall outlets facing onto dirt passages. The setting looked more antique than the items for sale.

The vendors, too, were an unfamiliar species. They certainly didn't behave like the poised and sometimes pushy sales staff in Europe. As often as not, they absented themselves from their shops or didn't bother making themselves known to potential customers.

My initial reactions to the local conditions ranged from distaste to dismay. Then, with resignation, I rolled up my sleeves and began rummaging through the dusty rubble. Many of the items were of dubious value but I reminded myself that one man's trash is another man's treasure.

At the bottom of a precariously stacked pile of 'trash', I exhumed some interesting 'treasures': an unusual wooden incense burner, an old wooden bowl with a crack that had been stitched with copper wire and a silver tray with etchings of Makkah and Medina. Each item spoke to me, begging me to take it home. After a timid attempt at bargaining, I became the proud owner of this grubby collection for the princely sum of 35 riyals, about 10 dollars. I cleaned and stained the wooden pieces and polished the tray. They had a new lease on life and I had a new hobby.

With increasing regularity, I wandered the dark, labyrinthine alleyways, practising my Arabic in lively conversation with favourite dealers. Gradually I shed the notion that disputing a price was rude. My blossoming skills turned shopping into an intellectual stimulation and, sometimes, a theatrical audition: I kept finely tuned reactions such as disappointment, shock and regret ready for quick retrieval.

I learned that the more I wanted something, the more I had to mask my enthusiasm. This might mean appearing to ignore an object that caught my attention and then asking the price with studied disinterest. "How can you bargain from a position of strength if you don't know what something is worth?" an astute Saudi friend had commented. So I tried to become more knowledgeable about items in anticipation of serious bargaining sessions. Equally important, I disciplined myself to walk away if the offer exceeded what I perceived the value to be. Finally, after much resistance, I abandoned my craving for instant gratification: some of my most memorable purchases have taken weeks of repeat visits in which the protracted negotiations were regularly interspersed with cups of refreshing mint tea and equally refreshing discussions unrelated to the transaction.

One of my hard-won treasures was a coffee-bean roaster. Several sets of the long-handled, shallow bowls with the accompanying stirring implement hung on a warped mud wall. The vendor displayed a particularly good selection but he was notorious for his inflated prices and his unwillingness to give much of a discount. Regretfully bypassing the beautifully ornate roasters crafted from three metals, I selected an attractive but modest set that would surely have a price that reflected the relative simplicity.

"How much for this one?" I asked with feigned indifference. I had already enquired about several other sets, hoping to put the deceptively disinterested seller off the scent.

Wily old Abdullah eyed me carefully, scratched his scraggly beard, and then made ineffectual adjustments to the red-and-white check cloth that covered his head in helter-skelter fashion. Was this charade one of his sales ploys? I suffered his silence without any show of emotion. Abruptly, without mercy, he pronounced his verdict: "One thousand riyals."

Smothering a gasp, I did a quick calculation: nearly 300 dollars!

"What would you say to an offer of 50 riyals?" My low counter offer was no more outrageous that his initial quote.

"I would say that there was no chance of you going home with what your heart so obviously desires," Abdullah replied with calm confidence.

Experience had taught him to be a good judge of human nature but he had miscalculated my tenacity.

"Take it," he relented six weeks later, after yet another long session of haggling. I was now the proud owner of a charming coffee-bean roaster for the reasonable price of 120 riyals. Beneath Abdullah's gruff manner, I sensed amused delight at my perseverance. I have no doubt that both of us profited.

Once in a while I could achieve the same results in only one morning.

"What on earth is that?" I asked with idle curiosity, pointing to a large object on an uppermost shelf in the cluttered shop.

My sales friend called it by an unfamiliar Arabic name. My acute short-sightedness precluded visual identification.

"Shall I get it down for you to examine?" he kindly offered.

"No, no, please don't bother. I'm sure it's special."

Whatever it is. Although not interested in buying anything that day, for form's sake I asked the price.

"Ah, this is a rare item but I can make a sacrifice and offer it to you for only 380 riyals," came his quick and eager reply.

"My friend, that seems an ambitious price. Perhaps I misheard you?"

"Please, make me an offer, any offer. You are a favoured customer and I don't want you to walk away empty-handed."

Oh well, what harm could there possibly be? Besides, it would achieve my main objective of keeping the Arabic banter in play.

"All right then," I agreed amiably, "would you consider taking 45 riyals?"

"*Ya sadikati,*" the poor man sputtered, "you don't seem to understand that this is a unique find."

"Forgive me. Perhaps I shouldn't even be considering the purchase of something whose value I cannot fully appreciate."

"I want you to have it. Think carefully and make me another offer, please."

By the time I had shared several cups of tea with him and discussed the local news in detail, my offer had risen to the grand total of 72 riyals. Since I had no idea what it was I was bargaining for, the amount seemed reasonable.

Eventually it was time to go. He was either desperate to rid himself of the mysterious 'unique find' or else he truly wanted me to claim it as my own. No sooner had I left his shop than he came after me, attracted my attention and gave a barely perceptible nod of his head. A sense of honour made me agree to the sale. Unwittingly, I had bought a… whatever it was.

We returned to the shop and he clambered over the disarray to retrieve my purchase.

"Good grief, what on earth is this?" I asked once again, viewing a broad-based, narrow-necked, silver coated, beaten copper, lidded and handled container that stood as high as my waist.

Realising that I had never understood in the first place, the merchant used mime and simplistic vocabulary to explain that this was a shaikh's water jug.

Awkwardly, I lugged the monstrosity home. Later, the Museum of Antiquities verified the jug's identity and confirmed that, because of its size, it was indeed an uncommon piece. It looked as though I had a treasure after all. For an insignificant sum I had enjoyed a morning's entertainment that culminated in my very own much prized *objet d'art*.

The lessons bargaining taught me weren't restricted to the *suq*. They were a formula for life in general: dare to question instead of blindly accepting; don't always be transparent about objectives; have the strength to say 'no' and say 'no' from a position of strength; be less hurried for results and instead enjoy the process of getting the results.

Learning, accepting and applying the philosophy of bargaining brought me unexpected rewards, not to mention rainbows to my once black and white world.

* * * *

The *Suq Al-Hareem*, women's *suq*, secluded itself behind a noisy, smelly abattoir in the old city. There were no counters, no shop windows, nothing to immediately identify this as an area of commerce. The women sitting cross-legged on the ground with their backs to a wall looked like a group of friends taking a break from the rigours of shopping. Those in the know could seldom resist the temptation to make a detour to the otherwise unsavoury destination to sift through the inviting piles of merchandise stacked in front of the black-clad, hennaed women. If an old woman liked a customer, she might ferret out an item from a rusty biscuit tin in which she stored favourite merchandise like a turquoise-studded Bedouin bracelet, old Maria Theresa *thalers* formed into a heavy necklace or jet-black *kohl* to adorn the eyes.

"The thing to buy here is Bahraini pearls," advised my companion Carolyn Wilkinson. Carolyn and I had gone from being tennis partners to forming a solid off-court friendship. "Bahrain was famous for its pearling industry. It's pretty much dried up now but they still call them Bahraini pearls, even though they usually come from lakes in Japan."

We walked past the row of seemingly indifferent vendors, looking for items of particular appeal.

"Be sure to bargain," Carolyn whispered. "If you're timid, they're likely to toss your purchase at you!"

An old woman whose seated height matched her generous width attracted my attention. She flashed a toothy grin and beckoned me to sit with her. She looked me up and down and grunted. Then her stubby, gnarled brown fingers pried loose the lid of her tin and unearthed a small bag of umber-coloured powder from her cache of goodies.

"Perfumed incense. For hair. Good for bedroom."

Her cryptic description confused me. Was I supposed to put it on my hair or scatter it around the bedroom? She shook her head at my obtuseness.

"Rub on hair. When in bed with husband… good time."

Her companions laughed in appreciation of her ribald humour. I made the purchase. The product worked as advertised.

* * * *

Beautiful hand-woven carpets were on everyone's shopping lists. Arabia's new wealth served as a magnet to traders from all the carpet centres in the region: Iran, India, Pakistan, Afghanistan, Turkey and the Soviet republics. The eye, trained or untrained, feasted on the vibrant colours and complex patterns.

Frequently, carpet dealers brought large selections to the house. Lingering over a particular design always prompted the salesman to make a hard-to-refuse offer.

"Keep the carpet for a week. See if it suits your home. If not, you can return it, no problem."

In our case, the chosen carpets seldom got returned. They just lived with us happily ever after.

Our favourite carpet salesman was a delightful Pakistani called Hassan. His short, muscular body had an energy that constantly kept him on the lookout for the next deal. We had introduced many of our friends to Hassan. In appreciation, he often gave us first refusal on unique carpets.

"Great news. I find three piece all same. These set very, very rare. You take."

And we did. But only because they complemented the colour scheme of our bedroom, we told ourselves, not because we were carpet pushovers.

One day Hassan told us that he had sent his carpet-buying brother on a quest.

"He have instruction to find bestest quality carpet for you. First-class wool, bestest weave, everything. Special for you."

"But Hassan, what if we don't like it? Or can't afford it? Please don't ask your brother to make an effort on our behalf."

Friendship could sometimes be a burden!

"No worry. You no like, you no take. And price will be very low for you. My way of say thanks you for bringing me so many business."

The brother took his commission seriously. For a long time, nothing met the exacting standards he had been given. Then Hassan called.

"At last," he announced excitedly, "I have carpet for you. I bring your house tonight, *insha'allah*."

It had taken the brother almost two years to find a carpet that passed muster. The wait was worthwhile. Hassan proudly presented us with a beautiful specimen woven in the finest lamb's wool.

"It feels like silk," Sean said admiringly, walking on it in his bare feet.

"The dyes are so intense," I remarked, standing at each end of the carpet in order to see the dark and light effects of the weave.

True to his word, Hassan offered us the carpet for a fraction of its retail price. For us, the greatest value of the 'thanks you' carpet lay in the sentiment we attached to it.

* * * *

We had a couple of friends who, over the years, had bought hundreds of old carpets at the junk *suq* for bargain prices. They shipped the cleaned booty to Switzerland and sold it at a significant profit.

One Friday, for a family outing, we checked out the possibilities for ourselves. The four of us sifted through mountains of broken wheels, armchairs without arms and a cornucopia of damaged or obsolete items. The junk *suq* was well named.

"Mommy, I think I've found something," Tara called excitedly from a few feet away.

We all rushed to help her free a corner of fabric from under boxes of cracked crockery. A quick inspection revealed an ugly machine-made carpet. We kept searching. And searching. Suddenly I spotted a potential flash of colour.

"This looks good," I grunted, lifting engine parts off the thickly folded rug. "It's definitely hand woven."

After concentrated effort we released the carpet from its cramped prison only to find another disappointment: much of it was in shoddy condition, hanging together by threads. We eventually decided to abandon our quest and revert to the convenience of having dealers come to our home. On the way back to the Suburban, we crossed a central area with several potential piles of rubble. We looked at each other, shrugged our shoulders and agreed to have another try.

"Eureka!" I shouted. "I've found something. And this time I think we've struck pay dirt!"

Sean ambled over to my pile of boxes and fabrics and leaking shampoo bottles. With justification, he treated me like the boy who called wolf. We pulled and lifted and pulled some more until the carpet came free.

"Let's open it up for closer examination," Sean suggested. He wasn't prepared to buy just any piece of junk. It had to have merit.

"The design looks promising," I said, hoping that Sean would choose to ignore the dried animal dung and other assorted filth that obscured much of the carpet's potential. "And it's definitely the size we're looking for, don't you think?"

Sean paced about five feet along the carpet's width and seven feet along the length. I took his faint grunt to mean that we should ask the price. A tough-looking old fellow sat nearby in the shade. His body arched forward as though it leaned against a phantom cane. I approached him, reasoning that his proximity made him the owner of this pile of junk.

"One hundred fifty riyals," he declared tersely. His grey beard bobbed back and forth, as though affirming the quote.

This was the equivalent of less than 50 dollars. In the parlance of Riyadh's booming economy and hand-woven carpets, this was a steal, even considering the rug's unkempt condition. The frayed fringes didn't detract from its good condition and still vivid colours. Nevertheless, thinking that if his starting price was 150 riyals, then it must be worth considerably less.

"One hundred riyals," I countered confidently.

The man was apparently not in the mood to quibble.

"Two hundred," he retorted with diminishing tolerance and a silencing glare. I reluctantly admitted to myself that, with his humourless attitude, the price would probably continue to rise. I paid him his 200 riyals. We still had a bargain.

"You might be interested to know," his raspy voice volunteered, "that this carpet was originally in the palace of King Abdul Aziz."

True or not, it took the sting out of the abbreviated negotiations and added a bit of romance to the purchase. After we had the rug air-hosed and cleaned, an expert on Oriental carpets identified it as an antique tribal carpet from Shiraz. We had bought a real Persian carpet for less than 70 dollars!

* * * *

To help pay expenses on their journeys to and from Makkah, *hajis* brought with them carpets and other valuables to sell along the way. The large *haji* camp outside Riyadh buzzed with the excitement of people looking for bargains on interesting items from colourful characters. We love the carpet we bought from a battle-scarred Afghani as much for the story as for the quality workmanship.

"Each year I come, sell carpets, get money, go home, buy guns. War is difficult for my people but Afghanis will not surrender. Foreign invaders will not win."

He referred to the Russian occupation. I wonder if he still comes to Saudi to earn enough to buy guns to rout the latest assailants?

One year at the camp, I spotted an extremely large carpet in the back of a Toyota pickup. I couldn't resist the opportunity to negotiate. To my astonishment, the young man eventually agreed to my low bid. Just as I was handing the lad a wad of cash, his father showed up.

"Are you crazy?" he shouted at his son. "Do you know how much this carpet is worth? You're selling it for less than we paid!"

The transaction had already been made but I didn't want to be responsible for a family rift.

"Please," I said, "take the carpet back. I see now that it's too big for my home."

The father gave a curt nod and silently shook my hand – and I missed out on the carpet deal of the century.

* * * *

The wonderful Tamer Pharmacy on Thumari Street in old Riyadh was an important exception to the predominant *suq* shopping. Friendly staff and a comprehensive selection of perfumes, cosmetics and pharmaceutical items gave Tamer a loyal clientele. Admittedly, the many free cosmetic samples with every purchase were an important part of the appeal.

After a summer absence of three months, I visited my Tamer buddy.

"Well, what samples of miracle potions do you have for me today?" I asked.

"Very special things for you today, Madam. This one Age Smoothing Cream. Can cure even difficult cases. And this Rejuvenating Night Cream work while you sleep so skin no have chance go back natural state. And this for saggy skin under eyes. Very good for older ladies. This newest cream…"

The poor man stopped dead in his tracks when he paused for breath and happened to notice my paling face.

"I don't mean you need these now, Madam. You save them in your cupboard for a long while and then they prevent you maybe needing them."

He quickly got on safer ground by dropping miniature perfume bottles into the bag. It took me a while to accept that I had moved into a new stage of cosmetic requirements. On the plus side, I knew my friend at Tamer would always have exactly what was needed to solve any beauty problem that might come my way.

* * * *

Unexpected prosperity inspired Saudi businessmen to take an architectural leap from the traditional market format. Stand-alone specialty shops offered customers air-conditioned alternatives to the *suqs*. In response to the growing trend among Saudis to have European-style furniture, large furniture stores appeared. Their dizzying inventory ranged from gorgeous to gaudy.

"Can you believe that hideous pink seashell bed?" I exclaimed to Sean nearly every time we passed the expansive window of a furniture store that stocked only the outrageous. The bed remained an eye-catching feature for many months.

"My personal favourite...," Sean would respond, adding any of the new display pieces that caught his fancy. It might be the fuchsia and purple lip-shaped velvet sofa or the multi-mirrored bed. Many of Riyadh's furniture shops were like cinema: fantasy and Technicolor.

In the late 1970s, Christian Dior opened an elegant boutique on Airport Road, at that time the main thoroughfare of modern Riyadh. The new building was fashionably pleasing outside and pleasingly fashionable inside. Nothing this trendy, this chic, had appeared on the local market.

What added to Christian Dior's uniqueness was the fact that no man could enter the women's department, a sacrosanct area staffed entirely by female personnel. Men who wanted to buy a Dior gift for their wives had to have suggested items passed across a curtained threshold. Conversely, women could come and go in the men's department.

Dior's attractions weren't restricted to its *haute couture*. Here, women could try on clothes before buying them, something unheard of in Riyadh. The *mutawwa* considered women's changing rooms to be beacons for potentially immoral activities. Mirrors, too, were *haram* because they might reflect women's faces to passers-by, inducing further temptation.

Salesmen usually skirted around this prohibition by hiding a mirror under a counter or in a back storeroom. Mannequins and 'suggestive' ads also fell into this cluster of *harams*.

Another of Dior's draws was the lingerie section. The variety of pretty, high-quality items was only part of the appeal.

"What a joy to at last be able to buy my underwear from a saleswoman," I said to Sean when we met up in Dior's men's department. "It utterly astounds me that this is the only store to have women clerks."

"That's easy enough to understand. The religious people here, in this home of Islam, believe it's important to keep the sexes separate as much as possible so that morality isn't jeopardised."

"So it's all right for women to be served by a male clerk but it's taboo for men to be served by a female clerk?" I asked in mock confusion.

"Don't try to incorporate reason, Kathy. You should know that fanaticism and rationale seldom mix."

"Fine. But just try to explain to me how anyone who's so zealous about keeping women and men apart can condone having men sell underwear – intimate apparel – to women!"

By now I was on my soap box. "It is disgusting to me to have to buy a bra from an oversexed man who glares lewdly at my chest and tells me he knows what my cup size is!"

Despite the fact that most women had a similar complaint, the religious guardians made no concessions on this point. Perhaps they were moonlighting as underwear salesmen?

* * * *

Dior, with its female staff and isolated women's section, was the precursor of 'doorbell' shops. Fed up with the various restrictions, women began to open clothing and lingerie businesses beyond the invasive reach of the religious police. The *mutawwa* cannot enter a dwelling without clear evidence of impropriety. The female owners avoided unlawful raids by installing cameras at the entrance and by keeping the door locked at all times. Only visitors passing the video screening were buzzed into the building. Once inside they could enjoy the pleasure of browsing without having to suffer lecherous looks of salesmen. Nor were they subjected to trying on clothes surreptitiously in dark storage areas or public toilets. Because the doorbell shops had no storefronts, finding their discreet locations was by word-of-mouth. Generally, though, this was how life in Riyadh operated. The *mutawwa* frowned on most pleasures, however insignificant. Even something as simple as trying on clothes in a dressing room in front of a mirror had to go 'underground'!

Chapter Nineteen

By 1980, the first stage of housing and support facilities had been established on the vast 240-square-kilometre Riyadh airport site. These would accommodate construction and management teams during the building phase and house maintenance staff when the airport became operational.

Once Bechtel began relocating its personnel from the city to the desert, Sean took the family on a pre-move tour. Part of his motive was to reassure me that we'd be upgrading our living conditions.

"It feels like we've stepped from the pages of a Sears catalogue into a feature story in Architectural Digest," I enthused as we inspected the house we had chosen for ourselves.

"Well, it's not quite that standard," Sean laughed, "but the improvement is *almost* headline worthy!"

To my delight, Bechtel had hired an interior designer to select tasteful, coordinated furnishings and curtains for the compound's 120 villas. I wasn't happy about uprooting to the middle of nowhere but this pleasant environment would ease the transition.

In addition to tidy rows of two-storey homes, the new Family Housing compound had tennis courts, an Olympic-size pool, an elementary school, a playground that got a resounding thumbs up from Tara and Kieran and a recreation centre with a restaurant.

Still under construction was Community Facilities. This extensive open area adjacent to Family Housing would comprise a supermarket, fire station, theatre, small hospital, indoor and outdoor pools, tennis courts, apartments and more houses. This was the epitome of a 'company town'. I was glad we already had an active social life. It would have been difficult to establish a niche in the Riyadh community from the distant confines of this gilded cage.

* * * *

In response to the requirements of its multi-national population. Riyadh offered a number of educational options, including French, British, American and Japanese. Nothing corresponded to the Irish or Canadian curricula we would have preferred. The move to the jobsite solved the immediate dilemma of choosing a compromise system. The large population of mostly American children warranted a satellite branch of the American Saudi Arabian International School – Riyadh (SAIS-R) within the compound.

I already had resigned myself to the reality that a Saudi learning experience was neither available to nor suitable for Tara and Kieran. My initial inclination had been to enroll the kids in a local school, at least for pre-school and kindergarten. This would enable them to learn Arabic and meet other Saudi children. No one encouraged the plan.

I invited my Lebanese friend Salwa for coffee one morning. Surely with her Arab heritage and high level of education she wouldn't foster the same prejudices as Western friends?

"If there was even such a thing as early learning here, your kids would be excluded: they aren't Muslim," Salwa pronounced.

"What on earth does religion have to do with toddlers playing together?" I asked in astonishment.

"This is Saudi Arabia. Everything relates to religion."

"And how can there not be kindergartens?" I continued. "It's inconceivable that Saudi mothers don't incorporate this mini salvation into their lives."

Salwa laughed at my naivety and helped herself to another brownie. Her svelte good looks belied the fact that she had an unquenchable craving for sweets.

"First of all, *habibti*, there's no need for organised playgroups," Salwa explained. "Large Saudi families always have plenty of kids around. The older ones teach the younger ones. Secondly and more importantly, secular education is a new concept here. Universal education is even more recent. The first girls' school opened in 1956. It's only since 1970 that women have been able to go to college."

"Wow. I had no idea the situation was quite so… rudimentary. The few

Saudis we've met seem pretty savvy."

"Don't confuse a lack of formal education with a lack of inherent intelligence," Salwa said, already eyeing her next caloric gratification. "Saudis have many honed skills but most are not yet academically equipped to meet modern challenges. The existing system focuses on rote learning; non-religious subjects take second place and there's no room for lateral thinking. Not the best preparation to participate in and contribute to the economic and technological needs of today's world, is it?"

Evidently Salwa didn't approve of Saudi education at any level in any circumstances.

"What happened?" I asked. "The early advances of Arab astronomers, doctors and mathematicians form the basis for so much of today's knowledge."

"That's right. Islam emphasises the importance of learning – for everyone. In Saudi Arabia, however, implementation has fallen short of the original intention."

"Education is a country's greatest resource. It seems ludicrous not to match the investment they're making in the physical infrastructure with an investment in quality teaching. And to marginalise women? That's a bit shortsighted, don't you think? If they're serious about reducing dependency on foreigners, the government will have to properly train and make use of their full population."

"Absolutely," Salwa agreed. "But few men are willing to have women in any decision-making roles outside the home. Religious conservatives oppose 'dangerous' progress. This translates into anything that threatens their control. They believe females should focus on being good wives and mothers. In their view, religious studies sufficiently provide the groundwork for these duties. Saudi Arabia is still a tribal society. Honour rests on the chaste shoulders of its women. Many elders worry that female freedom equates to potential family shame."

"Other Arab countries are Islamic and tribal and they have educated women," I argued. "You're educated."

I poured fresh coffee.

"Yes," Salwa admitted. She added sugar and an indulgent helping of cream to her cup. "Riyadh is different. This area is the birthplace of

Wahhabism, the most conservative form of Islam. That doesn't bode well for change. The government's trying to alter public perception but these things take time, especially in a deeply traditional culture. Many men fear strong women. They'll keep them subjugated for as long as possible. One day, though, they'll lose the battle. In Prophet Mohammed's time, women could be warriors. The time will come when they'll fight again."

Salwa and I raised our cups to toast what we viewed as an inevitable event.

* * * *

Our move to the jobsite meant that I had to endure a 50-kilometre commute, much of it over unpaved roads, to work each day. After a year of doing this dusty, bumpy drive, I regretfully quit Al-Sharif.

Once again I was faced with the problem of satisfying my keep-busy nature. Leila, a Lebanese friend who loved food as much as I did, suggested that we start a small take-away venture with an East-West theme. In order to keep the business at hobby level, we limited the menu choices and confined our delivery area of Gourmet To Go to jobsite families. My days still needed filling. Weekly French-language coffee mornings were stimulating but I was looking for a more regular challenge. Eventually, I enrolled in correspondence courses from Queens University in Canada. This all-consuming effort gave me the intellectual inspiration I craved.

As an added bonus, the studies indirectly expanded our social horizon. Queens suggested the Canadian Embassy as the locale for an upcoming Spanish exam. My enquiries got a positive response from the Embassy.

"You might be interested to know that the Ambassador's wife, Beverly Valentine, is a university professor. One of her specialities is Spanish," the counsellor told me.

After the exam, Beverly invited me for coffee in the adjacent residence. She and her husband Doug had recently arrived in Riyadh. I had racked up six years' experience in the Kingdom so I was a useful source of information. We became good friends. The Valentines included Sean and me in many events, helping to establish our presence in the burgeoning diplomatic community.

In a possibly unique situation, embassies originally were not based in Saudi Arabia's capital city but in Jeddah, on the west coast. Jeddah's location on the well-established ancient trade routes, its role as an important Red Sea port and its proximity to Makkah and Medina made it a logical choice in the Kingdom's first days of statehood.

In the early 1980s the embassies began to relocate to Riyadh. The stylish Diplomatic Quarter, more popularly known as the DQ, had been created to house all the foreign missions in a newly-developing suburb on the edge of the now sprawling metropolis.

As a result of this cultural infusion, the city's already lively social scene began to glitter. It was as though the men straightened their ties and the women threw on some extra jewels and another splash of perfume. 'Society' had arrived; Riyadh had come of age.

Apart from an elegant ambiance and interesting guests, embassies could be counted on to have relatively unstinting supplies of alcohol. Officially, they weren't on Saudi soil, so the usual constraints didn't apply. An invitation to an embassy function meant an enjoyable evening of legal drinking. Those who exploited the privilege might be taken off future guest lists.

Most embassies respected Saudi restrictions about the general availability of alcohol. They made certain their supplies went no further than their own compounds. A few notorious diplomats, however, acted as black market agents. Some paid for the running costs of the embassy through illegal booze sales. More often the profits went straight into the pockets of the sellers. For the unscrupulous, a Saudi posting contributed nicely to their standard of living.

Incoming diplomats were advised to include in their household effects, but not list on the inventory, enough beer, wine and spirits to meet their entertaining needs for the duration of their posting. Many years previously, when the British Embassy was located in Jeddah, the newly arrived Ambassador received an urgent message from Saudi customs. They politely requested him to make arrangements as soon as possible to collect his shipping container from the docks because his piano was leaking.

* * * *

The influx of embassies augmented Riyadh's already rich mix of cultures. What the city lacked in outward refinements, it made up for in international experience. Social gatherings were often an exotic blend. At one of our dinners, our 12 guests represented 11 nationalities.

Although English served as a common language to these polyglots, words often had different meanings to different people. Chris Troke, a friend from the British Embassy was at one of Riyadh's famous multi-national dinner parties. From somewhere down the table he heard a Finnish guest mention 'squash'. Chris's ears perked up. He was an expert squash player and felt he might be able to contribute something to the conversation. Suddenly an Italian clarified the name of the vegetable for the Finn, saying, "No, that'sa really a *zucchini*." A Frenchman immediately jumped into the conversation, correcting the Finn and the Italian. "Non, zee true name for zees vegetable eez *courgette*." "I thought a courgette was a large cucumber," said a confused English lady. "And I," said Chris, at last making a contribution, "thought it was something I drank after playing squash."

Not all misunderstandings were so benign. Intractable prejudices between races or religions can be heightened in adverse situations. Labourers, who often live in trying conditions, sometimes expressed their hostilities physically. Periodically, tales of brutal recriminations shocked the community.

Exemplifying these deep, cross-cultural animosities was the incident of the Korean worker involved in an accident during construction of the airport. Fortunately, he had been wearing his hard hat, otherwise the heavy object that fell on his head would have killed him. Instead, the force pushed the hat down and its inner frame cut off his ears. Man and ears were rushed to the jobsite hospital where surgeons successfully rejoined them. The patient was recovering well until a British friend visited him. Besides the obvious language barrier, there was an inconsistency in their senses of humour.

"Hello, Mr. Kim. How are you feeling now?" asked the concerned friend.

"Velly so head. Pain no good," responded the suffering patient.

"Not to worry, old man. You'll be out of here in no time. And when you do get out, you'll be the star of the show with those new Filipino ears."

Mr. Kim's otherwise sallow complexion turned purple. Then he went berserk and attempted to rip off the offending ears. Nurses managed to sedate him before he could do serious damage. The horrified friend realised too late that what he had intended as an amusing comment was interpreted as a gross insult.

* * * *

Like so many businesses, the medical field was feeling the pinch of the country's reduced oil revenues. Instead of continuing to hire top Canadian, American and European doctors and nurses, companies recruited staff from developing countries. Many lacked adequate qualifications for their positions.

Too often, the complex equipment – and even some simple machines – far exceeded the skills of the inexperienced operators. Test results might be confused, either because of administrative mix-ups or because of badly maintained machinery. Our small jobsite hospital had not escaped the endemic staffing and stocking cutbacks. I suffered first-hand experience of this reality when I was taken there with a back injury seven years after my blissful maternity experience at the King Faisal Specialist Hospital. The differences in comfort and competence couldn't have been more dramatic. The first indication of a lack of professionalism came after I had X-rays taken.

"My God, my God, have you seen your spine?" the Filipino radiologist excitedly asked me.

I painfully turned in the wheelchair to try to get a better look at the film he was waving at me.

"Look at this, look at this." His compulsion to speak in echoes momentarily distracted me. "Your spine is all twisted. My God, my God. I am sorry for you."

A doctor arriving on the scene hastily banished the alarmist technician. He assured me that the slight curve at the base of my spine was nothing to worry about.

"Nevertheless," he said strictly, "you've managed to slip a disk. You should remain immobile for a few days. I'm recommending a stay in hospital. It'll be a nice break from the kids," he added with a wink.

I gave in to temptation.

It was Thursday afternoon and only a skeleton staff remained on duty for the weekend. Someone eventually found sheets for the bed but I had to go without washing for nearly two days because no one could find a key for the linen cupboard.

"Not to worry, dear," a nurse consoled. "There probably aren't any towels or nightgowns in the cupboard anyway."

The dietician didn't work on the weekend, so the Korean cook delighted in doing his own gastronomic thing. For lunch he served a disappointing version of bulgogi, one of Korea's national dishes, in lieu of the beef stroganoff listed on the menu. Other weekend meals featured unrecognisable food, except for breakfast: eggs boiled for such a long time that they were burned under the shell! The return of the dietician brought marked order to the chaotic kitchen but not even she could work miracles with shoe leather masquerading as meat.

After a week of Keystone Cops care, I could take no more.

"Please, doctor," I begged. "Let me go home. Medical treatment is obviously not conducive to my good health. I've lost weight, I have friction burn on my bottom from combative bed-changing methods, and an allergic reaction due to the administration of the wrong medication. To add insult to injury, the nurse put an analgesic cream on the allergy instead of on my back. What was she trying to do, ensure pain-free blisters?"

The doctor shook his head in disbelief and released me to the safety of my family.

* * * *

Medical attention wasn't the only aspect of jobsite living to show deterioration. What had been a relaxed environment became uncomfortably conservative by Western standards. As the project neared completion, Saudi staff stepped into airport maintenance jobs. The gradual integration of these Saudi families into the community resulted in drastic changes to our once agreeable living conditions.

The first new rule was a strict dress code – for women only, of course. I had always been circumspect in my dress, so it particularly annoyed me to be hauled in front of Bob Schnaible, the Bechtel project manager, to be chastised. Bob's wife Nan and I had been at a coffee morning that day. Nan, who didn't always approve of my free spirit, reported my unacceptable attire.

"Quite frankly, I'm surprised you would have the nerve to show up in the same outfit that got you in trouble in the first place," Bob said as Sean and I appeared in his office that evening.

"According to current Saudi standards, there's absolutely nothing wrong with this outfit," I argued. "The trousers and the top are loose-fitting and the sleeves are below the elbow. I wanted you to see that for yourself."

Bob didn't like rebels but he couldn't admit I'd done anything rebellious. Times were changing and we were all caught up in how far to go – or not to go.

"Look, Bob, the coffee morning was for a few expat women one street away from my house in a walled expat community. Was there really a need to cover myself from head to toe in such circumstances?"

"The 'need' is to follow the site's dress code, not your interpretation of it," Bob said strictly. "You've been warned, Kathy. Take it seriously."

I guess I got off lightly. Not too long afterwards, Bob fired an employee and sent the family home because he and his wife were out walking one evening and she didn't have her arms fully covered!

In this increasingly orthodox atmosphere, it was inevitable that the swimming pools would be segregated. In addition to the pronouncement of general separation of the sexes, women could no longer use the outdoor pools at any time on Fridays, the day the men had off work. Nor could any of the male lifeguards work during women's swimming hours. Worse, mothers could no longer go to the pools with sons above the age of 6. Seven-year-old Kieran was right at the cut-off point. Needless to say, I opted to take the risk and continue to let Kieran swim with Tara and me in the afternoons after school; needless to say, I got caught and reprimanded once again. Kieran had to restrict himself to swimming with Sean during men's hours.

Other annoyances included the cancellation of the piped TV and the closure of the local tape library.

"It makes no sense," I argued to my neighbour Jeannie Brownrigg. "There are plenty of tape libraries in Riyadh. What's the problem with having one here? Now everyone will have to go into town to get movies."

Jeannie was a pretty, smart Southern Belle who had started a manicure/pedicure service to keep herself busy. She was in the process of trying to make my desert-toughened feet presentable.

"It does seem extreme, doesn't it?" Jeannie said. She paused to concentrate on her work. "I heard the problems arose because the Saudis on the site were upset with the coverage of the Olympic games," she continued. "They didn't like to see all those scantily-clad women running races and throwing javelins."

Jeannie shrugged at my look of astonishment.

"Are the Saudis being hyper-sensitive to our ways or are we becoming hyper-sensitive to theirs?" I asked. There was no clear-cut answer.

In a further move to infringe on a harmless lifestyle, the children's Christmas party was cancelled. One aspect of our lives that absurd rules and regulations couldn't dampen, however, was the private celebration of Christmas.

Contrary to my initial fears, Christmases in Riyadh were exceptional. The pronounced lack of commercialism gave more significance to the season.

Riyadh's community of diverse cultures created a happy amalgam of traditions enjoyed by all. The desert was the scene of many Christmas-related events: concerts, Christmas Eve carol sessions and, between Christmas and New Year, a fantastic car rally.

We spent one of our more remarkable Christmases in the desert at the invitation of the inveterate party givers Liz and Michael Moore. We congregated with other guests at a designated landmark just outside the city late on Christmas morning in order to travel in convoy to our destination. The uncharacteristically cold, grey weather dampened our enthusiasm.

"I don't know about this, Kathy," Sean grumbled from behind the wheel. "You know how I love my home-cooked Christmas dinners."

"I know, sweetheart," I said soothingly. I tried to hide my own misgivings. "I wonder how Liz will manage a hot dinner for so many people in the middle of the desert?"

We drove for more than an hour and saw no other off-road traffic except our own line of 4-wheel drives. We crested a final dune. There, in a large depression, we noticed a number of expats industriously erecting tents. We had arrived.

"Merry Christmas and welcome," Liz and Michael said cheerfully as we got out of the Suburban. Oscar eagerly explored his new territory, manfully marking its boundaries along the way.

"You can put your things in the drinks tent," Liz said, pointing to a medium-sized, square structure on the perimeter of the camp. "We'll set up the cots in there when the kids are ready to go to bed."

We didn't have our own camping gear at this stage but the Moores, as experienced at camping as they were at entertaining, had extra equipment for us to borrow.

After unloading the car, we helped with various chores before dusk fell. Wood needed stacking. The fire would be an important source of warmth as the already cool temperature dropped further in the night. There were hors d'oeuvres to be laid out in the drinks tent and tables to be set in a dining tent that would accommodate 30 adults and assorted children at dinner. Entry to this main tent was restricted at this stage to only a couple of assistants.

When all the preparations had been made, everyone retired to dress for dinner. With spectacular incongruity, this was a black tie affair. At the appointed hour, the scruffy gaggle of campers reappeared in the guise of elegant dinner guests. We had drinks and amused ourselves with the game of matching baby pictures to the adult guests. Then Liz invited people to the previously off-limits dinner tent.

As we made our way past the canvas opening, each of us had the same reaction: Wow! Strings of fairy lights on the tent walls and ceiling augmented the romantic lighting of the candlelit tables. Holly and other decorations completed the festive scene. A tape of Christmas music played in the background. After a delicious, traditional turkey dinner with all the trimmings, we sang carols accompanied by Sir Patrick Wright, the British Ambassador, on an electric keyboard. The magical evening ended around an enormous campfire. We all felt we had partaken of the true spirit of Christmas.

The next morning I awoke with the sensation that I had alcohol for blood and cotton wool for brains. I hadn't drunk *that* much the night before, so what was the problem? It took no more than a deep inhalation to discover the cause.

"Jeez, Sean, this tent smells like a brewery. The canvas must have absorbed the fumes and we've been sucking them in all night! Remind me never to sleep in a drinks tent again. The poor kids will think they've been gassed!"

On our way to breakfast, we passed Sir Patrick digging a hole in the sand. He dumped all the empty bottles from the previous evening into the shallow grave and then smashed them.

"Just a precaution," he smiled.

No one thought the destruction of all evidence of our illegal – and considerable – consumption of alcohol extreme.

By midday everyone had dispersed.

"What do you think, guys?" Sean asked on the way home. "Was that one of the best Christmases ever?"

The kids and I shouted a resounding Yes. Oscar added a happy bark.

Expats came and went; new Christmas traditions took root or new people took on the responsibility of established ones. In the absence of blood relatives, we were each other's family – a family without squabbles or jealousies, a family of friends determined to celebrate the most important date in our calendar in the best way we could, despite the restrictions.

Chapter Twenty

The $3.2 billion King Khaled International Airport (KKIA) was construction on a grand scale. In addition to obvious components such as terminals, runways and a control tower – at 81 metres, one of the tallest in the world – the contract included almost 800 kilometres of roads and 20 bridges. Bechtel managed dozens of contractors and subcontractors from all over the world. For nine years we had been part of the ups and downs surrounding this impressive project.

Now construction was complete. Sean and I had been apprehensive for several months. It looked like we would leave Saudi but we had no certainty about where we would go – or if Sean even would have a job. It was 1985 and the world was still reeling from the effects of the recent recession. We guessed that Bechtel would send Sean back to the San Francisco head office to await an assignment but this presented a schooling problem: children weren't allowed to register at school unless they had a permanent address. We would have to settle first and then find a school well into the school year. Did we want to 'settle' if there was a chance that Sean would be transferred soon?

Oscar, too, was a concern. He was more than 10 years old. We worried that a long flight would be too much for him. Then, as though Oscar understood he was adding to our anxieties, his health suddenly and quickly deteriorated. One Friday afternoon, he gave us a final flap of the tail and lick of our hands and then died. Our lives, already in flux, now felt empty.

Lynn Wilcox, a former Bechtel colleague of Sean's, offered a possible solution to our situation. Lynn recently had joined an American company called CRSS & Metcalfe & Eddy. They had been awarded the contract to manage the construction of five massive, reinforced, underground command centres and 17 long-range radar sites around the country. Lynn was trying to recruit Sean. Sean expressed cautious enthusiasm.

"The job itself sounds interesting," Sean said when he related this latest development to me. "The problem is they're looking for someone with mechanical-electrical experience. I've only got electrical. I'll go for the interview but don't get your hopes up."

"How would you feel about leaving Bechtel?" I asked.

"I'd have to give it a lot of thought," Sean said after a momentary pause. "I've been with Bechtel for a long time; they've been good to me. Quitting wouldn't be an easy decision."

"On the plus side, transferring to CRSS would mean minimum disruption. The kids could continue school here."

"And there would be job security for a few years," Sean added. "As I said, though, don't get your hopes up."

* * * *

The emotional turmoil of our private lives didn't slacken the pace of our social life. We maintained our tradition of holding Friday brunches for jobsite personnel. At one of these brunches, an acid-tongued guest annoyed me with a bitter barrage of unfounded, negative comments about Saudis.

"I'm fed up with that woman's narrow-minded judgments," I complained as Sean and I cleaned the kitchen after everyone had left. "What's worse, she's not the only one who thinks hers is the only acceptable way of life and that her lifestyle should transfer seamlessly to any culture or locale. I'm going to write a bloody article about this counterproductive attitude."

Sean turned on the dishwasher and refilled his glass of wine.

"Go for it," he encouraged. "You'll never know how much you can achieve if you don't accept new challenges."

I loved the idea of being a writer. In equal measure, I hated the idea of the inevitable rejection slips that came with trying to get published. Our seemingly imminent departure made me less inclined to worry about rebuffs: with Saudi Arabia's erratic mail system, I'd probably be out of the country before a rejection slip could catch me – if the newspaper even bothered to send one.

In tongue-in-cheek style, I used medical terminology to describe ethnocentrism, the evaluation of other cultures by the standards of your own culture, as a social disease. Before I had time to change my mind, I mailed the article to the *Arab News*, one of the Kingdom's three English-language newspapers. In the midst of our other distractions, I forgot about the submission.

A week later, Sean arrived home for lunch with a huge grin and the words "I have news". It looked like our uncertainties had been resolved. I was excited to know what the future held in store. Then the phone rang.

"Yes, this is Kathy Cuddihy," I responded to the accented query at the other end of the phone.

"Good afternoon, Kathy. My name is Khaled Al-Maena. I'm the editor-in-chief of the *Arab News*. I wanted to call you personally to tell you how much I enjoyed your article."

Sean signalled me from the kitchen doorway, obviously impatient to reveal the latest job developments. The timing of the phone call couldn't have been worse but my ego wouldn't let me consider cutting short *this* conversation. Khaled's words were music to my writer's ears.

"It is an excellent piece of writing. In fact, I'm going to put it on our medical page."

Oops. Khaled had missed the whole point of the article. I tactfully tried to explain the nuances to him but he wouldn't be swayed.

"It will be in tomorrow's paper," he said. "And please let us have more articles."

I felt like shouting my achievement from the rooftop.

"Oh, sweetheart," I said to Sean after giving an emotional victory yell, "I know you have something important to say. But this phone call means I have the opportunity to be a writer, a published writer!"

My eyes shone with the possibilities. Sean's moment of glory had been robbed but his generous spirit allowed me to enjoy my little triumph. Finally I got my feet back on the ground.

"OK, tell me. What's the news?" I asked, giving Sean my full attention.

"The job with CRSS has come through. I'm on the management team. This means we'll be in Riyadh for a few more years. We'll have to move to Al-Yamama compound, the best in the city, where you'll have access to all sorts of non-company people. Can you cope?" he teased.

The glow of pleasure on my face gave Sean his answer.

* * * *

Al-Yamama lay on the still developing, mostly Arab, north-eastern edge of Riyadh. There wasn't much in the vicinity that was commercially interesting except a wholesale vegetable market. After our five-year stint in the desert, however, this was 'in town' to us, with not a dusty road in sight.

The compound deserved its reputation as a first-class oasis of Western living. Well-spaced two- and three-bedroom ranch-style houses sat on wide, winding streets and cul de sacs lined with gardens and large green spaces. A friendly, international ambiance flourished. Although we lived in company housing, this wasn't a company compound. This was a real neighbourhood whose residents worked for a cross-section of Riyadh's employers.

CRSS adopted a *laissez-faire* attitude towards the families under their sponsorship. They organised corporate events such as the annual St. Patrick's Day compound 'pub' crawl, or periodic barbecues but otherwise people were left alone to get on with their lives. In such a normal environment, there was no need for rally-the-troops coffee mornings and few of the women had the time or the inclination to play company politics. I felt that I could breathe again. This was the atmosphere I had subconsciously yearned for. At last I could be my own person – whoever that might be.

* * * *

One good thing about Al-Yamama's otherwise remote location was its proximity to the main American SAIS-R campus. The ten-minute bus ride meant the kids wouldn't have to endure long, hot commutes, like many of Riyadh's children.

The international school truly lived up to its name in the diverse nationalities of its students. In my day, names like Susan, Peter, Jane or Jimmy prevailed. When I asked Tara and Kieran to name some of their classmates, they rewarded me with a cornucopia of unfamiliar syllables. Sounds like Nizzilla, Wona, Irem, Baran, Coy and Yanki gave little indication of whether they belonged to boys or girls.

Muslim names were distinctly absent. Initially, even children who had Islamic names but no Muslim background were pressured to register at Muslim schools. Authorities could close a foreign school that did not comply with the directive. Muslims whose children previously had been educated out of the country had to fight to enrol them in foreign schools. Eventually the Ministry of Education relented and didn't force non-Saudi, non-Arab Muslims to attend Saudi schools. These students were nevertheless expected to keep up with their studies of the *Qur'an,* usually six days a week.

The Ministry was equally intent that foreign schools remain non-denominational. They made periodic spot checks to ensure the children's exposure was strictly secular. Remarkably, this included counting the points on snowflakes made by the children during the 'holiday' season. Six-pointed snowflakes were forbidden: too much like the Star of David.

* * * *

School was always a trial for hyperactive Kieran – and his teachers. It became a challenge for all of us to get through each day with a minimum of trauma and drama. The school was aware that he had been diagnosed with hyperactivity/attention-deficit disorder (HADD). Although HADD had been recognised in the West, Riyadh had no suitable support groups and little available information. Few educators had adequate training to deal with HADD children. At the beginning of each school year I met with Kieran's teachers to explain how to get the most from him.

"Get him involved," I advised. "Give him little chores to do that make him feel good. For instance, pretend you don't know how to put staples into your stapler, or that you can't open a bottle. He has an amazing talent for figuring out how things work. He just needs to be kept motivated."

Usually my suggestions went unheeded. To most of them, Kieran was just an unruly child who didn't fit neatly into the mould. Disciplinary notes were inevitable, numerous and usually stressful; on occasion, though, they made me admire Kieran's inventiveness.

Dear Mrs. Cuddihy,
I have to admit, my curiosity has finally got the better of me. Have you signed any

homework sheets/permission slips/absentee forms for your son lately? The reason I ask is that due to a recently discovered talent displayed by Kieran, we are led to believe that 'your' signature is not actually yours.

Today we caught the boy submitting a forged note to his gym teacher excusing him from class due to health reasons. We got suspicious when the note was written on scrap paper with frayed edges… and when it cited 'pre-minstral tenshun' as the cause of the illness.

We are alarmed that the forgery is such good quality. We feel you should be informed urgently. We have taken disciplinary action at school but you will probably agree that parental involvement is also required.

Dear – ,

Did you really send me a note yesterday or was that one of my son's clever tricks?

Aside from the fact that yours is supposed to be a progressive school that should encourage any and all talents in the children under your care, I do feel that your concerns are misplaced. Who cares about forged homework slips, etc.? What I have to find out is whether or not the little genius has been using my chequebook!

As well as notes, I periodically received phone calls from school. Our phone didn't have caller ID so I always feared who might be on the other end: friend, business contact or yet another teacher reporting Kieran's mischief. One day a teacher called with a benign request.

"Would you consider talking to my class about writing? It would mean so much to the children. We've been discussing books and authors. When Mickey told me that his mother is a writer, it seemed like a perfect opportunity to give the children some first-hand contact with a real author."

Mickey? Our conversation continued for a few more minutes. All of a sudden 'Mickey' reappeared. At this point I felt it necessary to make a correction.

"My son's name is Kieran. Are you sure you're calling the right person?"

"It's funny you should say that. His name is Kieran in other classes, according to some of his teachers. In my class, though, he's Mickey, not only to me but to everyone else."

Interesting. Did I have a little changeling on my hands?

"What gives with the Mickey business?" I asked when Kieran came home from school.

He looked a little sheepish at first and then confessed.

"At the beginning of the year, the teacher asked if anyone had any nicknames. I raised my hand and told her she should call me Mickey."

"And none of your friends make fun of you? Or does everyone have pseudonyms?"

"I'm the only one with a different name but no one makes fun of me. I'm Mickey in three classes. Everyone is used to it by now. As soon as we go into a Mickey class, everyone forgets that I'm Kieran."

It's extraordinary how resilient kids are. Or maybe they knew Kieran well enough that nothing he did surprised them.

* * * *

Writing is a solitary sport. The circumstances of life in Riyadh, where most expat activities were unadvertised and 'illegal', made it particularly difficult to discover other writers. If I could ferret them out and get us together, it would surely benefit everyone. We could exchange information on the business of writing such as new opportunities, what publications to avoid, who paid well and who didn't pay.

To my pleasant surprise, these efforts revealed a number of previously unknown colleagues. The newly formed Writer's Group met twice a month. Only a couple of us had been published but everyone had enthusiasm.

"I do my best writing after these meetings," Pam Daugavietis confessed. She echoed the sentiments of all of us.

Pam and her husband Andy had recently come to Riyadh. They both worked at the King Fahad Hospital, Andy as a doctor, Pam in public relations. Like many others in the group, Pam had a surfeit of fervour and a dearth of experience. These gatherings gave her the confidence to express her writer's voice.

Several people in the group despaired of ever getting past the rejection letters. I decided to give them a project.

"Let's do our own book. Everyone can contribute a chapter, either fiction or non-fiction. It will be a collection of thoughts from women living in Riyadh."

No one dismissed the idea but neither did it receive unanimous support. The unknown world of publishing intimidated some of the novice writers.

"Sometimes you just have to take matters into your own hands," I insisted. If nothing else, life in Riyadh had taught me that lesson! "Andre Gide said you can't discover new oceans until you have the courage to lose sight of the shore. Come on, girls, let's push the boat out."

The group finally agreed. Lisa Greenburg came up with the clever title of *Sandscripts*. After the usual nagging to meet deadlines, a book was born. Riyadh had a new flock of published writers. The Writer's Group had achieved its objective of bringing like-minded people together for the advantage of all.

Chapter Twenty-One

As far as health matters went, I was the weak link in our family's otherwise robust medical chain. Thankfully, my illnesses were few and far between but they tended to be accompanied by a bit of drama.

My latest problem started with stomach cramps. The pains were becoming worse. And more frequent. Something was definitely amiss. I returned to the Lebanese gynaecologist I'd seen a couple of weeks previously. He ran a series of tests but could find nothing wrong.

"Let's try a colonoscopy," he suggested.

Ignorant of exactly what the procedure involved, I readily agreed.

The doctor had a superb bedside manner but nothing could distract me from the garden hose-like tube that he planned to stick up my bum.

"Don't worry, my dear," he soothed. "Everything will be fine." He patted my hand in confirmation.

But it wasn't. I'd had no anaesthetic and my body didn't enjoy the invasion.

"Your problem, my dear, is that you're too much of a lady. We get old Bedu in here and the tube slides in easily. It's not such a novelty for them, if you know what I mean."

These Lebanese doctors certainly have a way of getting the mind off pain!

Although the doctor assured me that I had "a colon like a baby", the pain dilemma remained unresolved. I presented myself at his office and told him I wouldn't leave until we could find a reason for the severe cramps.

"Are you happily married?" he asked, no doubt assuming a negative answer would provide the elusive cause of the problem.

"Yes. And I've got a great family. I don't think this stems from emotional upset."

"What is different in your life?"

"Only the hormone replacement therapy you prescribed," I responded firmly.

"It can't possibly be that," he insisted. "You have the mildest dosage."

My silent stare told him I wasn't going to be brushed off. He got up with a sigh of resignation and walked over to his large bookshelf. His long fingers passed over the spines of several medical tomes before they settled on the one he was looking for.

"I don't believe it," he exclaimed a moment later, reading the small print. "In extremely rare cases, this medication causes your symptoms."

I stopped taking HRT. The pain disappeared but I could never quite erase the image of what those old Bedu were getting up to.

* * * *

Dental incidents for me were sometimes no less extreme than medical incidents. In the course of a general check-up, Bill Fisher, a long-time dentist friend, made an unexpected observation.

"You know, Kathy, you should really consider getting braces – for therapeutic reasons." Bill's bulk hovered over me as his meaty hands skilfully manipulated the probing instruments.

"Goo geef, Bill," I slurred, before managing to free my mouth of his prodding fingers, "I'm 37 years old! Braces are for kids... aren't they?"

I shuddered at the thought of the ordeal.

"It's your choice. You can either go through the hassle now or wait until you're in your 50s. But eventually you're going to need to correct a problem that's getting worse. We have a good orthodontist in the office."

Although it had become trendy in North America for adults to get braces, the fad hadn't reached Saudi Arabia, where there were few dentists and fewer orthodontists.

With moral support from Sean and an oh-what-the-heck impulsiveness on my part, I made the commitment. The designated teeth were pulled and the embarrassingly conspicuous silver braces applied. The orthodontist had lulled me into a false sense of security when he assured me that "orthodontics is not painful". I'm not quite sure where he drew the line between pain and strong discomfort. In retrospect I have to admit that his psychology was effective. Every time I dosed myself with aspirin or felt tempted towards self-pity, I realised it could be worse: instead of feeling utterly miserable, I could be in pain.

"Does my adult status give me any reprieve in how long these wretched things have to be on?" I asked, desperately wanting some good news.

"Not a chance, Kathy. Count on having a tin grin for a good two years."

Despite a growing impatience to have the braces removed, disappointment tinged my initial reaction to the New Me. It was certainly a relief to be rid of the birdcage in my mouth. And there was absolutely nothing wrong with the orthodontist's handy-work but – no matter how hard I smiled – I just didn't have that gleaming movie star look about me. Always quick to defend his expertise, the orthodontist bluntly pointed out the reality of the situation.

"The teeth are fine, Kathy. I think it might be the hair and the body that need a bit of help."

And I thought I was through with humiliation.

Chapter Twenty-Two

Unlike Family Housing, which had no servants' quarters, Al-Yamama's houses had a small ensuite room in the house to accommodate help. Now that we had got out of the habit of live-in maids and the children had grown beyond the need of constant supervision, I preferred to use the space as an office. Sean claimed the bathroom portion as his winery.

Choosing not to have a live-in maid meant relying on part-time help. The young men the compound management sent for interviews always looked capable and acted confident. Only after hiring them would I make unsettling discoveries. Like when I noticed my charming Sri Lankan houseboy going through furniture polish at an alarming rate. We didn't have that much furniture! A surreptitious check on his work revealed he used it not only to polish the wood but also the tile work and porcelain in the bathrooms and the counter tops and sink in the kitchen! I caught him just as he stood contemplating whether or not to Pledge a bathroom mirror.

On another occasion, I ran through all the instructions with a houseboy who, as usual, assured me of his abilities. Two days later I caught him industriously engaged in cleaning the toilet bowls with Calgon dishwasher powder.

"Try to remember, Kathy, that most of these people are illiterate or semi-literate," Sean reasoned as I angrily showed him the tin of Pledge and bottle of Mr Clean that a houseboy had exhausted in one session. "Those who do have an education might only read Arabic or Hindi or some other non-European language, none of which appear on American or European cleaning products."

"You're right," I admitted. "I just get so frustrated. What's the point of having help if I always have to chase after them?"

"Perhaps the answer isn't to chase but to lead." Sean gently took the empty cleaning containers from my hands and threw them into the garbage. "Invest the time, reap the benefits. Accept that a humble houseboy probably isn't going to achieve your high standards in a couple of days. Show him how you like things done, let him try and then be prepared to show him again... and again, if necessary. Rome wasn't built in a day."

I clenched my jaws, hating to have my failings so succinctly brought to my attention. I realised that I needed to try to correct this character flaw but the ongoing skirmishes continually tested my resolve.

One day I came home to a worried houseboy.

"Madam, explosion today in house."

"Explosion, Lintu? Good grief, where? Are you all right? What happened?"My eyes darted around the room, seeking evidence of the reported calamity.

"Big bang. Big mess. Powder shoot everywhere, Madam."

"Bang? Powder? Shoot? WHAT HAPPENED? Show me where the explosion occurred. Show me what exploded," I said, hand on heart, fighting the panic that threatened to take hold.

He guided me into the living room. Beside a table lay the gutted remains of… a vacuum bag.

"Lintu, don't you realise that you have to change the bag regularly?" My relief expressed itself in exasperation.

"No, Madam. In all my years cleaning, I never see this before."

"But, Lintu, don't you wonder where all the dust that you suck up from the carpets goes?" I asked incredulously.

"Oh no, Madam. I know where it go," he replied confidently. "Dust get sucked into special place in sky. When enough stock, it come back here as dust storm. Everything in life come back."

What a delightful insight into the workings of reincarnation. The logic might be a bit fuzzy but it sure changed my attitude towards vacuum bags.

After I carefully explained the mechanics of vacuum cleaners, we both vowed to pay more attention to these small but important details.

When I told Sean the story that evening, he enjoyed an appreciative laugh at Lintu's philosophical attitude but then reminded me to keep things in perspective.

"You have to understand, Kathy, that no one, least of all Third World servants, is born knowing how to operate modern appliances and gadgets.

What we think of as essential, labour-saving devices are unheard-of luxuries in many parts of the world."

I could certainly relate to that. I refused to have anything to do with technological wonders that arrived in our home until someone else read the instructions and then gave me an idiot-proof tutorial.

Not all help has an exaggerated learning curve. A few grasp concepts with a zeal – an embarrassing zeal.

Canadian friends Jeri and Peter McArthur were thrilled to receive a dinner invitation to the home of Sir Frederick Rosier, the head of British Aerospace. In their anxiety not to be late, they arrived slightly early. They rang the bell and were greeted by a formally dressed, gloved, Indian butler who perused the invitation card they handed him.

"Come this way, please," he said with superiority.

He led them into the house, past what was obviously the living room, and up a main staircase. *Strange that these people don't entertain in the downstairs living room*, thought Jeri.

They came to a closed door. The servant tapped lightly, opened the door with a flourish and announced in his best Master of Ceremonies voice, "Dr and Mrs McArthur."

There stood Sir Frederick and Lady Rosier in the privacy of their bedroom, he in boxer shorts and gartered socks, she in a slip. Instinctively, Sir Frederick extended his hand in the finest British tradition and said "How do you do."

Putting the strange situation down to the idiosyncrasies of British aristocracy and remembering that the invitation said casual, Jeri and Peter gamely walked into the bedroom. Lady Rosier quickly cleared up the misunderstanding when she frostily asked the servant to take the guests downstairs and give them a gin and tonic.

"No, better make that a double," she corrected with clipped clarity.

* * * *

Taking the time to properly train help can be demanding, but communication is usually the ongoing stumbling block. Giving clear instructions is only one part of the equation. It doesn't mean a thing if they're not understood.

Of course, communication should work both ways. Deciphering foreign English could be perplexing.

A houseboy once surprised me with a colourful but cryptic query: "No marshmallow sink, Madam?"

I stared blankly, mulling over the possible translations. We didn't have any marshmallows in the house. Could that be the problem? If so, what did he plan to do with them? Wash them in the sink? Or perhaps our sink was too hard? After a series of hand signs and other clues, I eventually discerned that he simply wanted to know if I had a sponge with which to clean the bathroom!

The communication breakdown comes to the fore most blatantly, and most frustratingly, in the relaying of messages, particularly telephone messages. Not only is the name likely to be garbled but the same possibility exists for the caller's phone number.

A houseboy once informed me that a Mr Abu Rashid had called. Abu Rashid? I had never heard of the man. Feeling rather foolish, I dialled the number, identified myself and asked if anyone there had tried to phone me.

"Kathy," came the amused reply, "it's David Ashley! Liz and I wanted to invite you and Sean to dinner but your houseboy seemed to keep saying you were in the Philippines! It didn't make much sense so I left my contact details on the off-chance that you had gone no further than into town."

Sometimes the mixed messages were almost appropriate. When I called my friend Jan Quinn one evening, her young daughter told me she had gone out. I left my name and number. Eventually Jan returned my call.

"We got a mysterious message that Katie Clutterhead had called. We racked our brains trying to figure out who it might be. I'm not sure why, but you were the best candidate. Did you call?"

To the Quinn family, I remain Katie Clutterhead.

Chapter Twenty-Three

The publication of my first article in the *Arab News* introduced me to local editing practices. Not only did the features editor not seem to understand the concept of satire, he scrapped the vital punch line. Each of my subsequent articles appeared with new editorial foibles. Sometimes space restraints meant deleting paragraphs. Instead of making sensible cuts, however, they often started from the bottom up, leaving a story without a logical ending. With time, and as a result of my vocal complaints, editorial gaffes decreased.

Having got in the door of the newspaper world, I suggested writing a humorous weekly column about life in Saudi. The *Arab News* turned down the proposal. Perhaps they feared a backlash from readers who might not see the funny side of expat living. The *Saudi Gazette* had no such compunction. After approving a couple of sample copies with illustrations by my neighbour Mimi Cousart, they introduced Kathy's Korner.

I had discovered Mimi, another CRSS wife, on the compound shopping bus. Her mop of unruly red curls suited her pleasantly bohemian attitude towards life. Mimi, I learned, played the role of Clownie on Saudi TV's popular children's show. When I found out that this amusing character also had an art degree, the entrepreneur in me immediately wanted to find an outlet for her talent. Kathy's Korner seemed perfect. Mimi agreed to give our creative partnership a try. Her professional training in presenting the artwork and her clever cartoon depictions of my text impressed me. We were in business.

Regular newspaper exposure gave me the confidence to seek new outlets. Magazines now lured me into their orbit. The drawback was that Saudi Arabia didn't have any national English-language publications. Then I remembered *Ahlan Wa Sahlan*, Saudia's glossy in-flight magazine.

The editor Khalil Ziadeh phoned me from Saudia's head office in Jeddah to give me the go-ahead for an article on Riyadh's unique dairy industry. I was delighted – until he told me their rate.

"We usually pay 100 pounds for an article," Khalil informed me.

Jeez. It's a good thing I didn't have to support myself on the Saudi pay scale. Apparently the boom benefits didn't extend to writers.

"Actually, I was thinking more in the range of 1,000 riyals."

This was almost three times Saudia's offer. Khalil Ziadeh didn't show any interest until I said I was willing to negotiate.

"Instead of cash, what about giving me a first-class return ticket to London for every article?"

Suddenly he found cash to be a preferable option. We came to a compromise that definitely favoured Saudia but that wasn't impossible for me to accept. After writing a couple of well-received articles, Khalil presented me with a surprise bonus: first-class return tickets to London. This cloud definitely had a silver lining.

As my contributions to *Ahlan Wa Sahlan* increased, Saudia regularly gave the family and me upgrades – another unexpected bonus. This meant checking in at short first-class lines. Young Kieran obviously thought this was the norm. Once, when we were in transit in Frankfurt, we joined the long, slow-moving economy line for our non-Saudia connecting flight.

"Mom," Kieran complained in a loud voice, "what are we doing so far back in the line?" Then, in an even louder voice he ordered, 'Just tell them who you are!'

A number of eyes discreetly glanced at us, no doubt hoping to recognise a famous celebrity. I smiled meekly, mutely apologising for their disappointment.

* * * *

Personal experience illustrated the fact that writing is the world's worst paid profession. There are even more writers below the poverty line than actors, for goodness sake. I was determined to be an exception to this reality.

"I've set myself the goal of at least doubling my writing income every year," I announced to Sean over breakfast.

He took a slow sip of coffee, probably giving himself time to wipe the smile off his face.

"That's not going to be too difficult for the first couple of years, is it. You've hardly earned anything!"

"True," I replied with just a hint of impatience, "but that's going to change. I'm going to become as creative about marketing as I am about writing."

The obvious first step was to recycle my work. It seemed silly to invest maximum writing effort for minimum financial return. If I could tweak articles and then sell them several times, this would make the endeavour worthwhile.

I already enjoyed a measure of success recycling the magazine articles. Could I do the same for the weekly column? A marathon session of writing query letters to every newspaper and magazine in the Gulf brought favourable responses from Kuwait and Dubai. I was now a syndicated columnist.

The ultimate recycling exercise would be to collect column articles into a book. I finally found a local publisher and pitched my idea to him.

"Yes," the Saudi manager told me with a smile, "I follow your column in the paper each week. It is very funny."

"That's great. I'm so glad you like it. I'd like to publish a book of all the columns that refer to adapting to living in Saudi. I'd call it *Familiarity Breeds Content.*"

He rewarded me with a glazed stare and a slack smile.

"That's a play on words," I continued gamely. "In English we have a saying 'familiarity breeds contempt'. I'm giving the book a positive spin."

He remained bewildered. His long, bony fingers nervously worked his worry beads, as though this exercise would give him a solution to his quandary. Then he made a strange pronouncement.

"But your book would be funny, yes?"

"Yes," I confirmed. "Just like my columns that you enjoy."

"Ah, that is the problem, you see. Saudis don't have a sense of humour. Who would buy the book?"

He shrugged his shoulders, as though dismayed at his countrymen's failing in this matter.

I was back at square one.

"There's got to be a way around this," I grumbled to Mimi.

She had stopped by to deliver illustrations for the column. And to sample the banana bread that I'd just taken out of the oven. Mimi tried to avoid going into her kitchen but her sense of smell was quick to pick up signals when something good was happening in mine.

"Why not publish the book yourself?" she asked between bites.

In addition to her TV career, Mimi was well known in Riyadh for her Christmas card and t-shirt designs. She worked with a local printer.

"I can introduce you to my contact. If the quote is decent, you just have to present him with a camera-ready copy."

After indulging in yet another slice of banana bread, Mimi phoned her printer. We had an appointment for the following morning.

Mustafa, a burly, hirsute Lebanese, clearly enjoyed the unusual circumstance of having two women in his office. He dragged out negotiations over several cups of tea and then agreed to an astonishingly fair price.

"You happy with work, you come back. We be friends."

Mimi and I smilingly agreed but mentally rolled our eyes.

"It's the X chromosome," Mimi assured me when we got to the car. "His genes are screaming 'I'm available' but he's actually a big teddy bear. I've never had a problem. In fact, once he gets past trying to make the impression that he's a lothario, he's quite the gentleman. The important thing is that he does decent work and he delivers on schedule."

Now I just had to provide him with a camera-ready copy – whatever that was. In my limited writing experience, editors handled all the behind-the-scenes stuff. I was still loyal to my faithful old Selectric typewriter. My computer literacy extended no further than playing a detective game with my children. To propel myself into the age of technology, I had just ordered a state-of-the-art Macintosh, the creative world's best friend.

The technician arrived a few days later to install the computer and laser printer. He gave me a quick tutorial and then got ready to leave.

"Wait," I said, frantically grabbing his arm. "How do I turn the machines on and off?"

Despite this rocky start, I produced the required manuscript. The next hurdle was getting it approved by the Ministry of Information. Without their certification, the book legally couldn't be printed or sold in the Kingdom.

I made an appointment for Mimi and me with Mohammed Nouri, the Director of English-Language Publications. This seemingly simple task gave us more than a little anxiety. After all, this was the department that ruthlessly defaced foreign newspapers, magazines, books and recording covers. Moral guardians blacked out any offensive word or image on all copies before they appeared on the stands. Particularly resolute censors would impose the dreaded black marker on exposed female necks and wrists. Few imported publications remained unscathed. If ever there was going to be an example of a humourless Saudi, this would probably be the man.

Our driver dropped us in front of the Ministry's stark building. A young fellow delivering a load of papers pointed towards the stairs and told us, "*Sayed* Nouri on floor three." We arrived, knocked and entered *Sayed* Nouri's large office with trepidation.

Our fears were unfounded. Mohammed Nouri was typically courteous and decidedly unmenacing. After some introductory chitchat, he called in Ahmed, a tall, gangly Egyptian who had Male Chauvinist written all over him. This, alas, was the man who would read the manuscript.

"Tho, what have you little ladies done?" he lisped. "A cookbook?"

Ahmed gave a condescending smirk as he scanned us from behind heavy eyelids that hung at half mast. Boy, had this guy misjudged his audience. In order to avoid what suddenly might deteriorate into an embarrassing clash, the Director quickly thanked Ahmed and said he would send the manuscript to his office.

Because everything in the book had already appeared in a national newspaper without repercussion, Ahmed's objections didn't get past our new friend Mohammed.

Two weeks later, having survived both the Ministry and the stress of producing camera-ready copy on an unfamiliar computer, I held my first book in my hands. Peregrine Publishing was born.

Eventually I would self-publish five books. Anticipating Ahmed's need to flex his censorial muscles, I sprinkled future manuscripts with sentences I knew would raise red flags. I would agree to delete these inserted bargaining chips if the rest of the text got approved. Even censorship was negotiable.

* * * *

My journalistic career came about by accident, without benefit of formal training. Nevertheless, it progressed quickly and steadily – in a country with an aversion to journalists.

My acceptance was mainly due to the fact that I often showed interviewees a copy of the article before publication. I had two reasons for doing this: linguistic difficulties on their part and comprehension errors on mine.

A visiting journalist from the hallowed halls of Washington DC was appalled to learn of this practice. We had been having coffee together, discussing the ins and outs of working in Saudi.

"*Real* journalists *never* show their work to *anyone*," she drawled.

"Not all my interview subjects speak good English," I explained. "They sometimes choose an unsuitable word or accidentally reverse the order of numbers. Looking at the text allows them to correct honest misunderstandings."

"That's just *no* excuse." Donna flipped back her long black hair in a business-like manner and glared, hoping to impress on me the severity of my transgression.

"Mistakes don't always come from the Saudi side," I said in defense of this unorthodox behaviour. "I might be assigned a story on new technology, local agriculture methods or banking. In case my best efforts to understand the unfamiliar terms fall short of the mark, the original source can clarify. Besides, not a single person has ever tried to persuade me to change the article, except to correct mistakes. They simply appreciate knowing in advance that I haven't misinterpreted what they have to say."

"I guess you *won't* be persuaded. You'll just have to *live* with the fact that you'll *never* be a *real* journalist."

True, perhaps, but my reputation gave me easy access to just about everyone in the Kingdom – something my visiting colleague couldn't achieve, much to her annoyance.

Chapter Twenty-Four

I was always looking for new story ideas. Surely the Arabian horse would have wide reader appeal? I mentioned my nascent thought to our good friend David Ashley. His successful picture framing business gave him access to a wide spectrum of Riyadh's population. Maybe he had come across someone with expertise in this field.

"You should speak with Abdullah Al-Sweilem. He works as a deputy minister in the government but his passion is horses. He has some beautiful Arabians on his farm just outside the city. Abdullah knows as much about horses as anyone. He's also quite a character. I think you'd like him."

This sounded encouraging. David made contact with Abdullah and phoned back with an intriguing invitation.

"Abdullah is cautious around writers. Too many times, foreign journalists have misrepresented Saudis. He'd like to meet you before making a commitment about an interview. He's asked all of us to dinner at his farm on Thursday. Come to our place first for drinks."

I was surprised at such a friendly response from someone who wasn't sure he could trust me. Then I remembered the Bedouin rule of the desert: treat even your enemies with hospitality for three days.

When Sean and I got to the Ashleys', Abdullah had already arrived. Saudis can be notoriously relaxed about time, so punctuality was a point in his favour. But where was the man David was so sure I'd like? This solemn figure of authority that David introduced unnerved me with his dark, forbidding stare. We made small talk over drinks but Abdullah never dropped his iron guard. When he announced that we should head to the farm, I felt relief at temporarily removing myself from his almost brooding company.

"I don't think I want to do an interview with this man," I said to Sean as we followed Abdullah's car into the desert. "He actually intimidates me… and you know that almost never happens."

"Backing out isn't an option at this stage, is it? Surely you don't find him that impossible."

"Actually I do," I responded with uncharacteristic meekness. "All I can say is that his horses had better be more appealing than he is or this story is getting binned before it's even written."

To our astonishment, the Abdullah who greeted us at his farm was a different person from the one we'd met over drinks.

"*Ahlan wa sahlan*," he said warmly. "Welcome. Let me introduce you to my friends and then I'll show you around."

Interesting. On his own turf and in the role of host, Mr Unapproachable had morphed into Mr Congeniality.

Sean and I met Abdullah's cousin Abdul Mohsen and his three other male guests. Then we met the magnificent equine residents.

The Arabian is said to go back 4,000 years but its recognition as a distinct breed came about with the spread of Islam, from the 7th century AD. A favourite Bedouin myth states that Allah gathered the forces of the four winds: spirit from the north, strength from the south, speed from the east and intelligence from the west. Then he proclaimed, "I create thee, Oh Arabian. To thy forelock, I bind Victory in battle. On thy back, I set a rich spoil and a Treasure in thy loins. I establish thee as one of the Glories of the Earth... I give thee flight without wings."

I'd read about the beauty, endurance and intuition of Arab horses. Desert hardships had weeded out the weak until the gene pool comprised loyal, hardy beasts able to survive extreme temperatures and frequent food shortages. Abdullah's stables housed prime specimens. He had made it his mission to restore authentic bloodlines to Arabia, the original home of the Arab horse. Abdullah searched the world for pedigreed descendents of established strains. Now he proudly owned some of the finest stock. Abdullah caressed the welcoming muzzles. I could feel the bond between man and animal.

With darkness falling, we returned to our two-legged companions. We sat on the ground around a wood fire, using firm cushions covered in Bedouin weavings as support. Tall date palms surrounded the cosy camp area. Soon a field of bright stars became visible through an opening where the treetops didn't quite meet. In this little oasis, it felt as though Riyadh was many miles and many centuries away.

Abdullah was an inexhaustible host. He constantly made sure everyone had enough to eat and drink but also took the time to chat. His Saudi guests were equally charming and attentive. I felt like a queen.

As the night air chilled, Abdullah presented everyone with *farwas*, the long, sheepskin-lined wraps that the Bedouin use to keep themselves warm. I felt snug, content and pampered. I didn't want to go home.

Eventually, Sean gave me a quiet signal that we should say our goodbyes. With reluctance, I unfolded myself from my cosy position in front of the glowing embers. Abdullah walked us to the car. To express my gratitude for Abdullah's graciousness, I impulsively hugged him and gave him a kiss on each cheek. With equal impulsiveness, he returned the hug and kisses.

"This has been one of the best nights I've had in Riyadh," I said with feeling. "Thank you, Abdullah."

An encounter that had started out with so little promise had turned into an impossibly romantic evening – and a new friendship.

* * * *

Abdullah had an impressive track record when it came to providing me with memories of 'best nights'. He regularly invited us to the farm in Diriya for evenings of stimulating conversation and delicious food. The fact that Abdullah's gatherings were usually men only suited me perfectly. I was at last back in the milieu where I felt most comfortable. The country's restrictions on mixed company inspired in Abdullah's Saudi guests an old-fashioned appreciation of female companionship. As the sole recipient of their spoiling attention, I was in my element.

Not too long after we first met, Abdullah found out that it would soon be my big Four-O birthday. He was surprised to learn that I had never had a birthday party. As the date approached, Abdullah decided this deficiency had to be remedied.

"You prepare the guest list. Invite as many people as you like. I'll take care of everything else," he announced to me during one of our phone conversations. Saudis don't attach much importance to birthdays so the gesture was particularly thoughtful. "We'll have the party at the farm."

Abdullah's farm had become one of my favourite places. I was thrilled that my Western friends would have the opportunity to experience this peaceful retreat.

Having a Saudi host surely meant we had to honour the greatest Saudi tradition: language. I asked each guest to write a birthday poem or, for those with a musical flair, a song. Abdullah might be bringing the food, but I'd arrange the entertainment.

Abdullah, our mutual friend David Ashley, and myself formed a small organising committee to make sure we covered all the bases for the event. A few nights before the party, I invited David and Abdullah to the house. We needed to go over final arrangements.

"Would you like me to bring something to eat?" Abdullah offered.

I often teased Abdullah that it was time to have dinner at his place because he had a cook and Sean and I needed a break from the kitchen.

"No, thank you," I replied. "I think I can manage to feed you guys tonight."

At the appointed hour, there stood two of my favourite men on the doorstep. Abdullah held a large box with Pizza Hut emblazoned on the lid.

"This should go in the oven right away to keep it hot," Abdullah announced as he handed me his offering.

"Abdullah, I said I'd do dinner. Are you trying to tell me something about my cooking? We're *not* having pizza tonight!"

Abdullah just laughed.

"Give it to the kids when they come home," he said nonchalantly.

I relegated the offensive pizza to the kitchen table and forgot about it. About half an hour later I heard a yelp of delight from ever-hungry Kieran.

"You can thank Abdullah," I said as I went to the kitchen to supervise the disbursement of the snack.

Kieran rubbed his hands together, anxious to get his teeth into the gooey cheese topping. I opened the box. And gasped.

"Abdullah, what on earth have you done?"

From the cardboard container I pulled a stunning silk carpet.

"Happy birthday, Kathy. It's a Qum. I picked it up on the way over here but didn't have any gift-wrap. As I passed a Pizza Hut outlet it occurred to me that one of their boxes might do the trick."

Abdullah beamed at the success of his deception. The treasured gift was forever after described as the Pizza Hut carpet.

The birthday party was no less memorable than the gift. Abdullah enchanted us all with his unstinting hospitality, idyllic setting and his own guests. For most of our friends, this was their first opportunity to meet Saudis informally.

"I invited a prince," Abdullah whispered to me. "I wanted your evening to be really special."

Abdullah then introduced me to Prince Abdullah bin Faisal bin Turki bin Abdul Aziz, the personable head of the Royal Commission for Jubail and Yanbu. Prince Abdullah, I discovered, was also known as the PR prince. Because he got on so well with foreigners, Prince Abdullah was often trotted out as an official voice. He displayed his charming social skills to the fullest that night.

Although the setting was simple, it nevertheless seemed exotic to those of us who weren't used to socialising in a desert. The indoor seating area, in a small, house-like structure, had abundant quantities of food and drink. Most of us preferred to remain outside, under the palm trees and bright stars. Here everyone gathered around a fire to sing amusing songs and recite sometimes irreverent birthday poems. *Was this what it was like to be a Bedouin camped at an oasis?* I mused.

With reluctance, I eventually brought the festivities to an end.

"Thank you so much, Abdullah," I said with no small amount of emotion. "This has been the birthday of a lifetime."

I knew with a certainty that for all my remaining birthdays, nothing would ever match this magical evening.

Chapter Twenty-Five

"It's time to spread my wings."

My pronouncement received a cautious glance from Sean. He thought we were simply taking a pleasant evening stroll around the compound. Instead, it looked like another one of my mould-breaking schemes might be about to materialise.

"We've been all over the world," I continued, "but we haven't explored Saud i Arabia."

"When I have vacation time, I prefer to get *out* of the Kingdom," Sean reminded me.

"I know. And I understand. That's why I'm going to do this on my own."

Sean halted, almost afraid to know what new strategy I had hatched.

"And how do you intend to accomplish this?" he asked, giving me a fixed stare. "Touring a region with virtually no infrastructure for tourism is difficult in the best of circumstances, particularly for women, who aren't allowed to stay in hotels by themselves."

"I know all that but I have A Plan. I'm going to give Saudia the opportunity to fly me around the Kingdom. In places where we don't have friends or contacts, there must be some way to get around the hotel glitch."

Sean looked incredulous at first and then chuckled.

"Let's see if Saudia looks upon this as an 'opportunity'."

Sean's scepticism was well placed. Khalil Ziadeh, my Saudia editorial contact, responded favourably when I suggested an article on Abha, a lively market town in the Asir mountains. As one of Saudi Arabia's few tourist destinations, this seemed like a good place to start my discovery of Arabia. His enthusiasm evaporated, however, when I suggested Saudia sponsorship.

"Kathy, this has never been done before. Who knows what the reaction would be from the… more conservative elements in our society. What if something went wrong?"

"Khalil, what could possibly go wrong? You just have to get me there and back and arrange for a guide. I'll stay with friends in the area. 'Conservative elements' won't even know I'm in town."

After an inordinate amount of planning, Khalil assured me that Saudia's Abha station chief would meet me off the plane and provide a car to take me to the major sites.

No one met me. When I finally located Saudia's airport office, the manager seemed surprised that this lone woman authorised by the Jeddah head office had actually appeared. Making a quick recovery, he snapped his fingers at an agent occupied with paperwork and assigned him as my guide and driver.

"Do you know if there's somewhere I could get a press kit on the area or professional photos?" I asked.

The manager's lower jaw slowly separated from the upper in slow-motion astonishment.

"Madam," he enunciated carefully, "this is the undeveloped province of Asir, not the Tower of London."

'Undeveloped' also referred to my tour. The itinerary included nothing more than the Visitor Centre at the Asir National Park and, due to the imminent noon prayer, an abbreviated visit to the famous market.

To compensate for the disappointment, my unrehearsed guide suggested lunch at the impressive Abha InterContinental Hotel. The building originally had been constructed as a guest palace and retained a regal ambience. After lunch, I explored the hotel. Searching for tourist brochures, I came to the office of Willie Da Cunha, the hotel's affable sales manager.

"We're always eager to promote the area," Willie said as he handed me all the available information on the region. "Why not let us arrange a VIP tour for you tomorrow? Our driver could pick you up at your friend's place. Then, I'd like to invite you to be a guest of the hotel." Anticipating my query, he added, "It's not a problem to stay here without your husband if we're sponsoring you."

Aha. So there was a way around the veto against women staying alone in hotels. I immediately accepted the rescue plan.

The following morning the hotel driver picked me up punctually.

Willie had arranged a comprehensive excursion. The antique villages and watchtowers enchanted me. Mud houses were cleverly constructed with protruding tiles on the outer walls. This deflected the rain, preventing erosion. When we entered one of these houses, I was astonished to see bright glossy colours covering walls, floors, ceilings and stairs – not in solid blocks of paint but in wonderful geometric patterns. A couple of women in the region had become well known for their imaginative interior work.

The terraced fields clinging to the mountainsides grew an abundance of crops. Here, the women working the land wore wide-brimmed hats, not veils.

Thanks to Willie's timely assistance, I had enough material for a couple of articles – and a determination to discover more on future visits.

* * * *

Despite the fact that my Abha article appeared with numerous incorrect editorial changes, Willie recommended me to a colleague in Al-Baha, another western province.

Because the Abha trip had no repercussions, Khalil was easily persuaded to send me a ticket to Baha, especially since a local hotel would be responsible for me.

The Motel Al-Baha Frantel's incongruous structure sat like an eagle's aerie at the top of a hill dominated by tall, wrinkled mountains. Each of the freestanding igloo-shaped rooms overlooked miles of unblemished beauty. Mischievous baboons lingered nearby, adding to the feeling of being in wilderness.

It was Ramadan, a month of fasting from dawn to dusk. Instead of lying low during the day like most people, I was on yet another magical mystery tour. Tony Kuhnen, the hotel manager, and his wife Mari-Lynne invited me for the traditional *iftar* supper that evening. After going without food and drink all day, my growling stomach welcomed the sumptuous display: *samboosa* (deep-fried pastries stuffed with cheese or minced meat), *chorba* (a minestrone-like soup with chickpeas and meat), *foul* (a bean dish, pronounced 'fool'), fresh dates, and an enticing selection of other unfamiliar fare. After taking my first few bites, I had one of those 'ah-ha' moments.

"I get it! Break fast! That's what we do when we have our first meal of the day after going without food all night: breakfast!"

Tony and Mari-Lynne nodded absently. I put their lack of appreciation of my revelation to the fact that English wasn't their first language.

The highlight of the visit to Al-Baha was meeting Mohammed Atiyah, the mayor. Mohammed wanted me to see as much of the region as possible. Excursions took me along lush valleys, up difficult escarpments, down to the humid coastal plain, to ancient villages and archaeological sites. The colours and smells of the Thursday market tantalised the senses. Homemade ghee in kidskin containers, wild honey from the coastal region called the Tihama, old musical instruments, daggers, Bedouin jewellery, spices, baskets – the inventory of the stalls was as endless as it was fascinating. Al-Baha was a hidden gem.

Mohammed and I bumped into each other at the motel later that evening and spent several hours chatting about everything and anything.

"When I studied engineering in the US, I loved having animated talks with male and female friends," Mohammed remembered fondly. "As you know, mixed gatherings with non-family members are not the norm in our society. You've made me realise how much I miss this small pleasure. Please come back and visit us. Bring your husband with you the next time."

I was already planning a return trip – but first I'd have to get home. For some inexplicable reason, passengers could not leave Al-Baha airport until they passed through a bureaucratic equivalent to immigration, but in reverse. There had been no such check on arrival.

"Show *iqama*," the official ordered.

"I don't have an *iqama*. The government issues identity cards only to people who have work visas."

The man must have been familiar with this regulation. Presumably he just wasn't used to seeing a women travelling on her own. A Saudi woman can't travel without a male family member or a letter of permission from her husband. Maybe he thought the rule applied to foreign women as well.

"No *iqama*, no go."

And no negotiation, evidently. Showing my passport with its valid residence visa didn't help. Eventually Saudia sorted out the problem. Mohammed's intervention ensured that future visits to Al-Baha presented no such disruptions.

* * * *

Word of a travelling woman journalist percolated through the Kingdom. One day I received a phone call from Bassam Badra, manager of the Hyatt Hotel in Jizan.

"My friend in Al-Baha has told me how you've helped his business. I wonder if I could persuade you to write an article about this region?"

Khalil Ziadeh readily agreed to the story idea. This remote south-west corner of the Kingdom was a low-traffic destination. Giving the place some exposure might help everyone.

This time I brought 9-year-old Tara with me. It would be a good opportunity for her to see more of Saudi Arabia and to witness the research side of my articles.

The heady, tangy smell of salt air blowing in from the nearby Red Sea welcomed us to Jizan. Not all impressions were as positive. Oblivious to their otherwise beautiful surroundings, the local population used the sides of the dirt strip road between a fishing village, curiously located several miles inland, and the sea as a garbage dump.

What the people lacked in environmental awareness, they made up for with their generosity. On the way to a covered market at the village of Abu Arish the hotel guide brought us to a local farm. The charming old farmer patiently explained his agricultural methods. Then he presented me with a kid – of the goat variety.

"I would be so honoured to accept this gift," I sputtered, taken completely off-guard, "but he looks too young to be taken from his mother."

What on earth would I do with a kid? The farmer assured me it was already weaned. I needed another strategy.

"We live in a city and the goat wouldn't be as happy with us as he is with you."

Surely the man would accept this argument.

"But Mom, we have a huge grassy area behind the house. The goat could live there," Tara pleaded.

Tara definitely wasn't helping matters.

"Unfortunately, I wouldn't be allowed to take him on the airplane."

Success at last. The man accepted my third awkward refusal of his hoofed offering. Although I believed his sincerity, he probably was relieved not to have to deplete his small herd. At that point, I remembered that it was considered polite for a host to make an offer three times. My refusal would have been less stressful if this point of etiquette had come to me sooner.

The next day we visited the governor's office. We required a permission letter to travel in the remote areas of this feudal province. Foreigners were a rare site; unveiled, blond, blue-eyed females were totally alien. The letter from the prince guaranteed safe passage.

An armed guard led us into a spacious office. I waited for the man sitting behind the large desk to finish writing. Then I launched into the little welcome I had prepared in Arabic.

"Your Highness, thank you for taking the time to see me. It's an honour to be a guest in your beautiful province."

The man's heavy black eyebrows dipped into a frown over his beaked nose. Had I said something wrong? Ignoring me completely, he turned to my companion, a minder from the hotel.

"Who is this woman?" he asked impatiently.

"This is the journalist from Riyadh," the intimidated minder replied. "She has an appointment to see the Governor."

His memory jogged, the man brought his tall frame to a standing position and led me to an office even larger than his own. There sat the Governor, a more amiable character than his secretary had been. I made a mental note not to be fooled again by big offices. After the requisite cup of cardamom coffee and smalltalk, the Governor instructed his secretary to prepare the necessary permission letter. The province's doors were now open to me.

Jizan represented a land that time forgot. Away from the populated areas, the countryside was magnificently unspoiled. The mountains straddled the border with Yemen. Although the Saudi government didn't like to admit it, this was *qat* country. The Saudis took serious measures to prevent the illegal drug from getting a grip in Saudi as it had in Yemen but they had little control in this rugged corner so close to a porous frontier. Chewing *qat* leaves produces a soporific effect and eventually turns the teeth black. One of the guides gave Tara and me a couple of leaves to sample – for taste rather than effect. Neither of us liked the bitter flavour. Or perhaps we just didn't relish ruining our expensive dental work.

The province was justifiably proud of the recently-built Wadi Jizan dam. Homes and land were now safe from periodic, devastating floods. In my honour, they opened the floodgates. The site engineer admonished me for trying to take photos.

"This dam secret. Same rank as military installation," he told me nervously.

"Secret from whom?" I asked. "Haven't you heard about satellite photography?"

Evidently the man had not been updated on espionage techniques. And if it was 'secret' why was I allowed to include it in my article? I waved the prince's letter in front of him and proceeded with picture taking.

A visit to an isolated mountain village illustrated too clearly what it meant to be a stranger in a strange land. Tara and I walked ahead of the entourage of five men from the prince's office and the hotel. The camera bag on my shoulder and the camera hanging from my neck sent distress signals rippling through the population. Photographing Saudis was discouraged and often forbidden. Some held the superstitious belief that taking a picture stole the soul. Others didn't want to risk having the photos appear in inappropriate places. It was particularly *haram* to photograph women. My journalistic role usually allowed me to circumvent these taboos. This remote village, however, seemed intolerant of photography and photographers. The natives were definitely getting restless.

A few curious onlookers soon swelled into a threatening mob that began to close in, separating Tara and me from our minders. The situation was turning ugly; any sign of fear on our part might incite violence. Tara gripped my hand tightly.

"Mommy, I'm scared. I don't like all these people pushing me," she said, her voice quivering.

"Just pretend you're a movie star, Tara. Hold your head high and think of these people as your adoring fans."

"I don't *want* to be a movie star any more, Mommy. I want to go home."

Just as poor Tara was about to break into tears, the man carrying the

Prince's letter reached us and shoved the vital authorisation into the face of the nearest man. The seal on the back of the envelope immediately turned the mood. The angry mob became a welcoming community.

Suddenly everyone fought to have his picture taken. It was impossible to get a shot without the intrusion of smiling faces. I pulled out the newest addition to my equipment: a Polaroid camera. The villagers had presumably consigned the possibility of soul theft to the ranks of myth. Instead, they enjoyed the gift of keepsake photos.

During my travels throughout Jizan no one ever opened the Prince's letter but the seal was always carefully inspected for authenticity. They may not have been able to read but they recognised every squiggle of the raised stamp.

* * * *

A couple of months later I was back in the tamer province of Al-Baha. By now Mohammed Atiyah and I had become good friends. He was an excellent source of Saudi lore and article ideas.

"I'm hosting a special lunch with several important people," Mohammed told me shortly after my arrival. "Please join us."

"Thank you, Mohammed, but isn't that suggestion a bit liberal, even for you? It's all men and they might feel uncomfortable having a woman in the midst of their business lunch."

Mohammed gave me a look of genuine astonishment.

"But, Kathy, how could there be a problem? Everyone knows you're an honorary man."

My reputation for being 'safe' had its uses in this strict culture but is that really how a woman wants to be described?

The following day, Mohammed arranged a meeting with the province's new governor.

I was escorted to a small anteroom in the administrative building and told that the Governor would be available in about 15 minutes. Less than five minutes later, a tall, muscular, bandolier-burdened guard led my group of hotel and government reps and me into the next room. Once again, I was in a large office with a man busily writing at a desk. This time I wouldn't be fooled into giving silly speeches to secretaries.

I was invited to sit in front of the desk. No one talked. No one moved, except the man at the desk, half hidden by a stack of books. I broke the awkward silence by chatting with the guard who towered over me.

"That's a really nice belt you've got," I said, pointing at the thick cinch embroidered with gold-coloured thread only a few inches from my face. "Is it typical of the region?"

The guard gave me a look of surprise and then cast a nervous look at the man behind the desk. He was given a short affirmative nod so he told me about his belt.

"The handle on your beautiful *djambiya* looks rather special," I continued, admiring the curved dagger at his waist.

The man behind the desk had stopped writing and began to take an interest in my questions. His anecdotal contributions impressed me.

"You know so much about these things," I said. "What do you do? And what is your name? I'd like to mention you in my article."

"I'm the Governor," he said with an amused smile.

Oops. No one had bothered to introduce us because everyone thought I knew who he was!

A year later, Sean and I met Mohammed in London for dinner. We were deep into reminisces when Mohammed laughingly brought up the subject of the *djambiya* event.

"Your visit became one of the Governor's favourite stories. He loved the idea that a woman had come into his office and thought he was the secretary."

* * * *

Success brought me a measure of fame outside the borders of Saudi Arabia. In 1989, the government of Oman invited me on a first-class one-week visit to promote their tourism. This was the kind of offer I'd been waiting for: expenses-paid travel to exotic locations.

After a few days in and around Muscat, Oman's stunning capital, I flew to Salalah, the country's second largest city and a popular summer destination. The manager of the Holiday Inn was eager to impress. He organised a premier guide to show me the sights.

"Bill's a local British fellow. He's been here for years and can answer all your questions. We use him to escort our VIP guests." He gave an ingratiating smile as he said this. "He'll pick you up after breakfast and show you around for the day."

Bill met me in the lobby.

"We can take the air-conditioned hotel car or we can travel in my Land Rover, which will allow us access to more remote areas. The Land Rover is pretty rough, but you'll see some great scenery."

I'd been in numerous Land Rovers. These were the Rolls-Royces of 4-wheel drives. How rough could rough be?

Bill led me to a beat-up vehicle that had open sides in lieu of air-conditioning. The canvas roof had straps to hang on to if bumpy terrain threatened to dislodge passengers from their seats. The old but reliable Land Rover both suited and complemented Bill's own solid appearance. A rugged, sun-weathered face made it difficult to pinpoint his age. Judging by his full head of fair hair, piercing blue eyes and fit physique, I guessed he was probably in his early 40s.

Bill lived up to the manager's hype. This seasoned expat had encyclopaedic knowledge about everything Omani that he shared willingly, despite his natural tendency towards British reserve.

Our tour took us to the usual sites: the ancient fortified port town of Sumharam, markets selling a bounty of frankincense and myrrh and the spectacular beaches and coastline which host an impressive variety of migratory birds during the winter months. In addition, we received first-hand instruction on the business of incense from a farmer who grew acres of the precious trees.

"That covers all the main places of interest in these parts," Bill announced as we bounced along the rutted roads several hours into our journey. Then he proposed a brief detour before returning to the hotel.

"Look, it's not on the itinerary but there's a really beautiful spot up in the mountains that you might enjoy. The panorama is pretty spectacular. Few people make the trip because it's a tough climb, even in the Land Rover."

I'd been tossed and joggled on the regular roads. How much worse could it be? I accepted with enthusiasm.

"Oh, just so you know. There's been some tribal fighting in the region but that won't affect us, not this close to Salalah."

Hmm. That put a different spin on things. Potential carsickness *and* stepping into a battle zone? The lure of adventure overruled common sense. We were on our way.

Somehow Bill and his trusty vehicle managed to negotiate the steep drive. As far as I could discern, there was not even a track, just bolder-strewn scrub. Eventually we reached the summit. Bill was right. The views were unlike anything I had seen so far – including the quiet, sudden appearance of a man with a long, antique rifle pointed directly at us.

"We have to pretend we're married," Bill whispered urgently.

"How... how married do we have to be?" I responded equally urgently. Bill was a nice guy but he wasn't *that* nice.

Bill was taking this new development seriously so I thought we'd better get our stories straight.

"How many children do we have?"

Bill threw me a confused look and then turned his attention back to the nervous young Bedouin who cautiously approached us. He signalled with his rifle that we should get out of the vehicle and proceed on foot. With the help of our captor's monosyllabic directions and the occasional prod of his rifle, we soon arrived at a majestic copse of trees under which gathered the elders and other male members of the tribe. *What a way to go* was the fatalistic thought that flashed through my mind as I surveyed the romantic setting. I certainly didn't want to die but if that was going to be my fate today, this exit sure topped options such as disease or a traffic accident.

We were ordered to sit on the smooth earth. I had the place of honour beside the head of the tribe, a man with a long, feathery white beard, sparkling brown eyes and a creased face that reflected his long, hard life. I was smitten! I loved the company of the older generation of Bedouin with their character-lined features and inherent sense of honour.

Despite the possibly dangerous circumstances of our situation, my natural inquisitiveness couldn't resist taking advantage of the unique opportunity that presented itself. In passable Arabic, I began to interview our hosts. Initially they were reticent to succumb to this strange turn of events. *They* were supposed to be in charge, not me. What was kidnapping coming to these days if the hostages took control?

Suddenly the old shaikh gave a deep chuckle, shook his head and signalled to the womenfolk who had remained out of sight that they should bring refreshments. At least we'd be fed before being shot!

Instead of the anticipated cup of tea or coffee, I was offered a large, hand-hewn wooden bowl full of fresh, still warm… camel's milk. Stifling a retch, I heard my mother's voice warning me about the dangers of drinking untreated milk: *Milk is a magnet for germs.* I knew those little brown and black specks floating amongst the froth couldn't be nutritious additives. What to do in this circle of gun-toting, knife-wielding mountain men?

Giving a deceptively enthusiastic thank you, I brought the smelly bowl to my lips and pretended to drink, making sure I had a milk moustache as evidence of consumption. Everyone smiled and nodded. I did the same again. Surely, they'd soon notice that the milk level wasn't lowering. Then Bill gave me a subtle nudge and whispered through clenched teeth, "Go easy, Kathy, it's for everyone." Of course. How could I have been so remiss? With the greatest relief, I passed the bowl to Bill. Our 'capture' worried me less than the prospect of consuming a bowl of blood-temperature camel milk.

"What are you doing in this remote area," the leader asked. The social niceties had passed. Now it was time to discover the motive for our incursion into their territory.

"I am a writer," I explained. "My 'husband' said that if I really wanted to get the feel of the region, we should visit its most beautiful place, somewhere that most people don't go. And here we are." I shrugged my shoulders and smiled. "You are privileged to live in such a special area."

The old man nodded in agreement.

"But how did you find this particular spot?" he persisted. He still suspected that we were not just tourists.

"Maybe Fate guided us here. After all, everything happens for a reason." Warming to my topic, I continued, "I know this experience has certainly made my day more exciting! I will go home and write about the good people I met at the top of a mountain."

Bill's better-to-say-nothing-than-to-incriminate personality – as well as my chatty monopolisation of the conversation – had kept him quiet for most of the time. He couldn't avoid a shudder, however, when he heard my corny explanation. But Bill had underestimated the Arabs' love of words. Although nomads don't carry books on their long journeys, they treasure the rich vocabulary of the Arabic language. They love to craft these words into poetry and stories about even the most mundane events. This group could easily relate to the afternoon's activities being recorded for posterity.

Then the leader made a dramatic decision.

"I would like to kill a goat for you."

This was indeed an honour. Livestock was precious, especially in such mountainous terrain. The pronouncement also revealed a positive possibility: surely they wouldn't waste a goat on someone they were about to execute? Maybe, while everyone was feeling so magnanimous, this would be a good time to try to leave?

"My 'husband' and I would love to join you for a meal," I said sincerely. "We truly appreciate the invitation. Unfortunately we have to get back to our two young children. I'm sure you understand."

Our host smiled and affectionately patted my shoulder with his gnarled hand.

"Of course," he said with a twinkle in his lovely eyes. Then he continued in a pensive tone, "You are right. There are no accidents in life. Allah has brought you to us for a reason. I'm not sure what it is but I do know we haven't had such entertainment for a long time. Go in peace."

We said our goodbyes. A guide led us back to the Land Rover, this time with the rifle carried over his shoulder, not pointed at us.

* * * *

From Oman, the source of frankincense, through Yemen and along the length of Saudi Arabia's western corridor as far as Rome, once existed one of history's most famous trade lanes. For 500 years, the Frankincense Route witnessed the passage of some of the greatest riches of the ancient known world. Increasingly heavy taxation by tribes who controlled the various sections of the road eventually pushed traders to switch to sea lanes.

In an effort to expand inland tourism, the InterContinental hotels in Abha and Taif and the Motel Al-Baha Frantel in Al-Baha joined forces and initiated the Frankincense Route Tour. They asked me to write the accompanying guidebook. I had become well informed about the route as a result of my visit to Oman, the starting point of the lucrative journey, and my extensive regional research.

One day, Munir Ahmed, the InterCon's Riyadh sales manager, invited me to his office. To my disappointment, Munir didn't offer coffee and some of the InterCon's delicious baked goods.

"There's no time," he explained, rushing me out of his office. "We have to be somewhere else right now."

He wouldn't give any more details. As we walked briskly through the hotel, I saw a notice for a gathering of the British women's group.

"Who's the speaker this month," I asked absently.

By now we had arrived at our destination, a large meeting room. As Munir pushed open the door he turned to me and announced, "You are."

I froze in place.

"Munir, I've never given a speech in my life and I really don't want to start now."

"I know, Kathy," Munir said with a mischievous smile and unbending resolve. "That's why I didn't ask you. I knew you'd refuse. Now there's no going back. You'll be fine."

And I was – eventually. Munir made a flattering introduction – no doubt intended to butter me up as much as present me. A warm audience quickly dissolved my mind-numbing fear. My extensive knowledge about the subject matter gave me plenty to talk about. Munir's gambit had paid off – for both of us. The InterCon got sign-ups for their tour and I had a new activity. This dramatic and involuntary initiation into public speaking soon set me on the talk circuit in Riyadh and around the Kingdom.

Chapter Twenty-Six

Weekly trips to the Riyadh office of the Saudi Gazette to drop off my column brought me in contact with Peter Wilson. Peter, a gently irreverent American, worked as a reporter for the Gazette. He also was a stringer for Reuters, serving as their local source for Saudi news. We formed a friendship.

Because he was a 'real' journalist, Peter was a valued critic of my various writing endeavours. One day I asked if he would review the first chapters of a book manuscript I was working on. Peter agreed.

"This is good, Kathy," Peter said a couple of days later. He had a hint of wonder in his voice. "This is really very good. You've got to finish it. Stop accepting every job that comes along and concentrate on this."

Peter had a valid point. I couldn't resist taking on new assignments. Now I needed to make a choice: expend energy in starburst fashion or focus on one project.

On New Year's Day 1989, I resolved to work exclusively on my book. The following day, to formalise the decision, I bought donuts and went to Peter's office.

"Pour us some coffee, Peter," I said as I cleared a space and deposited the box on his messy desk. "This is a celebration."

Peter pulled himself away from his computer and eagerly opened the box of donuts.

"What are we celebrating?" he asked, poking the deep-fried artery cloggers to lay claim to his choice.

"Thanks to you, my friend," I explained, snapping the lid shut on his groping fingers, "I have made an important decision. All will be revealed when you put a cup of coffee in front of me."

"Jothi," he called to the tea boy. "Can you please bring two American coffees?"

Moments later I released my hold on the box of donuts and divulged my news.

"Well," I said between bites and sips, "I've decided to take your advice. As of today, I'm accepting NO new work. I'll complete my current assignments and continue with my weekly column, but that's it. Nothing extra. No exceptions."

Peter reacted to my proclamation with pleased surprise.

"Well done, girl. It's about time. I can't wait to read the next chapters."

The ringing of Peter's phone interrupted our discussion on the direction the book would take.

"Sorry, Kath," he said, moving piles of papers to find the phone. "Just give me a minute."

Although not intentionally eavesdropping, snippets of Peter's conversation began to alarm me.

"Thanks for considering me. I appreciate it. The problem is that I'll be leaving the Kingdom on an exit-only visa next month. It wouldn't make sense for me to start something I couldn't finish." Peter paused while the person at the other end of the phone tried unsuccessfully to persuade him to change his mind.

In order to boost generally low pay rates, most writers freelanced, accepting random commissions. This caller evidently wanted Peter to moonlight.

"Look, I definitely can't take the job," he continued, "but I can strongly recommend a colleague. In fact, she's sitting here in my office. I'll send her right over."

Peter studiously ignored my frantic hand gestures. He hung up the phone and took another donut, as though nothing unusual had occurred.

"How could you, Peter? How could *you*, of all people, do something like that?" I was beyond angry. "For months you lecture me to take more time for my book. Then, when I finally agree, you commit me to a job without even having the decency to ask me, for goodness' sake!"

Peter showed no shame.

"What exactly does this person want done? And how long will it take?" I asked reluctantly.

"It's the King Faisal Foundation. Something about press releases and a prize ceremony. They'll explain when you go there. This will be good for you, Kathy. And for them," he added cryptically.

"Why would they even agree to see me? A couple of years ago when the Al-Khozama Hotel wanted me to do their PR, it fell through because their conservative owners – King Faisal Foundation – wouldn't approve of them hiring a woman! We're talking darker than dark ages here, Peter. It doesn't sound like my turf. Not to mention the fact that I'm breaking my New Year's resolution before the words even have a chance to get cold!"

"They're waiting for you, Kathy," Peter said unsympathetically. He took the last donut and turned his attention back to the business of journalism.

Less than twenty minutes later I stood in the imposing headquarters of the King Faisal Foundation. Few women entered the building, so my arrival fascinated employees who crossed my path.

Instead of going immediately to my destination, I was first taken to an office to be vetted. Of course, no one used this term but that was what the interview amounted too. My 'interrogator' gave the game away when he finished our meeting with "I think you might be acceptable." It took all my willpower to remain calm and polite.

I was escorted to the Public Relations floor, the domain of Prince Bandar bin Saud bin Khaled, a grandson of the late King Faisal through his mother. A muscular, vaguely menacing-looking administrator called Ibrahim guarded access to the Prince. Ibrahim immediately ushered me into the office – one of those typically expansive spaces enjoyed by VIPs – and then disappeared, quietly closing the distant door behind him.

Prince Bandar's lanky frame stood to greet me. His easy smile and outgoing personality made him a good choice as the Director of Public Relations. But I was still angry and determined not to be charmed out of my black mood.

Prince Bandar introduced me to his aide, Farid Warsi, a tall Buddha-like Pakistani who stood by the side of the desk. As though he'd received an invisible cue, the tea boy, a slender Sudanese of uncertain age who discretely kept his eyes averted from me, appeared with the compulsory cups of cardamom coffee.

"Before we get down to business, we need to get things clear," I announced. "You would no doubt prefer to work with a man and I wasn't planning on taking on any new assignments at this time. Yet here we are.

And here are my terms. Tell me what you want done and I'll give you a quote. There will be no negotiating. And no extra work slipped in. That's the deal."

Saudis have an unfortunate reputation for either altering the agreed fee or terms of a contract in their favour or avoiding payment altogether. Breaking my New Year's resolution was bad enough. Not getting paid for my hard work would be beyond the pale.

A wave of astonishment passed fleetingly across Prince Bandar's features. With commendable poise in the face of my somewhat hostile onslaught, he agreed to the conditions. Farid remained silent; pursed lips betrayed his disapproval that I wasn't showing his prince the deference owed him.

"In three months' time we will announce the winners of the annual King Faisal International Prize," Prince Bandar explained. "Previously, a US-based PR firm has done the press releases and tried to promote the prize internationally. We haven't had the results we hoped for. This year we'd like to try doing it ourselves."

During the next hour, we enjoyed a surprisingly constructive and fun brainstorming session. Prince Bandar had indeed charmed me.

From start to finish, the project that I hadn't wanted to do was stimulating and often entertaining. I felt like part of a family. Once-scary Ibrahim revealed his zany side and became *habibi* (my darling). Khalid, the Prince's Pakistani secretary was as helpful as he was hardworking. He often came to my rescue by ferreting out obscure information and by working without complaint for as many hours as a job took. Farid's resourcefulness and Prince Bandar's enthusiastic support and PR shrewdness ensured the success of my creative output. True to their word, no extra work was added to the original proposal. Payment was prompt and in full.

With my now enthusiastic consent, Farid and Prince Bandar continued to come up with new public relations projects to keep me on the Foundation payroll.

The book manuscript retired to a bottom drawer.

* * * *

When I first started working for the Foundation, I had no idea what went on in the twin-towered building. The landmark 14-storey glass-faced headquarters was a mystery to most foreigners. My enquiries revealed some interesting insights.

Saudi Arabia's first king, Abdul Aziz Al-Saud, was remarkable for bringing together disparate, warring tribes throughout the extensive region that is now Saudi Arabia – Arabia of the Sauds. King Faisal was one of Abdul Aziz's 44 sons and the Kingdom's third ruler. His greatness came from moulding the recently unified regions into a modern state with a respected place in the international community. Through a blend of discipline, daring and wisdom, King Faisal managed the delicate task of moving his country forward while respecting and preserving traditional values. Not everyone agreed with his vision. A bullet fired by a resentful subject ended his life in 1975. By the following year, to preserve the memory of their father, Faisal's eight sons formed King Faisal Foundation, the Middle East's largest philanthropic organisation.

Despite this distinction, the good works of the Foundation were largely unknown in Western circles. This was primarily due to the fact that the inherent modesty of Saudis conflicted with the relatively flamboyant principles of marketing. In 1980s Saudi Arabia, public relations was still in the embryonic stages.

"Why would I place an ad in the newspaper about my company?" a Saudi friend said in response to my suggestion that he could increase business through advertising. "People who like my shop will tell others. This is the way to grow business, through excellence. If you have to tell people how good your company is, maybe it's not as good as you think."

Slowly, Saudi firms became convinced that informing the public about products and/or services could be advantageous and that self-promotion was not necessarily boasting. Prince Bandar's appointment in 1984 as head of the Foundation's PR department coincided with this growing change in perceptions. His youthful energy and positive outlook were important ingredients in the department's accomplishments. Prince Bandar's uncles, the Foundation's founders, had wisely given him latitude to push the boundaries of accepted convention. In such a conservative culture, almost any new idea was ground-breaking!

* * * *

As a former student of psychology and sociology, I found it interesting to observe how people behaved in a royal circle.

Generally, there were three categories of individuals: those who allowed themselves to be awed or intimidated by royalty, neutrals who did their jobs regardless of who their boss might be and, the most intriguing and prolific, the politicos.

Across the royal threshold marched the humble and the grand, the accomplished and the struggling. Everyone exercised a pleasantly elevated level of courtesy. Some of these 'nice' people, however, were simply trying to create a good impression and curry favour. It was all part of the age-old game of politics where individuals tried to better their positions. I witnessed skill levels of dizzying competence.

Almost everyone said only what they thought the Prince would want to hear, no matter how unrealistic or how far removed it was from their actual feelings on the matter. Incredulous at the constant flip-flopping, I asked one of Prince Bandar's regular visitors why he sometimes expressed one opinion to me but then stood on the other side of the fence with Prince Bandar.

"These people don't want to hear about what can't be done," he said, presumably referring to Saudi officialdom in general and royals in particular. "It's much easier to acquiesce on things like deadlines and costs. When the impossible doesn't happen, we offer plausible excuses and agree to a whole new set of usually unattainable projections."

"It seems dishonest and a waste of time and expectations," I countered.

"That's because you're equating 'opinion' with what someone actually thinks. In this part of the world, the only viewpoint that counts is that of the most important person or persons. Everyone else rallies behind them, whether or not they actually agree. Strong opposition would look disloyal. That's why people speak cautiously in a group. Chances are they'll have to change tack several times. If they haven't taken a firm stance, they have less compromise to make in bringing their views in line with the prominent voice."

It was an interesting concept – especially if you were the person in power. I consoled myself with the thought that 'these people' could separate the wheat from the chaff in conversations.

The fact that I disliked politics and had a strong disposition to say exactly what I thought made me an oddity in Prince Bandar's camp. My finesse was first tested when Prince Bandar's printer presented him with a sample business card. The Prince showed enthusiasm. Then, unexpectedly, he turned to me.

"What do you think, Kathy? Do you like the design?"

I looked at the gaudy, coloured card in paralysed silence. What could I say? I couldn't lie but to tell the truth would embarrass the printer and perhaps annoy this usually amiable prince. I prayed for diplomacy to make an intercession on my behalf.

"The design is… quite unique. I've honestly never seen anything like it."

The printer grinned proudly. Why couldn't I leave well enough alone?

"However," I blurted out, "you're a prince. You hold an important position. Perhaps the graphics don't yet fully reflect the image you want to convey?"

Prince Bandar told the printer he needed a bit more time to decide. The final card was classy and discreet – in black and white.

When I knew Prince Bandar better, I verbalised what he surely already knew.

"I'm really not good at all the heavy-duty tact that surrounds you. Because I wouldn't want to unwittingly cause offence, please never ask me anything unless you're prepared to hear something you might not like."

He took the advisory to heart. Sometimes I could feel him preparing for the worst when he asked me a question but he always accepted the answer with good grace. In meetings with outsiders, when he asked for everyone's views, he only had to look at my face. If I harboured the look of protest, he skipped me in the opinion poll.

"That's OK, Kathy. I know exactly what you're thinking."

* * * *

Although I normally worked in my home office, I frequently went to the Foundation to attend meetings or write press releases. The elegant Foundation offices had a buzz of energy. Sometimes this was generated simply by the imminent arrival of the Prince. "The Prince is coming" would inspire a flurry of activity in previously calm corridors. The pencil-thin, slightly stooped frame of lovely Mahmoud the tea boy would scurry off to fire up the coffee burners. *Habibi* Ibrahim would temporarily table his mischievous humour and put on his stern mask of efficiency when 'the Prince is coming'.

Once the Prince was in situ, he became available to all and sundry. Much of this stemmed from Prince Bandar's diverse administrative duties. Like most Saudis, he had his business fingers in many pies. Basically, though, personal involvement stems from the traditional *majlis* system of leadership where everyone has the right to meet with the boss. Problem solving is a basic job requirement. This paternal responsibility extends from king to tribal shaikh to corporate executive to the head of a family.

Meetings could be prolonged simply because of constant comings and goings. Only the most important appointments merited uninterrupted privacy. It was odd enough that people from other departments in the Foundation would wander into the office during a meeting to request decisions or signatures but sometimes they sat down and joined the discussion!

Initially, the Arab attitude towards meetings frustrated me. I understood the need for easy-going accessibility but the relaxed Saudi *insha'allah* approach to life wasn't always conducive to efficiently accomplishing objectives. On the rare occasions when we discussed and decided with directness, I would give a sigh and silently offer a fervent prayer of *ilhamdullilah*, thanks be to God. Eventually I felt compelled to talk to Prince Bandar about the problem.

"What do you think about having an agenda?" I suggested. "We could propose topics ahead of time and then make sure we cover those items first. It would save everyone a lot of time and ensure we addressed the main points before getting sidetracked."

"Sure, let's try it," Prince Bandar agreed with a smile. My efforts to organise his realm often amused him.

The new system worked like a charm – but at the expense of the meandering meetings for which I'd developed a love-hate relationship. This *über* efficiency lacked warmth. And, I admitted, the mystery of where a topic would eventually end up. With the unspoken agreement of all, our meetings evolved into an efficient blending of the order and chaos methods.

* * * *

King Faisal Foundation expends its time and budget on philanthropy, culture and learning. Scholarship programmes, lectures, libraries and a manuscript preservation department are among the organisation's many activities.

The most high profile aspect of the Foundation is the annual King Faisal International Prize. Committees composed of international authorities in each prize field select winners for Science, Medicine, Islamic Studies, Islamic Literature and Service to Islam. Each winner receives a 200-gram, 22-carat gold medal and US$200,000 during five days of ceremony and events in Riyadh. Because a significant number of the Science and Medicine laureates go on to win Nobel Prizes, the Foundation likes to say it recognises outstanding talent early.

As far as I was concerned, the best part of prize week was the desert picnic hosted by Prince Bandar. This festive outing in honour of the winners included the entire Foundation staff and special guests. Large Bedouin tents gave shelter from the sun and provided a *majlis* area to sit and chat. Camels and horses were available for those who wanted a more expanded Arabian experience. The day offered a pleasant escape from the office, the city and contemporary life in general.

At the appointed hour in late afternoon, the VIP guests were invited to a designated dining area. Down the entire length of the centre of the tent, a waterproof cloth on the ground served as a table to dozens of delicious dishes.

"You know, Kathy," Prince Bandar had confided with pride, "it's the women in my family who prepare all the food for the picnic. They're well known for their culinary skills."

Although I couldn't picture Prince Bandar's stunning wife Masha'el chopping vegetables, I had been fortunate enough to sample her cooking. Prince Bandar wasn't exaggerating. Almost the only place to find authentic Saudi food is in a Saudi home. Most foreigners never have the opportunity to enjoy these tasty dishes.

I joyfully indulged until there wasn't another centimetre of storage space left in my body. Except for a couple of companions and myself, everyone had gone outside. Then I felt a gentle tap on my shoulder. It was Khalid, Prince Bandar's secretary.

"The others are waiting to eat, Kathy," he whispered discretely.

Of course! We were the first wave. I had assumed that another tent accommodated the rest of the party – but I was sitting in the only dining room and the other guests wouldn't enter until I left. Rising from my cross-legged position, I quickly glanced at the remaining dishes to make sure the second sitting had enough food. In true Saudi fashion, there was reassuring abundance.

* * * *

HRH Prince Sultan bin Abdul Aziz, Minister of Defense and Aviation and third in line to the throne, sat on the board of the 'Service to Islam' prize. Because of his busy schedule, he was unable to come to Riyadh to help choose that year's winner. Instead, he sent his private jet and invited everyone to join him at his palace in the Eastern Province. As the Foundation's PR consultant, I got to go along.

I first brought myself to Prince Sultan's attention by inadvertently walking in on their selection process. Disoriented in the maze of palace corridors, I had hoped the unmarked door would lead me to the ladies' room. I'm not sure who was more surprised by my unannounced intrusion, the selection committee or me. Someone quickly shooshed me out but I noticed Prince Sultan had seemed amused by the distraction.

Later, in an almighty great audience hall that reminded me of Versailles, Prince Sultan made the rounds, shaking hands with many in the assembly of journalists and other interested parties. I was the only woman in the crowd. Suddenly an enormous bandoliered guard appeared before me.

"Go shake hand Prince."

Hating any hint of kowtowing, I declined the invitation. When the guard saw that I had actually moved back instead of forward, he renewed the command, this time a little more forcefully.

"Now. Go *now* meet Prince."

"Thank you but I'd really rather not. It's just not my thing."

Evidently Prince Sultan had asked the guard to make sure this sole female was easily accessible at the front. The Prince was closing in on us and the guard hadn't fulfilled his mission. He took matters into his own hands. Literally. Stepping behind me, he gave a sudden, vigorous shove in the direction of the Prince. Both my feet left the ground and I was catapulted into Prince Sultan's arms. For some reason, both of us had stuck out our hands to prepare to shake.

"Good evening, Your Royal Highness," I said as though this was always how I met royalty.

"Ahlan wa sahlan," he responded, our noses nearly touching. His eyes laughed at our unorthodox encounter.

Over the next few years I fell under Prince Sultan's gaze another couple of times. His little chuckle of recognition allowed me the fantasy that I'd once given the Prince a night to remember.

Chapter Twenty-Seven

Iraq's August 1990 invasion of Kuwait shocked the world. The success of the lightning attack encouraged Iraqi troops towards a bigger target: Saudi Arabia and its rich oil fields. For millions of people, life was taking an unpredicted and unwelcome turn.

While thousands of Iraqi troops stormed across blistering desert sands toward Kuwait, the children and I were on holiday at our home on Bantry Bay, Ireland. We had gone into town to enjoy the weekly market. As we paused at a stall offering irresistible samples of delicious homemade fudge, I noticed James Hegarty, the friendly, loquacious owner of a local supermarket, impatiently making his way toward me. James skipped the usual social niceties.

"Well, how are things in the Gulf? Is it hot enough for you?"

I assumed that he used the word 'gulf' to refer grandly to Bantry Bay and that the mention of 'hot' related to the uncharacteristic rise in temperature.

"It will have to get a lot hotter before you hear me complain," I responded.

We continued in this vein for a few more sentences until James realised that I didn't know what he was talking about.

"No, no," he said with concern in his voice, "the war, I mean the war."

"What war?" came my puzzled reply.

"Don't tell me you haven't heard. Iraq has invaded Kuwait and taken over the country. Saudi Arabia's their next stop."

James had barely finished speaking before I threw him a hasty goodbye, grabbed the kids and dashed across the street to The Paper Shop to buy an armload of newspapers – a habit I had neglected in the past couple of days.

Judging by the media coverage, the situation seemed serious indeed. Iraq's President Saddam Hussein threatened to make Kuwait a graveyard if outside powers interfered. In the meantime, a powerful segment of the international community had joined forces to condemn Saddam's offence – and to promise serious reprisals if he made further advances. A phone call to Sean in Riyadh dispelled my hope that the media was sensationalising events.

"Everyone is extremely nervous," Sean admitted. "Iraqi troops are only five miles from the Saudi border. It doesn't look good."

There is something about extreme situations that seems illusory. Or perhaps our brains devise a safety mechanism to cope with news of impending disaster. As Saudi expatriates, Sean, the kids and I were being swept unwillingly into the net of panic and confusion thrown over the entire region. My state of denial made me dismiss further talk of a preposterous war and concentrate the conversation on updates of Sean's new job.

In June 1990, Bechtel had offered Sean a management position on the new airport project in Hong Kong. The company that had been responsible for bringing us to Saudi Arabia in 1976 now lured us away. We both knew this was the right career decision for Sean but it broke my heart to think of leaving Riyadh and the unconventional but exciting life I was finally leading. I never knew what opportunities each day would offer. The thought of returning to a predictable existence, even in an exotic environment like Hong Kong, dismayed me.

Sean would complete the contract with CRSS, his current employer, in late September. We already had enrolled 14-year-old Tara at Ridley College in Canada. Boarding school for teenagers was the norm in Riyadh: unveiled girls attending non-segregated schools invited undue attention from the *mutawwa*. To minimise the added aggravation that a bunch of kids with raging hormones would cause, SAIS-R initially offered only kindergarten to grade 7.

For 12-year-old Kieran, the timing of the transfer, after the start of the school year, was awkward. Exceptionally, Bechtel agreed to provide housing and sponsorship for Kieran and me until I had wound up my various activities and it was convenient for us to leave Saudi, probably at the Christmas holidays. Despite the hostilities, it didn't occur to us not to return to Riyadh in September. Now that there was a chance of losing the peaceful and prosperous Saudi Arabia we had known and loved, we wanted it more than ever.

Sean phoned daily to report on the latest developments. By Monday, 6 August 1990, the political mood had deteriorated further. Tensions in Riyadh were palpable. Our comfortable world was unravelling at the seams but the enormity of events hadn't really sunk in.

"The Canadian Embassy has been in touch to say that we have to prepare for the worst. They've got evacuation plans in place."

Sean continued to elaborate. My numbed brain absorbed the details but refused to consciously interpret his words. My personal crisis with a faulty water pump seemed far more immediate. Suddenly my scattered thoughts honed in on a vital piece of the information Sean had tried to convey.

"Wait a minute," I said frantically. "Did you say that the Embassy evacuation policy is only one suitcase? This is almost as incredulous as the news of the war itself! How on earth can we put our lives into one suitcase? Fate is dealing a double whammy."

"A lot of the victims in Kuwait didn't even get the suitcase option, Kathy. Tell me as soon as possible what you want to include. No one knows how much time we have." Sean paused, unsure whether or not to share more details. "They say the Iraqis have scud missiles aimed at Riyadh." In a quieter tone he added, "There's a fear Saddam will use chemical weapons."

Now the man had my full attention. I felt sick with anxiety. After getting off the phone I burst into tears. Would Sean get out safely? Would we ever see our expat friends again? What would happen to Saudi friends who stayed behind?

Between sporadic crying spells, I attempted to carry on with day-to-day routines. Not only did the children need looking after but we had a couple of Australian house guests. These activities helped to distract me from the crueller realities.

Then I remembered that Sean urgently needed a list of things to put in the one allowed suitcase. Saudi Arabia definitely inspired packing dilemmas. Fourteen years earlier a lack of information forced us to rely on instinct about what to include in our limited shipment. Now, from a distance of thousands of miles, I had to choose what to take away – in a severely edited format.

What should I keep and what should I leave behind? I worried that I might forget to list something that looked insignificant to Sean but that would hold strong sentimental value for me. My mind's eye went through every drawer and cupboard in our Riyadh home. An eclectic list began to emerge: the treasured 'Pizza Hut' Persian carpet from Abdullah, my collection of favourite recipes that had been prepared at our many dinner parties and, most important, the contact information of friends who would soon be scattered around the world. Each new item I mentally selected brought a flood of precious memories of our Saudi adventure, from hesitant start to hastened finish.

* * * *

The escalation of events meant there could be no question about Kieran returning to Riyadh. With so little time left until the start of the school year, the only solution was to find a boarding school for him in Ireland. We chose St. Gerard's in Bray. Its proximity to Dublin meant he would have his grandparents and other family nearby.

Reluctantly, Kieran and I went shopping for school necessities. Kieran rationally understood the circumstances but he still couldn't accept them emotionally.

"But, Mom, it's not my time to go to boarding school," Kieran pleaded as we took the escalator to the boys' department in a large department store. "And it's not fair that I can't say goodbye to my friends."

The look in his eyes and the anguish in his voice made me want to weep. He loved Saudi as much as I did. Now he had to face a premature separation from his family and enrol in an unfamiliar school system. It was a lot for a boy to cope with.

"Life often isn't fair, sweetheart. You're learning this lesson in a particularly harsh way." We arrived at our floor.

"I know, Mom, but it doesn't make it any easier, does it? I feel so helpless, like my life is out of control."

"We all do, my darling. One thing I'm certain of, though, is that you're going to survive this mess and be stronger for it." I kissed the top of his head to reinforce this belief. We continued our shopping with a sad air of resignation.

I needed to keep to my original travel schedule for taking Tara to boarding school in Canada and then returning to Riyadh. Jenny Gilmartin, an English friend living outside Dublin, offered to keep Kieran for the short period before he started school. She had two children roughly the same age as Tara and Kieran. The environment of Jenny's large country property with horses might take his mind off other worries.

Tara, Kieran and I had discussed the pros and cons of my return to Saudi. The kids had given their blessing but that didn't make saying goodbye any easier. We hugged tightly and fought back the tears.

"I love you, my darling," I said to Kieran. "Daddy and I will visit you on our way to Hong Kong. It will be Christmas in no time and we'll all be together for the holidays. In the meantime, be good. Make the most of this unexpected experience."

I tousled Kieran's hair and gave him a final hug. Then Tara and I drove down Jenny's long driveway. For different reasons, each of us was about to enter a new phase in our lives. We had feelings of uncertainty in common.

Years later, Tara and Kieran revealed that this farewell was more painful than they let on.

"Kieran and I talked things over. We knew how much you wanted to go back to Saudi and we didn't want you to stay away because of us," Tara confessed.

"We pretended that everything was OK but really we thought we would never see you and Dad again," Kieran added.

Their altruism shamed me. Even in the midst of their own distress, they thought of me more than they thought of themselves. I had a lot to learn from my children.

* * * *

No sooner had I got Tara settled into boarding school than Sean threw another curve ball.

"There's talk that CRSS won't allow dependents back into the country. Head office will let us know later this week."

"I've got to get back," I cried. "It's bad enough the country is about to go to war. I need to at least be able to say goodbye, to have some sense of closure."

It was now my turn to echo Kieran's heartfelt sentiments.

"If you disregard the company decision, I'll be fired immediately," Sean warned. "We'll be without sponsorship and without a roof over our heads. That's probably not the best situation with a war looming."

Despite his valid concerns, Sean wasn't insensitive to my need to return.

"Look, you're already scheduled to fly in a couple of days. Unless I hear from head office within the next 24 hours, keep to your plans. I'll just tell them I can't contact you."

Sure enough, the edict came through. I had already arrived in London and was incommunicado as far as the company was concerned. At this point, I was determined that nothing would stop me travelling to Riyadh.

CRSS management was not impressed that I had slipped through the net, especially since most of them had wives who also wanted to return. They gave me 48 hours to leave the Kingdom.

When I told the news to Prince Bandar, he immediately went into can-do mode. Like Sean, he usually had a solution.

"Fly to Bahrain," Prince Bandar told me. "As far as CRSS is concerned, you'll have left the country. I'll have a visa waiting for you at the Saudi Embassy and you can come back under my sponsorship. CRSS won't have any recourse against Sean since you'll no longer be their legal responsibility."

Sean agreed to the plan. It didn't make him popular with his boss when I was back on the streets of Riyadh a couple of days later.

"The company's getting nasty because we've circumvented the system," Sean revealed.

"Don't they have more urgent concerns?" I asked. This unnecessary stress annoyed me.

"You'd think so," Sean admitted. "They're seriously considering not letting you live in the house."

Eventually the company backed down. Vindictiveness wasn't worth the long-term gamble: who knew what other cards I held up my sleeve?

I could now devote my attention to the job of getting ready to ship our household effects to Hong Kong. The one-suitcase threat still hung over us but we planned for the best-case scenario of an orderly departure with all our possessions.

The mood of gloom in the city was almost tangible. None of us was familiar with the protocols of war. Would Iraq plan a surprise attack like in Kuwait or would there be an official declaration of hostilities? Social conversations now focused on the benefits and availability of gas masks, stocking food and water and other emergency procedures. The howl of air raid sirens being tested filled the sky.

The only light relief came from Mimi Cousart. Humorously bowing to her Florida background, she had two wonderfully tacky, plastic pink flamingos on her front lawn. Their tall wire legs brought the birds above hedge level so everyone could enjoy their seasonal accessories: scarves in winter, sunglasses in summer, Halloween costumes, and the like. These days they wore gas masks.

After such a long stay in the Kingdom and with such a network of acquaintances, we had expected to leave on an exhausting crest of farewell parties, not the dramatic circumstances in which we found ourselves. In the current atmosphere, festivities were the least of anyone's priorities. A group of compound friends held an inevitably sombre dinner for us. Barring any unexpected events in the next few days, we at least knew when and where we were going. Few friends were so fortunate.

* * * *

Our final departure was no less memorable that our initial arrival had been. Fourteen years earlier we landed at a chaotic tin shack in a city with only two traffic lights and minimal infrastructure. Now we were leaving the modern metropolis of Riyadh from its architecturally impressive airport that Sean had helped build. The city had grown, the country had grown and we had grown. What a journey it had been.

Saudi Arabia had presented us with trials and triumphs, friendships and opportunities. We had been privileged to watch a once obscure kingdom emerge to become a powerful nation in less than a generation. But what would the future hold?

We boarded the plane with a heavy fear of the unknown, not for ourselves but for a country and people we had come to love. For a country on the brink of war. If we ever saw Saudi Arabia again, would we recognise it?

Chapter Twenty-Eight

The pilot skillfully maneuvered between mountains and highrises. We could see the TV screens in apartment blocks the plane narrowly avoided as it made the infamously dangerous descent onto the runway at Hong Kong's Kai Tak airport.

We had come to live in one of the most vibrant cities in the world. Finding accommodation, getting settled and making new friends occupied much of our time and energy. Yet even these distractions could not prevent us from focusing on more urgent concerns: hostilities in the Arabian Gulf.

Sean bought a small portable radio to keep informed of developments while he worked. His frequent phone calls updated me at home. So far, there was just a lot of political posturing. The intense mobilisation of US troops left little doubt that matters would soon escalate beyond diplomacy. Talk of scud missiles armed with deadly gases and aimed directly at Riyadh kept me awake at night. Concern for Prince Bandar particularly distressed me.

"I'm going into the army," Prince Bandar had told me shortly before our departure from Riyadh.

"You can't," I had replied fearfully. "You're… you're a prince." My search for a valid excuse failed. "Your family needs you. I need you. Please don't go."

Every pacifist cell in my anti-war body shuddered at the thought of young men enlisting for potential death. Prince Bandar had become like a brother to me. I couldn't bear the possibility of losing him.

"I have to go," he quietly stated. "You know that."

Yes, deep down I did know. But I also guessed that, like most young bloods, signing up was as much about that male response to a good fight as it was about defense of country. After all, how often did a war come along? He wasn't going to sit this one out! I did what generations of women have done through the ages: prayed for a soldier's safe return.

Relations with Iraq deteriorated. On 16 January 1991, coalition forces from 34 nations conducted an extensive aerial bombing campaign on Iraq.

The Gulf War had begun. Then, with breathtaking brevity, on 27 February 1991, it ended.

By March, Prince Bandar considered it safe enough to invite me back to Riyadh for a couple of weeks. The Foundation had decided to proceed on schedule with the King Faisal International Prize ceremony. Prince Bandar wanted his full public relations team in place. I was thrilled.

I returned to a Riyadh pulsating with euphoria. Everyone was giddy with victory and with the relief of eliminated danger. The market was flooded with war souvenirs commemorating the short-lived event. Photos of incoming scud missiles over Riyadh sold like hotcakes. My favourite memento was the brainchild of Kim Fisher, the wife of our dentist. She and a friend made an impressive income selling... condoms. A picture of Saddam Hussein beside the word 'Saddam's' graced the front of each package. The inside of the cover carried the immortal words: *For the man who just doesn't know when to pull out.*

The physical changes to the city were more sobering. I noticed that an unfamiliar grime covered the outside of my hotel room window.

"That's oil," the Al-Khozama manager told me. "Saddam adopted a scorched earth policy. He ordered retreating Iraqi forces to set fire to the Kuwaiti wells. They mined the area, so it's even more dangerous for fire-fighting crews. Winds spread the soot and oil droplets all over the region. They say it might take years to fully extinguish the flames."

In fact, it took months. By November 1991, experts had capped the last well. The ecological damage was more long term. Fish and wildlife populations were decimated.

Military personnel who were camped in the desert outside Riyadh spilled into the city to explore the *suqs* or attend meetings. Hotel lobbies looked more like the Pentagon than a base for traveling businessmen. Battle fatigues prevailed over *thobes* and *abayas*.

Military vehicles crowded the roads. These transports, as often as not, had female soldiers as drivers. I applauded this progress. Surely Saudi driving licenses for women must be imminent? I soon learned that this crack in the door to liberalisation had been slammed shut in no uncertain terms a few months previously.

The long-awaited sight of women driving inspired in many Saudi women an if-they-can-do-it-why-can't-we attitude. It was a time of national emergency. With so many men enlisting, the continued ban on driving left families vulnerable. Women fleeing Kuwait – driving themselves – fueled this justified concern.

In November 1990, 47 women, accompanied by their husbands or male relatives, drove in convoy through the streets of Riyadh.

"It was a peaceful protest," one of the women explained. "We did nothing disrespectful of Islam. Nevertheless, the *mutawwa* were vicious. They called us whores. They told lies about us and whipped up public opposition. For simply trying to claim a right that every other woman in the world has, we were vilified. Those of us who had jobs were suspended or fired. Our passports have been taken away, so we can't travel."

Months later, when visiting Riyadh once again, I met another of the participants. She had been a prominent, well-respected photographer. Now she was an angry, broken woman.

"As if they hadn't already done enough damage to careers and reputations, the *mutawwa* raided my home. They destroyed my entire photographic history. Every picture, every negative. My life's work. Gone. What they did was unjustified – and immoral. Yet no one criticises their actions. Our sin was to deviate from the collective norm. For that we are persecuted."

As a result of this courageous but defiant action, the unofficial ban on women driving became official.

* * * *

I continued to work for the Foundation from my home office in Hong Kong. Once or twice a year I commuted to Riyadh for prize-related events.

In 1992, King Faisal International Prizes for Science and Medicine celebrated their 10th anniversary. The Foundation wanted to mark the occasion in a special way. They chose London as the venue. This major hub would be a convenient meeting point for the many international winners of the past decade.

I flew to Riyadh to help with the last-minute details. Actually, in true Saudi fashion, it was pretty much all last minute, relatively speaking.

Somehow or other, though, despite occasional panics, the Foundation, with the help of London-based planners, had managed to put together a glittery schedule of festivities.

"We need you to write a couple of speeches for Prince Khaled," Prince Bandar told me at one of our pre-departure meetings. This request wasn't a major surprise. Periodically I wrote for Khaled Al-Faisal, one of the Foundation founders. "One is the welcome speech at the gala dinner."

"Not a problem," I replied, mentally adding it to my substantial to-do list.

"The other," he continued, "is a speech for the Royal Society. Prince Khaled has been honoured with an invitation to be the first non-member ever to address the Society."

"But we're leaving for London in a couple days," I said, feeling weak. "This speech is… historic. It needs to be done well, not rushed. You know how I like to let my work cook for a while. This doesn't leave me any time. Surely there must be someone else who can write well and doesn't have a million other things to do! Please don't ask me to do this."

Prince Bandar wavered. Normally I took heavy workloads in my stride. If this task distressed me, there must be a good reason. Farid quickly interjected before Prince Bandar could relent.

"No," he said with finality. "It has to be you. You know Prince Khaled. We trust you."

High stress levels and copious infusions of caffeine helped me to produce polished drafts in an astonishingly brief period of time. Everyone was delighted with the results.

"I knew you could do it," Prince Bandar said cheerfully.

I smiled, pleased at the praise and glad that the worst was over.

"Now pay attention, Prince Bandar," I said, shaking my finger at him. "In ten years there will be another big anniversary. You have plenty of advance warning. Don't leave things until the last minute!"

"And miss out on the fun of seeing you struggle – and perform?" he laughed. "Not a chance!"

We flew to London for the final preparations. I loved the glamour surrounding the events but this came with a worried anticipation of unforeseen glitches. It was a relief when the celebrations ended without mishap. They had been an unqualified success.

Afterwards, Yousef Al-Hamdan, the gentle-natured Secretary-General of King Faisal International Prize, approached me with an invitation.

"Prince Khaled asks if you would join him for lunch at his home. It's his way of saying thank you for all your hard work."

"How very kind of him, Yousef. I'd love to go. Thank you."

Yousef and I arrived at Prince Khaled's house at 1 p.m. A butler answered the door and guided us to a reception area. Cultured and creative Prince Khaled had decorated his beautiful home with taste. His collection of paintings and artifacts kept me happily distracted while we waited for the Prince. Suddenly I heard Yousef clearing his throat in that unnatural way people have when they want to attract attention. Prince Khaled's tall, athletic frame stood in the doorway. He looked like an aristocratic movie star in his finely tailored tweed jacket. He had been observing me studying the brushwork on an interesting oil painting.

"Welcome, Kathy. I'm so glad you could make it."

Like I would have missed this opportunity?

As Prince Khaled and Yousef escorted me into a dining room that achieved both a feeling of space and of intimacy, I reminded Prince Khaled of another lunch we had shared.

"The last time, we got together at your home in Abha. We had a rather... strong... discussion on the Iraq-Iran war. You disagreed when I suggested that Iraq might have been the aggressor. I held my ground but you were pretty intimidating."

Prince Khaled took a few seconds to recall the event. Then he threw back his head and gave a hearty laugh.

"Ah, yes. Now I remember."

"I promise just to appreciate the food and the company and not to introduce politics into the conversation this time."

We enjoyed a delicious lunch with lively conversation that kept to 'safe' subjects.

* * * *

As well as looking after the Foundation's public relations needs, I took care of the international prize winners during their stay. Various outings introduced them to Saudi culture.

In 1993 the official programme started on a Saturday. Several of the winners and their guests had chosen to arrive a couple of days earlier. For a visitor stuck in a Riyadh hotel, Friday could be a day of stultifying boredom. Farid, Prince Bandar's aide, had overruled me on making plans to entertain the winners on Friday.

"They'll be fine," Farid assured me. "Let them have a day to themselves to discover the city."

"We're not exactly in Paris or New York, Farid. This isn't the city that never sleeps. Everything will be closed on Friday afternoon and only the *suq* is open in the morning. We're the hosts. We should look after our guests."

Non-Arab Farid evidently didn't share the Arab trait of unwavering hospitality. The argument fell on deaf ears. I groused about the situation to my Canadian friends and long-time residents Pat and Andy Padmos. Andy worked at the King Faisal Specialist Hospital. His immediate solution was a desert outing.

"A group of us is going to The End of the World for a picnic. Why don't you and the winners join us?" Andy suggested. "Speak to the hotel about providing 4-wheel drives, drivers and a packed lunch."

What a great idea! For a pregnant moment I wondered if I should take on the weighty responsibility of absconding with these VIPs. *What can go wrong?* the little voice in my head queried. *Absolutely nothing,* came the firm response from the same source. *We're going with experienced desert travelers – and they're all doctors. We're in safe hands.*

The dramatic grandeur of The End of the World made it a popular destination for expats. Here the plateau suddenly ended at a steep escarpment high above the desert floor. This excursion would add an extra dimension to the winners' Riyadh experience. I made all the necessary arrangements for everyone who wanted to partake in an off-road, off-schedule experience.

After a fun afternoon, we headed back to the city. The overcast sky had turned threatening. A light shower started. We came to the *wadi* we needed to cross to get back to Riyadh. The narrow riverbed had been dry on the outward journey but now it flowed with shallow, fast-moving water. This was not good. Flash floods were a strong possibility. Deadly torrents of water could appear in minutes.

The lead vehicles drove across successfully. Ours got stuck and then stalled in midstream. The water continued to rise while companions on the other side quickly prepared to tow us out of danger. For a horrible moment a news headline flickered in front of my mind's eye: *Prize Winners Drown in Desert.* My well-intentioned effort was fast deteriorating into An Irresponsible Decision. If this story didn't have a happy ending, the Foundation would not be amused. *Better to concentrate on the problem at hand,* I told myself.

"The car's too heavy with all of us. We need to get out now and wade across," I instructed with urgency. "Hurry. There might not be much time."

Everyone immediately discarded shoes and socks in preparation for a wet walk. Except Steven Chu, the American co-winner of the physics prize. He thought it would be wiser to remain in the vehicle with his six-year-old son.

"It's only a few yards, Steven. We'll hold each other's hands. I think it's worth the risk," I implored.

We made it across. Steven Chu, a future Nobel laureate and US Secretary of the Environment, tagged along at the end of the line. Relieved of the extra weight, the vehicle was dislodged and pulled to safety.

"Well, that was a bit more adventure than I had planned for today," I said, thankful that everyone had survived unscathed.

Herbert Walther, the German co-winner of the physics prize, and his wife dried their feet and put on their shoes.

"Perhaps more exciting than a day in the lab," he acknowledged with a kind chuckle.

We arrived back at the hotel without further mishap. I made an executive decision not to inform Farid or Prince Bandar of the alternative Friday outing.

Chapter Twenty-Nine

The frenzied activity of Hong Kong stirred the blood. From the multinational conglomerates to the humblest street merchant, everyone seemed to be involved in some sort of commerce. This unrelenting busy-ness subtly roused my entrepreneurial nature. Anything could be made here, so why didn't I come up with a clever idea? Which market had a niche waiting to be filled? Inevitably, my thoughts drifted to Saudi Arabia. Although we no longer lived there, I felt such a strong bond with the country that I couldn't imagine trying to undertake such a project – whatever it might be – anywhere else.

No flashes of genius sprung to mind but I did know that the country had no cheap and cheerful touristy items. Mind you, it didn't have a tourist industry either but there were plenty of expat residents always looking for new selections of inexpensive gifts to take home.

On my next trip to Riyadh, I spoke to Mimi Cousart about the possibility of going into business together. She could do the design and artwork, I could handle the manufacturing and marketing and we could both find outlets for the sale of the products. Mimi enthusiastically agreed… in principle.

"Who's going to pay for all this?" sensible Mimi wanted to know.

"We need a money partner," I responded.

"Any bright ideas?"

"Actually, I was thinking of asking Prince Bandar. We already have a comfortable working relationship. I think he'd be perfect, if he's willing."

I prepared a business plan and made a sales pitch to my long-suffering prince.

"There's a demand for gift items with an Arabian theme. No one is doing this on a commercial scale – yet. There are already whispers of Saudi Arabia opening up to tourism. This idea would feed right into the industry. Apart from that, though, there's a huge expat base. I've made good contacts in Hong Kong; Mimi and I could set up sales teams here in the Kingdom."

After some discussion, Prince Bandar bought in. Design Arabia was born. The new partnership agreed to terms, drew up legal contracts, got an import license, designed a logo and received an injection of cash to start the manufacturing process. Then Prince Bandar went two steps further.

"This will be an interest-free loan, Kathy," he said as he reviewed the repayment schedule I had presented.

The astonished look on my face prompted him to explain.

"In Islam, loans should be made without interest. Ideally, the lender takes the same calculated risks as the borrower, sharing in the success or failure of the venture."

"Presumably this lender is counting on this borrower not to fail?" I asked rhetorically.

"That goes without saying, Kathy," Prince Bandar said with a smile. "One other thing," he continued. "I've asked my lawyer to make sure you have my share of the ownership of Design Arabia in case anything happens to me. Masha'el knows about this and agrees."

My first reaction was an instinctive concern that anything terminal might befall Prince Bandar. My second reaction was pure wonderment that he was considerate enough to think that far ahead. I was too emotional to utter more than a subdued 'thank you'.

* * * *

The fledgling company needed a man on the ground to clear shipments from customs, make deliveries and collect payments.

"Ramzi's out of work. You could ask him," Mimi suggested.

Ramzi had been our favourite driver at CRSS. We appreciated Ramzi's efficiency and reliability and Ramzi seemed to enjoy our spirit of adventure. The three of us had formed a friendship.

"He'd be perfect," I agreed. "He's smart and we both trust him completely. Do you think he'd want to work for two pushy women?"

I invited Ramzi to lunch at the Al-Khozama Hotel. Good food, I hoped, would help persuade him. Understandably, Ramzi was unsure about committing himself to our untried venture. My arm twisting and begging finally eroded Ramzi's resistance. Our small team was now complete.

* * * *

After poring over bulky catalogues issued by the Hong Kong Trade Council, I found several products that I thought could be adapted to suit the Design Arabia concept. Finally, I made a selection and put the idea forward at our first partners' meeting.

"What do you guys think of producing cookie cutters?"

My suggestion received bewildered stares. Whatever they were expecting me to come up with, it definitely wasn't something as mundane as cookie cutters. I should have anticipated the reaction: I was addressing two culinary neophytes who probably wouldn't know a cookie cutter if they fell over it. Mimi described a kitchen as 'the room with the big white appliances' and avoided the location as much as possible. Prince Bandar swore he had cooked but I sensed he had a limited, rarely practised repertoire.

"We could make a package of them in the shapes of camels, djambias, palm trees and crescent moons," I persisted. "They'd be lightweight for packing in suitcases and inexpensive, not just for us to produce but for customers as well."

"I guess I'll have to trust your judgment on this," Mimi said reluctantly. "Go for it."

"Do what you think is best," Prince Bandar agreed. He was clearly more comfortable making senior-level management decisions for large enterprises than determining whether or not to produce cookie cutters.

"There's just one thing," I added nervously. "Hong Kong manufacturers demand high minimums."

"How high?" Prince Bandar enquired suspiciously.

"Two thousand sets."

Worried silence met my response.

"I know what you're thinking: we don't know that many people who make cookies. I think this will work, though."

My conviction was real... but there was virtually no confidence to accompany it. I was a business novice trying to persuade my partners to invest in cookie cutters, for goodness sake. The notion sounded kooky, even to me. Just as the practical side of my nature was persuading me to suggest a more conventional alternative, like coffee mugs, Mimi and Prince Bandar gave a reserved go-ahead.

"I sure hope I won't be giving gifts of cookie cutters for the rest of my life," Mimi added pessimistically.

* * * *

Mimi and I survived the steep learning curve of manufacturing and importing our first product. Mimi had to produce camera-ready artwork to the manufacturer's specifications; I had to deal with a Chinese manufacturer whose English-language abilities weren't an awful lot better than my non-existent expertise in Cantonese. Equally challenging was navigating the paperwork jungle to ensure the product's timely and smooth departure from China and arrival in Riyadh. My next visit to Riyadh coincided with the clearance of 2,000 packs of cookie cutters. I announced the news as we sat around the fire before dinner at Abdullah Al-Sweilem's farm.

"How can that possibly be?" Abdullah's cousin Abdul-Mohsen asked. "When we met six months ago, this whole thing was just a vague idea. A bit of a far-fetched idea, I have to admit. Now you suddenly have a product delivery? It can take as much as a couple of years to do what you've done, from concept to completion. The red tape tangles a lot of good intentions. You don't even live here! How did you do it so quickly?"

"Ignorance," I laughed. "I had absolutely no idea what I was doing so I always took the most logical, direct path. I think my naivety brought out the chivalry in officials. They helped me to understand the process and then gave me what I asked for! Sometimes being a woman has its advantages in this country."

The cookie cutter gamble paid off. This initial product became a Design Arabia staple. Happily, it turned out that many thousands of people made cookies! Or at least bought sets of Design Arabia cookie cutters!

Chapter Thirty

On one of my Hong Kong-Riyadh commutes, Prince Bandar approached me about the possibility of Sean working for the Foundation.

"What would he do?" I asked with piqued curiosity. Sean had worked on some of the biggest projects in the world. I couldn't imagine him trading his construction management career for a desk job in philanthropy.

"The Foundation is planning to build a luxury complex that would include the city's first skyscraper, a 5-star hotel, apartments, convention centre and a shopping mall. Income from the property will help fund our various programmes. We think Sean would be perfect to look after the Foundation's interests and manage the construction of the entire project for us."

Prince Bandar had always impressed me with his problem-solving abilities. I knew he wanted me back in Riyadh but surely an undertaking of this magnitude was over the top, even for Prince Bandar. Seeing my perplexity, he explained.

"We've been thinking about this for a few years. Now the timing is right."

"You hardly know Sean," I said with surprise. "Meeting him a couple of times doesn't qualify him for the job."

As much as I wanted to live in Riyadh full time, the circumstances had to be right. I knew that Sean was more than capable of taking on such a challenge. But how could Prince Bandar possibly know this?

"Don't worry, Kathy," Prince Bandar smiled. "We've checked him out."

Of course. Prince Bandar wouldn't make such an offer without having done all the necessary background searches. I didn't need to know more on that score. I argued from a different perspective.

"You'd own me," I said simply.

"What are you talking about? Of course I wouldn't 'own' you!" Now

Prince Bandar looked perplexed.

"You'd hold my passport. You'd be able to control my comings and goings. You know how I hate being controlled!"

The law decreed that sponsors hold employees' passports. This precaution diminished the risk of unauthorised departures from the Kingdom. The rule was open to abuse. It gave unscrupulous employers leverage to mistreat foreign labour that couldn't easily escape unprincipled – and sometimes unpaid – work conditions. Well-intentioned labour laws didn't always succeed in protecting the most vulnerable workers. Considering Prince Bandar's indisputable sense of honour, my argument was unfounded.

"You and Sean can keep your passports," he assured me. "That's not an issue."

OK. Back to me again.

"Let me think about this. It's all been so unexpected."

My real concern was that employing Sean might change the dynamics of my special relationship with Prince Bandar. I wasn't sure I wanted to take the risk.

Armond Habibi, the Foundation's legal advisor, invited me to dinner that evening, presumably at Prince Bandar's behest.

"When I have a difficult decision to make," Armond counselled, "I write all the pros and cons in two columns on a piece of paper. Usually one side outweighs the other. This system might help clarify things for you."

I did as Armond suggested. I had a natural bias toward the 'pro' side. Shortly before returning to Hong Kong, I updated Prince Bandar.

"Thank you for making it possible for us to come back here. Career-wise, it's a big decision for Sean. I want him to be comfortable with the situation. We'll have to talk it over."

Sean received the news with guarded enthusiasm. He accompanied me on my next trip to Riyadh to meet Foundation officials and to learn more about the project and the offer.

As discussions moved in a positive direction, I announced to Prince Bandar that I had some conditions of my own.

"Go on, Kathy, let's hear them," he said amiably – and unsurprised that

I would have such a list.

"Sean never has to work on Christmas day. I know it's not a Saudi holiday but it's a special family time for us."

"Agreed," Prince Bandar answered immediately.

"I'd like to have my own driver, please. Someone who's exclusively at my beck and call, day or night, if need be. I'll need this freedom of movement for Design Arabia."

"Agreed."

"And lastly, I'd like to bring a maid with me from Hong Kong. This will let me devote myself to you," I teased. "We'd cover all her expenses, of course, but you would need to be her sponsor."

"Not a problem. As soon as you give me her details we'll start work on the visa."

All the bases had been covered. We couldn't find any negatives but we still weren't ready to commit. Sean felt a loyalty to Bechtel; he didn't want to keep changing companies. Persuasively, the Foundation assured Sean he'd have a job with them for as long as he wanted.

We returned to Hong Kong swayed but still undecided. Would our next trip to Riyadh be as returning residents?

Chapter Thirty-One

Negotiations between Sean and the Foundation finally reached a happy conclusion. After a three-year absence we were moving back to Riyadh.

We had to stop in Bahrain to collect our Saudi visas so we planned to spend three days with old Riyadh friends Derek and Hilary Barnes who had relocated to Manama, Bahrain's capital. A phone call less than 24 hours after our arrival interrupted the visit.

"It's for you, Kathy. Somebody called Khaled," Hilary said as she handed me the phone.

For years, Hilary had marvelled at my incursions into Saudi male society. An unfamiliar man calling me on their private phone didn't particularly surprise her.

"Hello, Kathy, my name is Khaled Al-Sharfa. I'm a Bahraini friend of Prince Bandar. He would like you and Sean in Riyadh by this evening so Sean can attend a meeting. I'm here to make sure it happens."

This unexpected announcement quickly snapped us into our new reality: availability 24/7, often with little advance warning. Upper-echelon Saudis have an extensive coterie of individuals to ensure that they achieve the seemingly unachievable but this might be a stretch.

"Hi, Khaled. We'd like to cooperate but we haven't received our visas yet. We've been told it will take another couple of days."

"Let me get back to you," he responded, unfazed. "In the meantime, I'll book your flights."

Khaled called back a short time later.

"There are no seats available on any flight from Bahrain until tomorrow. I got you on a flight leaving Dhahran in less than two hours. I'll pick you up in 30 minutes. Please be ready."

"But, Khaled, Dhahran is in Saudi Arabia. We don't have visas," I repeated, this time with more urgency.

Was this crazy stranger going to try to smuggle us into the Kingdom? "I'll handle that. You just be ready to leave the minute I arrive."

With the speed of Olympic athletes, we packed our bags and said hasty goodbyes to Derek and Hilary. So much for the relaxed reunion we all had looked forward to.

The hoot of a horn told us Khaled has arrived – and was impatient to make a quick departure. After hurried introductions, Khaled helped us load our suitcases into the SUV and whisked us away.

Khaled chatted amiably with us on the white-knuckle ride that got us out of Manama and onto the causeway that separated the Gulf island from Saudi Arabia. He handled the vehicle like this might have been his normal driving speed. He was probably a fun person to know but in these circumstances I wouldn't let his friendly personality distract me from the road that was flashing by faster than I was used to.

At the immigration checkpoint half way across the bridge, Khaled showed the official our passports and explained the unusual situation. The officer made a brief phone call, got the necessary approval and welcomed us to Saudi Arabia. The royal wand had been waved.

At Dhahran airport, the plane sat on the runway waiting for our late arrival. We got the two remaining seats. I suspected that a couple of passengers had been bumped to make room for us. If there'd been time to think about it, I would have felt guilty but everything was happening at warp speed. The half-hour flight barely gave us time to catch our breath.

"This is it," I said to Sean when we'd taken off. "We're back. It's not quite the orderly return we anticipated, is it? Who'd have guessed we'd be entering the country illegally?"

Sean at first made no response. He simply stared out the window at the endless desert below.

"They say you can never go back to a place," he mused. "I know we've discussed this but now that we're in the act of going against the maxim, I can't help but wonder what changes we'll see. It's not like the country has progressed at a natural pace. There's been a war. That's bound to have an effect."

"Nothing will distort our good memories, sweetheart. Look at this as a chance to build on them."

The pilot came on the intercom and announced we would be landing in Riyadh in a few minutes… *insha'allah*. I smiled to hear this favourite Arab expression. Used in this context I imagined the pilot sitting in the cockpit with his fingers crossed, offering a prayer to land safely.

A Foundation employee met us off the plane, collected our luggage and whisked us to the Foundation headquarters.

As usual, dear Ibrahim guarded the entrance to the Prince's office.

"*Habibi*," I said rushing toward him.

"*Ayouni*," he responded in our habitual exchange of endearments.

We shared a fond embrace. Then he led us into the Inner Sanctum.

Prince Bandar got the same hugs-and-kisses treatment.

Armond Habibi and Ahmed Salloum, another Foundation consultant, stood at a discreet distance. They smilingly observed the unconventional reunion.

"I thought when you shouted '*habibi*' that you were trying to get my attention," Armond joked.

"No," I laughed. "Only Ibrahim gets called *habibi* by me."

Sean, travelling in my emotional jet stream, greeted everyone with a calm and totally traditional handshake. He was no less happy to be back, he just didn't tend towards manic demonstration.

I left the men to get on with their meeting. As I closed the office door, I reflected on the chaotic events of the past few hours. Yes, it was good to be back in this untypical, ever-unpredictable existence. I felt at home.

* * * *

For the first month we stayed at the well-appointed Al-Khozama apartments located next door to the Foundation. Until Sean was given a vehicle, this proximity to the office made getting to work quick and easy.

"You're free to live anywhere you like," Farid informed us soon after our arrival. "The two Villas Rosas compounds, Al-Wadi and Al-Waha, are new. They're located near the Diplomatic Quarter. Tim Bird, a quantity surveyor who will work for Sean, has chosen Al-Wadi. You might want to check them out."

We looked, we liked, we signed a lease at Al-Waha. We chose a corner house with a large grassy area beside it that would nicely accommodate outdoor parties. The main selling point of the three-bedroom house was a separate downstairs den I could convert into an office. The fact that the house also had pleasing furnishings and comfortable rooms didn't impress me as much as the idea of having my own space. In this congenial cave I could work undisturbed to my heart's delight.

Compound living had definitely improved in our absence. Saudi investors competed to build Western-style housing for the extensive foreign community. An impressive selection of compounds now had upscale homes in a country-club ambience of welcoming pools and palm trees. One even boasted a nine-hole golf course. These upgrades, I happily noted, were a far cry from our creature-infested introduction to Riyadh in 1976.

The arrival of our shipment coincided with finalising paperwork on the house. We looked forward to getting settled. Alas, this came at a price.

"Customs is holding your container. There's a problem with a Christmas tree." Sean received this notification from Ahmed Salloum. "Why didn't you let us know you were bringing in a tree? We could have arranged for everything to come straight through. Now that customs has confiscated it, it will be very difficult to get it released."

The dreaded scrutiny of Saudi customs was one aspect of Riyadh life that evidently had not changed for the better.

"It's a fake tree, for goodness sake," I moaned to Prince Bandar. "It's not like we're importing contraband."

"Christmas trees *are* contraband here," Prince Bandar reminded me. "Give me a few days. I'll see what I can do."

Presumably favours were called in. The shipment was eventually released – but not before every single one of my computer discs had been taken for 'checking'. It seems customs was determined to exact petty revenge. In hindsight, I should have taken the precaution of carrying the discs in our luggage but the bulky stack took up too much valuable suitcase space.

Standing on principle, I pursued the daunting task of trying to retrieve everything. My efforts finally led me to a large room at the customs offices. Almost a third of it was filled from the floor to nearly ceiling height with every variety of computer disc. With dismay, I stared at the untidy heap.

There was no reference system, just squares and circles of plastic thrown on top of each other. They probably got shovelled up every couple of weeks and thrown away.

"You're welcome to have a look," the official said, shrugging his shoulders.

I walked away, defeated and outraged at such puerile aggravation.

The movers delivered the container to our new house a few days later. Prince Bandar popped over unexpectedly one afternoon to see how I was getting on. He found me in a serious state of upset.

"Look what they've done," I said, barely able to keep back the tears. "Why are those people so unnecessarily nasty?"

I pointed to a large, antique wooden duck and a T'ang dynasty horse on the dining room table. The duck had been repeatedly hacked with a sharp knife, scarring and gouging its once smooth back. The terracotta horse had had its ears and tail twisted off. Our three-year break in a more tolerant world had made us forget that orthodox Muslims disapprove of the portrayal of human and animal figures. We'd had the misfortune to come across a fanatic as an inspector.

"There's no excuse for this," Prince Bandar said. He seldom got angry but this spectacle annoyed him deeply. "I'm going to complain."

"No amount of complaining can undo this damage," I replied, disheartened. "I'm not planning to worship the bloody animals, for goodness sake. I just want to make a house a home."

I had a particular fondness for these items but what upset me most was the ignorance and bigotry at the root of the problem. People who refused to remove their blinkers would never be able to see the full spectrum of possibilities.

Rescue came from an unusual source.

"A friend of mine is the antiques restorer for the King," the agent for the mover informed me. "I'll ask him to have a look at the damage, if you like."

I gave him the duck. Miraculously, it came back looking unharmed. Despite the expertise, I couldn't bear to risk my beloved horse. I eventually found the tail in the packing box but, to this day, the 1,200-year-old antique remains earless, a reminder of the effects of religious excess.

* * * *

Remy, our live-in maid in Hong Kong, decided at the last minute that she didn't want to move to Saudi Arabia. A few days before our departure, a possible substitute appeared at our door. Marlen Silorio, a pleasant and practical Filipina, interviewed well. Riyadh's distance and venturing into the unknown didn't frighten her. We clarified all the conditions and came to an agreement. Marlen returned to the Philippines to have the required medical and to await her visa.

No sooner had we arrived in Riyadh than Sean received word from Marlen that her father didn't approve of her new job. Too many stories of abuse and/or unpaid salaries were associated with the employment of Filipina maids in the Kingdom. He didn't want his daughter exposed to unnecessary risk.

We felt particularly disappointed by this turn of events because Marlen had seemed so perfect. In his return letter Sean turned on the Irish charm and assured Marlen's father that we would take good care of her. The deal was on again. Then Marlen got sick just before her physical exam. More delays. Finally Marlen had jumped through all the hoops required by the Saudi Embassy in Manila. Still no visa.

"OK, Prince Bandar. I'm giving notice," I announced after more than a month of waiting for Marlen. " Either I get my maid here likkety-split or I'm going to have to stay home and do chores. It's your work or housework."

Marlen arrived in the Kingdom within the week.

Chapter Thirty-Two

Moving into our new home coincided with the arrival of a Design Arabia shipment of beach towels from Hong Kong. We hadn't yet signed a lease for a warehouse and Prince Bandar's basement was creaking at the seams with other Design Arabia stock. What to do?

"Don't even think about using our place as temporary storage," Sean warned just before he left the house for the office. This reminder came as a final punctuation mark to my repeated attempts to persuade him to change his mind. His tone of voice said he meant business.

"I guess we have to find another solution." Mimi said as we watched Sean's Land Rover Discovery pull out of the driveway. Mimi had moved to Houston after the Gulf War. Now she was staying with us for a couple of weeks to help me rev up the Design Arabia engine and develop it into a serious business.

"No, this *is* the solution, for the moment at least. We'll store the towels here. He'll never know," I said, giving Mimi a fixed stare. "And you'll never tell him."

"What do you mean he'll never know?" Mimi took a nervous drag on her cigarette and slanted her eyes at me through the exhaled smoke. "There are dozens of huge boxes. How can he *not* know?" She hated the idea of defying Sean – and the prospect of getting caught.

"We'll put them on the walkway at the side of the house. Even if he sees the boxes, he won't associate them with Design Arabia. He'll probably think someone is moving into one of the neighbouring houses and the movers have termporarily put stuff in the wrong place. It won't occur to him that we'd disobey."

Ramzi, Design Arabia's recently hired manager and delivery man, arrived shortly afterwards. He had a truckload of towels looking for a home. When Mimi updated him on the situation, Ramzi was no less reluctant than Mimi to countermand Sean's order. This was only partly because he respected Sean. The deeper reason was his inescapable marriage to tradition.

"Sean is your husband," Ramzi reminded me. "You have to do what he says."

Mimi quietly sucked in her breath at this dangerously chauvanistic pronouncement. Ramzi backed down under my determined gaze.

"Look, guys, we need to put this shipment somewhere. *Now*. If anyone has a better idea, fine. Otherwise, let's start unloading. We need to do this before Sean gets home."

The boxes stayed by the side of the house for a few days until we had access to a proper warehouse. Dear Sean was never the wiser. I felt only moderate shame for the necessary deception. Doing business in this tough environment, I told myself, demanded resourcefulness, not a happy housewife approach!

* * * *

We had returned to Riyadh in late October 1993. By mid December we began to think about entertaining. The kids would be flying in from boarding school for the holidays. We had a lot to celebrate.

"Let's ask Prince Bandar and Princess Masha'el to join us for Christmas dinner," I suggested to Sean. "It would be nice for them to be our first guests."

Sean agreed. So did Prince Bandar... eventually. The innocent invitation created a Potential Situation. How would it be perceived if a prominent member of the royal family participated in such an un-Islamic event? Attending a Christmas dinner could wave a red flag at the religious conservatives who might misconstrue his motives. Armond Habibi helped to overcome the dilemma.

"A housewarming dinner would be appropriate," Armond suggested to Prince Bandar. "You would simply be welcoming the Cuddihys to their new home."

So we invited them to a housewarming dinner – with turkey and all the trimmings.

As it turned out, Princess Masha'el had to travel to Cairo.

"Would you mind if I brought the two older children instead?" Prince

Bandar asked us.

"Not at all. It's Christmas. Children are always welcome," I responded.

To our surprise, a support force of two nannies arrived with the family. We set more places at the groaning table.

Everything about the day fascinated Prince Bandar and the kids. They had heard about this important Christian holiday but, like so many cross-cultural interpretations, reality bore little comparison to the myth.

"This isn't at all how I imagined Christmas," Prince Bandar commented. "It's so... non-religious."

In other words, he might have added, what are the conservatives making such a fuss about?

"Some people emphasise the religious aspect," Sean explained, "but most families celebrate it as a time of togetherness. Ideally, the Christmas season inspires peace and goodwill, irrespective of religious beliefs."

Our special guests ate turkey for the first time and enjoyed the new experience of Christmas crackers, those strange things that give a bang when pulled and then break open to reveal prizes and paper hats. We told the children about Santa Claus and his elves and explained the sometimes nonsensical lyrics of Christmas songs. It was an education for them and a reminder to us why we enjoyed the weird and wonderful traditions of this holiday.

The fat, gaudily-decorated tree intrigued the kids, especially when they each received a candy cane from it. Astonishment registered on their faces when Tara and Kieran found two gifts for them under the branches.

Prince Bandar, too, had brought a gift. We gratefully accepted the very large, beautifully wrapped box he offered us and put it aside to open after dinner.

Chocolates, I thought. *Why do Saudis bring such enormous quantities of chocolates?* We could have the chocolates with our coffee.

Now, with the filling dinner behind us, we sat and chatted comfortably in the living room.

"I like how you've decorated the house," Prince Bandar said as I carefully tore open the gift wrapping. "It feels so warm and welcoming."

"Thank you," I smiled. "It still needs a few finishing touches. I'd like to find an interesting hanging for that large wall space." I pointed to the area just below the two-storey living room ceiling.

As the paper fell away, an opaque plastic satchel-like object revealed itself. No cocoa odours filled the air. Had my assumption been wrong? Curious, I opened the folder.

"Oh My God!" I gasped. "How amazing."

I stood to unfold a large, beautiful, rare Suzani tapestry. Prince Bandar beamed at my positive reaction.

"How utterly perfect for the wall space!" I marvelled.

And how utterly unusual that, for once, I had said the right thing at the right time!

* * * *

When we first arrived in 1976, languorous Riyadh was awakening with some astonishment to find itself propelled into the late 20th century. Life was a bit like a camping trip: we couldn't necessarily run out and replenish diminished supplies or replace items missing from shipments. In those casual, make-do days, people learned to live without luxuries, borrowing was *de rigeur* and second-hand trade flourished. By 1993, this quaint snapshot had been relegated to history.

Throughout the 1980s, growth had been steady and evenly paced. During our three-year absence, the city had positively mushroomed. The term 'scarcity' was now obsolete in Riyadh's vocabulary.

My excursions into the retail world demonstrated that improved shopping had a downside: increased vigilence and intimidation from the *mutawwa*.

"They're positively toxic," I snapped at Sean in frustration after a morning spent sussing out some of Riyadh's new outlets. Sean thought I had dropped into his office for a quick coffee. Instead, the poor man had to listen to a protracted rant. I put my parcels on the floor, collapsed into the visitor's chair and continued my outburst.

"They've progressed from carrying long, thin sticks for rapping visible ankles. Now they shout 'cover up, cover up' to all and sundry, including foreigners who, for years, were asked *not* to wear *abayas*. And not only have they multiplied, they now travel in packs."

"That's an effect of the Gulf War," Sean reminded me, handing me a mug of American coffee. "There's a lot of anger at the presence of infidel Americans on Saudi Arabia's holy ground. The religious element is concerned that these liberal influences will erode the traditional base – and, no doubt, their control. As a compromise, the government is allowing them to have greater freedom."

"Well, it sure isn't freedom for women," I argued. "Times have changed. They'll soon find out the masses of youth don't want to be controlled this way. The religious elements may think they can continue to put a lid on progress but pretty soon that pot will boil over."

As soon as most women relented and 'covered up', the *mutawwa* issued a new demand: 'cover your hair, cover your hair'. Sometimes they tormented Saudi women for having ungloved hands. Angry conservatives never would be satisfied. As a matter of principle, I refused to be coerced into wearing an *abaya*. Other long-time residents felt the same. Perhaps the *mutawwa* knew that we knew they were on shaky ground. For whatever reason, they seldom targeted us. Whether or not a person was the victim of an attack by the *mutawwa*, everyone found the unrelenting harrassment unnerving. The city had progressed physically but it had taken a step backwards in outlook.

* * * *

It was the altered species of expat that surprised us even more than all the astounding developmental changes.

"They're operators," Sean explained.

"That sounds akin to 'con men' or 'cute hoors', as you Irish would say. Surely Riyadh hasn't deteriorated to such an extent?"

Ignoring my impertinent comment, Sean continued. "On any big project, the construction team comes first. They're no-nonsense people interested in getting the job done. Then come the operators. They run the projects. They're a different type of person. Saudi Arabia was the biggest construction site in the world. Now the job is pretty much done. It's time for the operators to take over."

A changed attitude subtly permeated the society. Part of it came from the Saudis themselves. The younger generation had come into its own.

They were usually rich, often bored and, for the most part, less prepared for life's responsibilities than their parents had been. Like the pampered Saudi youth, the legions of foreign newcomers were not interested in experiencing 'rough-and-ready'. An excess of consumer goods and cash meant that they didn't need the pioneer spirit of the city's original stock. Too many members of this new crowd complained about anything and everything.

"How can people who have so much feel so hard done by?" I asked Sean one Friday. We were working in our small garden at the back of the house. An encounter with yet another disgruntled expat the previous day had irritated me. "This bloody woman was whining about not being able to find skim milk. I told her to be grateful she had any milk at all! She got a glazed look when I told her that dairies are a relatively recent event here."

The trials of inter-cultural living inspired a grumble in everyone once in a while. The trick was to steer clear of the negative thinkers. Old friends still living in Riyadh helped us to widen our network of interesting people. We settled in easily and quickly.

Before long, we were fully back in the swing of endless social events. Here, too, there were slight differences. Except for the difficulty in getting ingredients, entertaining in the '70s and '80s had been pretty straightforward. No one in those days talked about food allergies. Vegetarians hadn't arrived on Saudi's sandy shores. The new crowd of expat brought with them a host of all the most fashionable dietary conditions: an aversion to cream and butter, an intolerance for onions and a moral objection to eating anything that once had eyes. The list was as imaginative as it was long. Only by keeping records of everyone's culinary likes and dislikes could I successfully plan dinner parties. Several 'special menu' guests on the same evening presented a challenge but the pleasure of great company always outweighed the difficulties of creating a universally-acceptable meal.

I couldn't always remember the names or even the faces of all the people we met but I had a great ear for voices. Once, while leaving my carry-on bag and coat in the cloakroom of British Airway's first-class lounge at Heathrow airport, the distinctive, gravelly speech of a woman caught my attention. I didn't recognise her but I definitely knew her voice.

"Excuse me. I'm sorry to disturb you," I said politely. "Have you ever been to Riyadh?"

"Yes. Many times," came the cautious reply.

"My name is Kathy Cuddihy. You seem so familiar. Have you ever been to my place for dinner?"

"I don't think so." She gave me a searching look to reassure herself. "I'm on TV a lot, so maybe that's how you know me. My name is Hanan Ashrawi."

Of course! This was the famous Palestinian politician, human rights activist, feminist and scholar. She had definitely been in our living room – on the big screen!

* * * *

Sean and I sat at a small table having dinner under the stars. Our companions were the former King and Queen of Romania, the Duke (Pretender to the Portuguese throne) and Duchess of Braganza, and Yousef Al-Hamdan, Secretary-General of the King Faisal International Prize. The Duchess had insisted that we join them because I'd taken the royal visitors *suq* shopping earlier in the day. This year, the Foundation had invited a dazzling cluster of European VIPs to the International Prize celebrations.

We were at Abdullah Al-Sweilem's new farm in a valley outside Riyadh. Abdullah had used his architectural training to full effect in creating a unique ambiance carved into rock face and the desert floor. The romantic setting complemented the heady company of royals, prize winners, diplomats and mere mortals like ourselves.

During dinner, Prince Bandar, now head of the Foundation, and Abdullah stopped by the table to say hello. As he so often did, Abdullah greeted me as *Shaikha*, an honorific title of respect. Suddenly the faces of our tablemates looked worried. Their aides had not warned them that I was a person of rank. It would be a dreaded lapse in protocol if they had not given me the recognition I deserved.

"Abdullah flatters me," I assured them with a laugh. "Believe me, I have no grand titles."

With the royals assured there had been no breaches in etiquette, we reverted to our lively conversation and continued to enjoy a remarkable evening. There was no doubt about it; the social life in Riyadh had gone up market.

* * * *

It wasn't just our own social life that had changed. Saudis were experiencing a new openness – but not in a way approved of by traditional society. Rapid advances in technology suddenly provided a world of possibilities. Satellite TV survived periodic bans and occasional attacks on the satellite dishes by conservatives armed with BB guns. Internet had become pervasive. Even under the weight of censorship, it introduced horizons undreamed of only a short time before. The most important kindling to this raging fire, however, was the mobile phone, a vital tool in making illicit contact with the opposite sex. With 84 per cent of the fast-growing population under 40 years of age, cell phone traffic boomed.

Determined to explore the forbidden, Saudi youth sometimes resorted to unusual methods in their pursuit of pleasure.

"Why on earth are those young people throwing papers at each other?" I asked Mohammed, my Sudanese driver, on a shopping trip.

"Telephone numbers," he responded. "The Saudi boy writes his number on paper, then throws at a girl, any girl. If she likes his look, she calls him. They start a phone friendly."

"But the boy doesn't know what she looks like. She's covered from head to toe."

"No matter. Often the bride and groom don't see each other before marriage. This is no different. At least the girl sees the boy. This happens all the time now."

Shopping malls became such a perfect outlet for this activity that guards had to be posted at mall entrances to keep out herds of salivating young men. Malls did more trade in phone numbers than in merchandise. The 'mall-crawlers', as they came to be known, tested management mettle and infuriated the outnumbered *mutawwa*. Sometimes fights broke out between young men and *mutawwa*. Worse, from the *mutawwa*'s perspective at least, many of the women refused to be intimidated by once effective bullying tactics. Times had definitely moved on.

Testosterone-charged males wasted no opportunity. They spent a lot of time in their cars, cruising the streets, hoping to find a stimulating distraction, preferably female. Here again, phone numbers came into play: papers pressed against windows begged for a positive response. Sometimes numbers were passed between moving vehicles. Desperate situations inspire desperate measures.

* * * *

In a society that still relies heavily on arranged marriages, 'love' isn't a publicly aired theme. Conventional wisdom dictates that, in the best scenarios, love within marriage grows with time. Love outside marriage is Strongly Discouraged. Valentine's Day, a day that modern commercialism devotes to the concept of love irrespective of where it might be found is, naturally, *haram* with a capital H. Every conservative in the land yearns to obliterate this 'immoral' day.

Once the *mutawwa* caught on to the red=love connection, they raided shops, seeking merchants and merchandise that they interpreted as circumventing their no-overt-hint-of-love rule. Florists fared worst of all. Red roses, then red flowers of any kind, disappeared (at least as far as the *mutawwa* knew) for days around Valentine's. Shops selling boxes of chocolate, too, suffered intrusive suspicion. Heart-shaped boxes and red wrappings were hidden from view.

Thanks to the Internet and satellite TV, Valentine isn't going away. Thanks to the frantic opposition by the *mutawwa*, Valentine's Day has become not just a day to celebrate love but an opportunity to plot and outwit the opposition.

Saudi-style dating vibrates with intrigue. The risks are real and the possible outcomes disturbing. In a society built so solidly on foundations of virtue, something as seemingly harmless as a photo of an unveiled girl can destroy her reputation and her chances of marriage. It's a harsh system, one that surely can't endure the swelling rejection of the new youth. The tsunami of change had begun. The moves are still unrefined but there can be no reversing the trend.

Chapter Thirty-Three

L iving in Hong Kong and learning the manufacturing ropes had been invaluable; for Design Arabia's day-to-day operations, being based in Riyadh was vital. Now I could devote myself to marketing, sales and distribution. There was always a new, more difficult aspect of the business to master. Never-ending work demands could be stressful but I loved the challenges – most of the time.

"What do you mean you need 15,000 riyals by Tuesday to pay for the next shipment?" Mimi shouted down the phone from Houston. "You've just told me we only have about 2,000 riyals in the bank! You make me crazy!"

"Relax, Mimi, we still have a couple of days."

Somehow or other at the eleventh hour I always managed to collect one more outstanding bill or make a large cash sale. Still, as often as not, it was business on a tightrope and it depended on me to keep pulling rabbits out of the hat.

Thankfully I had supportive business partners. Mimi was great not only for her creative ideas but also as a sounding board for the countless problems I ran into. Prince Bandar was always there if I needed him but otherwise he let me fumble along and make my own mistakes without a looming fear of recrimmination.

Many people couldn't believe that such a character existed in the form of a Saudi businessman. A dinner in honour of another visit from Mimi included Prince Bandar and his wife Princess Masha'el, as well as the Canadian Ambassador Peter Sutherland and his wife Jo-Lynne and the American Chargé d'Affaires Hugh Geoghegan. Peter and Hugh had been asking us questions about Design Arabia and the partnership. Hugh found Prince Bandar's role too good to be true.

"Are you telling me that you three are *equal* partners?" he asked.

Prince Bandar and Mimi immediately nodded their heads. I couldn't resist clarifying the situation.

"Actually, we're not *exactly* equal."

Astonished looks appeared on the faces of Prince Bandar and Mimi. What did I know about the partnership that they didn't know?

"Prince Bandar is just a man," I explained.

Princess Masha'el burst out laughing, evidently content that her husband was being kept in line.

* * * *

Both the Saudi and the expat communities loved the Design Arabia concept. We had fun designs, affordable prices and practical products. The company couldn't have grown, however, without the efforts of our valuable sales reps, a network which came about by unexpectedly. After giving a talk in Jeddah, a woman from the audience approached me. She mentioned that Lillie Arnaout, her friend in Dhahran, would be interested in selling Design Arabia stock in her store. Lillie was a business godsend. Her large, regular orders gave the company the boost it needed. The successful arrangement with Lillie inspired me to seek out women elsewhere. Step by slow but sure step the wholesale distribution spread throughout the Kingdom and into Dubai. Soon we had female agents in all the main centres. They welcomed an opportunity to have a business that kept them busy and gave them an income without having to compromise family life. I welcomed the fact that they worked hard and paid cash in advance for their orders.

Our strongest sales venues had been and continued to be bazaars. These markets took place monthly, except in November-December when there would be several each week in the run-up to Christmas. Behind the protective walls of large compounds, people could shop for gift and craft items without harassment from the *mutawwa*, who were automatically refused entry to the compounds.

I was constantly on the lookout for new outlets. Supermarkets fell into my line of sight. An interview with the manager of Al-Azizia, Riyadh's biggest and best supermarket, made me feel like a lamb in the company of a wolf. His ruthless professionalism dwarfed my relatively limited sales experience. The tough tutorials learned from Muteb Al-Johar in my old sheet-selling days helped but the business still had some surprises. My first meeting exposed the inner workings of the industry.

"*You* want to charge *me* a monthly fee to place my items on your shelves?" I was incredulous at this revelation. "Surely your commission on sales is payment enough?"

"Times have changed, Kathy," he said. "Now we create less obvious sources of revenue."

He slowly lit a cigarette and effectively managed to inhale and exhale without removing the cigarette from the side of his mouth. Meanwhile, he moved papers around his messy desk until he found what he was looking for: the current price list. Placements on eye-level shelves, ends of aisles and checkouts cost the most but everything was expensive and beyond my budget.

"Hel*lo*," I said with impatience. "This is not some multinational conglomerate you're speaking to. It's me. Just One-Woman-Show me. My products on your shelves will benefit both of us but I have no margin for these high charges."

Perhaps the Lebanese wolf sitting across from me had already eaten his prey for the day. After a lengthy pause and another long drag on his smelly cigarette, he decided to give this lamb a break.

"The best I can do," he said, brushing his thick black moustache with a stubby finger, "is to offer you a one-month rate for a three-month period. You'd have to pay in advance, though. Would that be manageable?"

The unexpected expense would still pinch but three months for the price of one was a concession I decided to accept. We shook hands and the manager gave a short laugh.

"I'm glad you're our only woman vendor. Otherwise, our profits might take a nosedive."

The investment didn't pay off as well as I'd hoped. Riyadh's population no longer relied on supermarkets as their principal shopping source. Still, a narrow profit margin was better than none at all.

Running Design Arabia introduced me to a repertoire of clichéd excuses why something hadn't, couldn't or wouldn't be done. *Bukra inshallah*, an integral part of the Arab vocabulary meaning 'tomorrow, God willing', was most frequently applied when I tried to collect money, although being a Western woman gave me a pretty high success rate on this score. After much trial and error, I learned to distinguish when 'no' meant 'yes' and 'yes' meant 'no'. Previously I'd touched on these cultural characteristics only peripherally. Now that I ran my own business, I endured them daily – and became more astute because of them.

* * * *

Once Design Arabia was on its feet, a new idea, inspired by my love of food, began to percolate in my entrepreneurial psyche. Arabian-theme gifts had been a success; why not promote Arabian-theme food? With Prince Bandar's blessing – and a suitably amended import license – Flavours of Arabia was born. A British company produced my recipes of date and orange preserves, chunky date chutney and honey with dates. Flavours of Arabia also did a range of spices packaged in bags made from Bedouin tent fabrics. This sideline always remained small but was no less satisfactory because of that.

* * * *

As busy as Design Arabia and Flavours of Arabia kept me, I still worked for the Foundation. They continued to pay me the retainer that had been established when I lived in Hong Kong. This setup worked well for everyone: I remained available to the Foundation but they had no problem with me taking whatever time I needed for myself, as long as their work got done. I had no office at the Foundation and, even better, no fixed work hours.

Having been on the same retainer for several years, I approached Farid about a raise. I had grown up in a society where annual salary increases were the norm. Saudi companies, evidently, didn't operate on the same principle. My request met with a strange response.

"Do you need the money?" Farid asked matter-of-factly.

What kind of question was that? And what business was it of his? For once, I remained speechless.

"Do you need the money?" Farid repeated.

When I actually thought about it, I had to give Farid an honest answer.

"I guess I don't need more income. I'd just like to have more. It would make me feel more valuable, more appreciated."

"As needs be," Farid said simply. "When you need an increase, it will be there for you."

I never asked again. And I never forgot to analyse the distinction between need and greed. This was but one of many lessons I learned from the example of my non-Western colleagues.

* * * *

'Saving face' is a particularly important talent in the Middle East. It is the deft practice of getting out of, or helping someone else to get out of, a sticky situation without compromising anyone's dignity or causing undue embarrassment. I experienced the skill firsthand many times but one situation was particularly clever – and prolonged. One year the Foundation received complaints from conservatives about a conspicuous blond woman in the audience at the King Faisal International Prize ceremony. Prince Bandar called me into his office to give me a heads up for next year's ceremony.

"You'll have to cover your hair, Kathy. The TV cameras are giving you too much attention and we're getting comments."

"I don't wear an *abaya*. Covering my hair is really a step too far!" I exclaimed.

"You have to, Kathy. That's it."

Prince Bandar's usually tolerant mind was inflexible on this point. But so was mine.

"Respect is a two-way street, Prince Bandar. I have always shown the utmost respect towards Muslims and Islam. It has to work both ways. These fanatics have to display respect for others."

Prince Bandar looked thoughtful. He may have agreed but he didn't give in.

"You'll have to cover your hair, Kathy."

"I won't."

"Yes you will."

After a moment of stubborn silence I made a decision.

"I won't go to the ceremony. It's a matter of principle. I won't let those people exert their negative influence over me."

Angry, I left Prince Bandar's office. It was the only serious disagreement we ever had.

Fortunately Prince Bandar had a better solution. The following year when ceremony time rolled around I waited for someone to remind me to cover my hair – or not attend. Nothing was said. It was as though the matter had never arisen. I was shown to a seat on the end of an aisle, well away from the centre. I found out later that the TV crew had been instructed not to pan their cameras in my direction. Problem averted. Everyone saved face.

* * * *

In 1997 the Foundation took the opportunity to invest in Riyadh's growing public relations awareness. The Foundation formed a local partnership with Burston-Marsteller, an international PR firm of renown. Ailamia came into existence.

"You won't be working on this floor anymore, Kathy," Prince Bandar informed me one afternoon after a meeting.

I had reconciled myself to the fact that Ailamia would handle the Foundation's PR work and that I'd be surplus to requirements. Now the moment of truth had arrived. Before I could feel maudlin, Prince Bandar continued.

"Ailamia will be located in the Foundation's north tower. You'll have an office there and will handle our account."

"But I'm not a PR executive," I exclaimed. "Those hotshot professionals would devour me. You're throwing me to the proverbial lions! I do my work for you by instinct, not by training. And that's going to become real evident real fast. I'm happy to help with the transition, but let these guys do what they do well – unhindered by an amateur."

Prince Bandar dismissed my concerns. I tried a new tack.

"It's a long time since I had a regular job where I had to keep proper office hours. I feel like I've grown beyond such convention."

"Make your own hours. We need results, not attendance."

Gradually, I got used to the reins of routine. More importantly, I loved the creative and fun environment provided by my talented, sometimes artistically eccentric new colleagues. The team included me in all the brainstorming sessions and welcomed my ideas for all the accounts, not just that of the Foundation. It felt good to be a part of this business and to have an acceptable and accepting outlet for my imaginative ideas.

"Working in an agency has been the equivalent of climbing another of life's mountains. I think I can finally see the peak," I said to Sean as we sat on our terrace one evening. I had just completed a difficult ad campaign. "I'm grateful to Prince Bandar for pushing me in this direction, despite my objections."

"The only way to develop self-confidence is to move beyond your comfort zone. Face your fears," Sean said wisely. "It seems you're becoming pretty adept at that."

* * * *

Ailamia became a communication point for visiting journalists and camera crews. We provided them with local information and contacts and they were a refreshing diversion for us. One day a team arrived from Condé Nast Traveller magazine. They were going around the Kingdom gathering material for a feature article.

"What's your itinerary?" I enquired.

They rattled off all the usual destinations.

"If you're going to be in the Asir, why not make a side trip to Najran? It's off the beaten track but I think you'd enjoy it."

"Sorry, it's not on the schedule," came the firm reply of the lead journalist.

"It's a worthwhile diversion," I pushed. "The mayor of Najran is a good friend of mine. I'm sure he'd arrange something special for you."

They discussed the idea among themselves.

"OK," they agreed, "let us know the details. We'll drive to Najran when we've finished shooting in Abha."

As soon as they left the office I phoned Mohammed Atiah, the former mayor of Al-Baha.

"Mohammed, this is a fantastic opportunity to promote your region. It's up to you to wow them."

"Great, Kathy," Mohammed enthused. "Thank you. Why don't you and

Sean invite a few friends and come as well?"

A week later, six of us were in the Kingdom's southernmost province. "The Condé Nast people won't arrive until tonight," Mohammed informed us as we checked into the hotel. "In the meantime, we're going to have lunch at the top of a mountain. But you have to climb the mountain to get the food!"

So we climbed. And climbed. When we finally reached our destination, all of us were happy to see that an advance team had lunch ready and waiting. The views were spectacular. An adjacent cave provided welcome shelter from the sun.

"During tribal wars, locals used these caves as refuge for themselves and their animals," Mohammed informed us.

"I can see why no one would want to follow them up here!" I was still recovering from the ascent.

We took a less exerting route back to town, had a brief rest and then went out for a dinner under the stars hosted by Mohammed.

The following morning we met up with the Condé Nast team. After a quick tour of Najran's main sights we drove in convoy into the *Rub Al-Khali*, the Empty Quarter, one of the largest sand deserts in the world. Most of our Saudi escort was of Bedouin extract. This was their turf. We felt safe.

When we hit the flat, hardened edges of the desert, the 4-wheel drives fanned out. Walkie-talkies suddenly crackled into life. Light banter soon evolved into clever, spontaneous poetry, each driver contributing a few improvised lines that the next driver continued. Even though we couldn't understand the nuances or many of the words, the cadence of the language touched a chord deep inside us.

Finally we arrived at the prepared camp.

"I knew you'd want everything as natural as possible, Kathy, so I told them not to bring generators. Or portable toilets," Mohammed laughed. "There are enough tall dunes that you can disappear when you need to."

Everyone eagerly explored the surroundings. The profound silence of the desert imbued in us a stillness that our busy lives normally lacked. The experience definitely wouldn't have been the same with generators!

By the time we got back to the campsite, dusk had fallen.

"What's that delicious smell?" I asked, nose sniffing the air.

"It's fresh bread," Mohammed said. "Come over to the fire and see the desert version of baking."

The young Bedu cook pulled an unleavened loaf from the ashes, brushed off some embers and proudly presented us with his creation.

"I don't think I've ever tasted more delicious bread," I said with admiration.

"The desert air heightens the senses," Mohammed explained.

He must have been telling the truth because the no-frills lamb stew approached Michelin-star quality according to my altered taste buds.

The camaraderie was pure magic. In typical Bedu fashion, story-telling followed dinner. The foreign crowd contributed their own tradition of singing around the campfire. Finally, gastronomically and culturally satiated, everyone said goodnight and headed to the communal sleeping tents.

Brad Davis, an inveterate adventure traveller and one of our neighbours in Riyadh, alerted us to a delightful incongruity.

"Don't you just love the wild patchwork colours of the tent interior? It really feels like we've stepped back in time. Until…" Brad pointed to ties on the cloth wall where people had hung bags and coats. There, suspended from one of the ties was an anachronism: a mobile phone.

We headed back to noisy, stressful civilization the next day.

"I can't believe we nearly missed this opportunity," one of the photographers told me as we said goodbye.

"You've just learned one of Saudi Arabia's most important secrets: the country is full of experiences that we sometimes think we'd prefer to avoid but which usually make us grateful we didn't.

Chapter Thirty-Four

Sean and I met Mike and Sandi Lee at a charity dinner at the Canadian Embassy. Mike had recently been hired as an emergency room doctor at the King Faisal Specialist Hospital. Sandi was one of those rare individuals who simply oozed talent. She sang, she acted and she painted, all with a high level of competence. Worse, she was beautiful. She could have been every woman's nightmare but, dammit, she was also a really nice person. Sometimes life wasn't fair to the rest of us.

Sandi had donated one of her paintings to the Embassy's silent auction. The lovely scene of a birch forest touched my Canadian soul. I started bidding – but so did a lot of other people. As the price approached my limit, I resorted to playful threats. I targeted my closest competitor Jim Stewart, another Canadian doctor and a good friend.

"Back off if you want to stay on our dinner list," I teased.

To my surprise, Jim took me seriously. Better still, he must have spread the word because my final bid won the painting. My pleasure at unexpectedly owning the watercolour outweighed the guilt I felt for having bullied Jim, even in fun.

When we got home that evening, Sean gave me an intriguing piece of news.

"Sandi is starting art lessons. She'll begin with basic drawing techniques. I'm going to sign up."

That was a revelation! I'd always been the major art lover in the family. I had no idea that Sean's companionable appreciation extended to wanting to learn the craft.

"You've never expressed an interest in a hobby before. Is this about art or about Sandi?" I asked suspiciously. Might Sean's unflagging loyalty waver in Sandi's orbit?

"She is gorgeous, isn't she? Sean laughed. "That's a bonus, though. I've always wanted to learn how to draw. This is a good opportunity – with an admittedly stimulating teacher."

I couldn't draw a straight line. I thought drawing was an inherited talent, not an acquired one. What if I could be taught? I briefly considered letting Sean be a guinea pig for a month. If he showed progress, then I, too, would take lessons. On the other hand, if Sandi's classes were effective, he'd be a whole month ahead of me in proficiency. My competitive nature couldn't allow that concession.

Sean reluctantly agreed to my request to join him. We became enthusiastic participants in Sandi's weekly evening classes. Our progress was rapid and, to me, astounding. The miracle of taking a blank piece of paper and covering it with a series of lines to create an illusion that everyone recognised never ceased to amaze me. Sandi had succeeded in taking our own blank canvases and creating budding artists.

* * * *

Although I was a happy workaholic, I acknowledged the healthy need for regular, non-business diversions. In addition to art lessons, I decided to brush up on my French. A friend invited me to join the city's most popular weekly conversation group. The participants were mostly ambassadors' wives but there were also a few Arab and French women. Numbers were kept to around 20 people, so I felt lucky to be squeezed into this richly diverse company.

Colette Liautaud, the inspiring French moderator, was the reason for the group's reputation. Colette was a delightful combination of striking good looks, fun personality and absorbing intellect. She had an innate ability to keep her group interested and interesting.

An invitation to the home of Colette and her charming husband Claude was much sought after and always rewarding, both socially and intellectually. Her guests might be treated to a French storyteller or a Saudi musician or a talented individual from one of dozens of other artistic backgrounds. Her devoted and extensive following included both Saudis and foreigners. Everyone loved Colette for her broad understanding of many cultures and for her seemingly effortless ability to eradicate divisions that might otherwise have surfaced. In 1995 the French government officially recognised her cross-cultural successes and awarded Colette the Medal of Arts and Letters, the country's highest civilian honour.

* * * *

Rita Kurth, a lively redheaded German friend whom I'd known since our earliest days in Riyadh, asked me an unusual question one day.

"Have you ever bought clothes at the second-hand *suq*?"

I stared at fashion-conscious Rita in disbelief. This was the Queen of Chic, my favourite choice for a shopping companion. Her unerring instinct could find trendy outfits in even the most unpromising circumstances.

"Are you telling me that your amazing wardrobe comes from the *suq*?"

"Of course not," Rita laughed. "But if you love fabrics – and the theatrical – this place is definitely worth a visit. It has to be seen to be believed."

I mentioned the conversation to Jan Quinn, another old friend.

"Oh yes," she enthused. "It's a really fun place to explore. I have some of the dresses. Come over and have a look."

Two of my most stylish friends knew about this place – and recommended it. How had I gone so many years without making this discovery for myself? I thought I knew about most of Riyadh's tucked-away treasures.

Because we both worked and had busy schedules, Jan and I got together less often than we would have liked. This invitation was a welcome excuse to indulge in her pleasurable company. After a chat and a cup of tea, Jan revealed her choice collection. My eyes popped.

"Do people actually wear these things?" I asked in astonishment.

"I'm afraid so," Jan confirmed with a shake of her head. "These are the cast-offs from the never-ending parade of Saudi weddings. No one wants to be seen in the same outfit twice so they get the tailors to whip up something different each time. The *suq* is a great option for people who go to a lot of weddings but can't always afford new dresses. Women often give their discards to their maids who then might sell them to a stall owner in the *suq*. If you hunt around you can find some exceptional gowns."

One of Jan's dresses in particular caught my attention. The frothy nylon turquoise opus with puffed sleeves had patterns of 'pearl' flowers sewn all over the front.

"This looks like something Cinderella would wear," I gushed.

I was in love. This gaudy fashion statement spoke to my fantasy side.

"Keep it," Jan laughed. "I can get plenty more."

"Really? Thank you so much," I said, clasping the one-of-a-kind creation to my breast. "Could I come with you the next time you go?"

"Of course. Why don't we plan an outing? Maybe a couple of other friends would like to come along as well."

Located on the outskirts of Riyadh, the *Suq al-Haraj,* or bargaining *suq,* covered acres of dusty ground. Everything from new refrigerators to old tires could be found here. Our destination rested in the midst of all the jumble. Thousands of dresses were crammed onto many hundreds of racks. The crowded clutter overwhelmed me. Fortunately, both Rita and Jan had trained eyes. They presented me with numerous interesting possibilities.

"You can't try anything on," Jan said. "That's why it's better to buy several at a time. It increases the odds that one will fit. And the more you buy, the cheaper the price. They average about 15 riyals each. That's less than 5 dollars!"

"My God! The beadwork on some of them is worth more than that!"

"And don't go to the expense of dry-cleaning them," Jan added. "Just throw them in the washing machine. They come out beautifully."

The irredeemably ugly dresses gave us as much pleasure as their must-have sisters. Our little gaggle of shoppers made an impressive dent in the stock that day. We could barely carry all our bouffant purchases.

"These creations demand a proper showing," I announced in the car on the way back to Rita's for coffee. "I'm going to have a party. I'll call it *The Best of Batha.* Everyone will have to get his or her outfit from this *suq* or the Batha *suq.* We'll have dinner, we'll dance and we'll let ourselves be unrestrained by the conventional boundaries of good taste."

Thus was born an annual event that had people clambering for an invitation. The kitschy décor complemented the outrageous clothing combinations. Each year the party got marvellously gaudier thanks to guests' increasingly eager participation in the spirit of garish fun.

Women's shoes, too, played an important role. I found a wonderful pair of glittery silver pumps with chunky high heels. They reminded me of something the Good Witch might wear in the *Wizard of Oz.* Evidently I had a dormant yearning to be a character in a fairy tale.

* * * *

On one of my excursions to find new fodder for *The Best of Batha*, I came across a stunning sequenced, black lace dress. There was no designer label but it could easily have been a copy from an expensive runway collection. It had a high neck, short sleeves and 29 small, covered buttons down the back. The front hem rose to just below the knees but the back hem trailed on the ground. The only flaws were two minor tears in the lace. These had been 'mended' with a large safety pin – and a staple! It was far too elegant to wear to *The Best of Batha* but, for only 20 riyals, I couldn't resist adding this gem to my wardrobe. An invitation to a formal dinner at the Canadian Embassy made me consider putting the dress to good use.

"You can not wear a *suq* dress to an embassy," Rita reprimanded.

"Why not? It's gorgeous. And," I admitted with a laugh, "it would amuse me to know that I'd given this discard the display it deserves."

Despite Rita's protests, I wore the dress. Never have I received so many compliments for an outfit. I was too honest to pretend that I wore the latest Balenciaga creation.

"Twenty riyals at the second-hand *suq*," I loved telling admirers. "The selection's great!"

Sometimes this comment met with stunned, disapproving silence. Most of the guests, though, simply enjoyed my eccentricity – not to mention the safety pin and the staple.

* * * *

My broad cross-section of friends and acquaintances included one of Riyadh's most high-profile characters. Describing Princess Halla bint Khaled as a square peg in a round hole was neither inaccurate nor unkind. Halla simply did not fit any of the regular moulds. This cute, quirky woman had a charmingly cheeky nature that I loved. Halla had become well known for the children's books that she wrote and illustrated. Not only did we have writing and a love of art in common but Halla was a niece of Prince Bandar and Princess Masha'el.

During one of Tara's visits from boarding school, Halla invited us for dinner. As usual, she had organised delicious food, stimulating conversation and interesting women. At the end of the evening, I walked one of the guests to the gate for a final goodbye. Tara stayed talking to Halla in the courtyard.

"If you want to see a really funny look on my mom's face, say 'rabbits' to her when she comes back."

"'Rabbits'?" Halla queried. "Why would I say that? What does it mean?"

"Just say it," Tara prompted. "You'll thank me. I'll explain later."

"Rabbits!" Halla announced as I returned.

She had no idea what she was doing but Halla was always game for a bit of fun. My face contorted into a look of shocked surprise.

"Rabbits, Mom," Tara added.

"You put Halla up to this, didn't you, Tara!" I laughed, accepting double defeat.

"Kathy, what on earth is 'rabbits'? Your expression was priceless." Halla still looked incredulous at the effect this single word had had on me.

"An English school friend first introduced me to the tradition. Good luck is supposed to come to whomever says the word first each month. It's silly but entertaining. I started doing it with Sean and then we got the kids involved."

Bright and early on the first day of the following month I answered my phone. Halla, merrily shouting "Rabbits, rabbits, rabbits, I got you!" into her mouthpiece, startled me out of complacency. The game was on. In future months, as a precaution, I said "rabbits" before saying hello. Usually the caller wasn't Halla, just a mystified business associate. It was more difficult to call Halla and succeed because her operator knew my voice and informed her of the caller.

"Just pretend you don't know who it is. Just this once," I would implore.

"No, Madam Kathy. No can do this. Princess would not be happy."

I resorted to deceit.

"'Allo? Zees eez Chanel. I call from Parees. Please I talk to *la princesse*?"

As well as French, my repertoire of accents included Chinese, Italian and Indian. Strategising occupied Halla and me for a couple of days before the first of each month.

Gradually the 'rabbits' circle widened to include competitive friends in several countries but no one ever matched Halla's mischievous panache.

* * * *

Everyone loved the anticipation of boarding school kids coming home for Christmas. For expat families, their arrival was the happiest time of the year. Young and old generations mixed comfortably and joined with friends to coalesce into one big clan.

During one of our dinner parties, the phone rang. It was Tara calling from school in Canada. After saying hello, she suddenly burst into tears.

"The Saudi Embassy won't give visas to Kieran and me until we get an AIDS test. There's nowhere around here to do that. Besides, I can't take time off school because we're having exams. We want to come home for Christmas, Mom."

This last statement produced a fresh burst of tears.

"Don't worry, sweetheart. This is just a glitch. We'll get things sorted out. I'll make a couple of phone calls. Just give me a few minutes."

I immediately tried to phone Prince Bandar but couldn't locate him. In a stroke of inspiration, I called his father's house and got hold of Prince Bandar's brother, Khaled. His senior position at the Ministry of Foreign Affairs might be useful. I explained the problem.

"Just have Tara call the Ambassador and tell him that I've given authorisation to waive the test requirement. Call me back to let my know that everything is OK."

Tara received her instructions and I returned to our dinner party.

A short while later the phone rang again.

"The Ambassador doesn't believe me, Mom. He told me to tell Prince Khaled to call him personally."

This was suddenly ballooning into An Incident.

"Stay by the phone, Tara," I instructed.

I called Prince Khaled and repeated what Tara had said. I could sense the Ambassador's insult hitting its target.

"I'll call you back," Prince Khaled said in a low voice.

"Please don't forget, Prince Khaled. You're speaking to a mother tiger who wants her cubs home."

"I'll call you right back," he repeated.

No sooner had I updated our curious dinner guests than the phone rang.

"Tell Tara the visas are ready."

Wow. That was efficiency. Then the phone rang again.

"Mom, you'll never guess. The Saudi Ambassador just called me to apologise for the misunderstanding. He's sending our passports by courier. We should have them tomorrow."

The dinner proceeded without further interruptions. The kids arrived home on schedule. We never knew what happened to the Ambassador's career path.

Chapter Thirty-Five

Since its inception in 1993, Design Arabia had restricted itself to the wholesale market. The completion of the luxury Al-Faisaliah mall, the retail portion of the $320 million Foundation project that Sean oversaw, persuaded me to take the leap into the retail market. Although it probably made better business sense to rent in a less expensive location, Al-Faisaliah was 'family'. British architect John Shenton, already connected with design work in the mall, translated my Arabian concepts into a fun shop with 'mud' walls and other 'authentic' touches that perfectly complemented our product line. In 2000 Design Arabia opened its doors for business. Being female, I wasn't allowed to work in the shop; my frequent presence was camouflaged as a browsing shopper when the roving *mutawwa* came on the scene.

In 2001, the September 11 disaster in the US brought an abrupt halt to Design Arabia's growing possibilities. Saudi Arabia went into shock; foreigners kept a low profile. This was the downside of a global community: the effects of the tragedy in New York rippled outwards and crippled commerce in Riyadh. Our high rent wouldn't get paid if customers continued to stay home because of the threat of terrorism. A challenging business was now struggling to survive. I felt the sun setting on Design Arabia.

The sun also seemed to be setting on a way of life that had made Riyadh so special. Sean and I were dismayed to see the subtle adjustments in attitude after the events of 9/11. Although most Saudis expressed sympathy and shame for the atrocities, a few believed that an important victory had been achieved. The actions of their Al-Qaeda brothers emboldened them to express long-simmering hostility towards Westerners because of the Allied occupation of Saudi soil during the Gulf war. They did not want their culture or their religion contaminated by outside influences. Economic decline and an unrelenting rise in the Kingdom's unemployment numbers fed the upsurge in homegrown, clandestine terrorist groups. The Government's cautious reaction to the rash of radical events emboldened discontented members of the population.

An incendiary device placed in a paper bag bearing the logo of a fast food chain and left on the hood of a Western man's car was the first serious incident we heard about. Then a bomb was left in a bin outside Jarir Bookstore. The explosion killed the foreigner who stood beside it having a smoke. Most people did not have first-hand experience of negative or dangerous events but everyone felt psychologically bruised. What was happening to safe, peaceful Riyadh? Warnings abounded and everyone remained on high alert. A once trusting population was forced to become street smart.

These small but fatal local attacks made everyone feel vulnerable. Compounds were now defended with a gauntlet of strategically placed concrete jersey barriers. Outside the larger compounds, police cars positioned themselves to deter would-be assailants. Cars that got past the approach had a bomb inspection at the gate: guards examined each vehicle engine and used an extended mirror to look under the chassis. They then verified the identities of the driver and every passenger. Coming and going for compound residents and their visitors wasn't as fast or easy as it used to be. The age of innocence had passed.

Although the social life did not diminish as a result of the new threats, people were particularly vigilant when leaving places located outside compound walls. Unprotected public streets were soft targets. Most expats now adopted an important new routine: searching for bombs under and around their cars.

One of the guests at a dinner we attended was the US Chargé d'Affaires Al Thibault and his wife Caroline. We both left the party at the same time. Because we lived near each other, we followed the same route home.

"Have you noticed that there's another car following every twist and turn taken by the Thibaults' driver?" I asked Sean. "It's been on their tail since we left."

"Yes, I've been watching the car." Sean increased his speed so as not to lose sight of our friends. "Those four fit Saudis make me nervous. They don't take their eyes off the Embassy vehicle."

Eventually both cars headed into the Diplomatic Quarter and we continued home. I was uneasy about what we had witnessed.

"Do you think those men were kidnappers? It all looked pretty suspicious, don't you think?"

"I don't know, Kathy," Sean replied in a worried voice.

"I can't sit here and do nothing. I know it's late but I'm going to call the Thibaults and make sure they got home all right."

My fears were relieved when Al answered the phone.

"Thanks for your concern, Kathy," Al said. "Everything's OK. That was our chase car. Because I'm the acting ambassador, the Saudi government provides protection."

This insight reinforced the realities of the world in which we now lived.

Chapter Thirty-Six

The nine-year-long Al-Faisaliah project was complete. Sean's position as project manager for the client was now redundant. With no other Foundation job coming up in the near future, we had to move on. Only foreigners with sponsorship could remain in the country and sponsorship usually came with employment. No matter how long they stayed, few foreigners enjoyed a feeling of permanence. We had lasted longer than most.

My jail experience a few weeks before our departure hadn't been part of our exit strategy. The brief interval behind bars had put my name on all the expat lips of Riyadh and earned me special *caché*. It also sent a tremor of anxiety through the community.

"If they can put you in jail, it means none of us is safe," my friend Averil worried.

I had been released from the women's prison a couple of hours previously. The adrenalin was still pumping – or was that shock setting in? At any rate, it didn't seem like a good enough excuse to back out of a dinner invitation from long-time friends Gerry and Averil Skea. My latest exploit was the main topic of conversation.

"The *mutawwa* are on the warpath but they're getting too bold," I insisted. "They'll soon have their wings clipped. You've been here long enough to know how the system works. The government lets them have their way for a while and then reins them in. It's the age-old political dance. The situation unravelled because I slapped the wretched man." The memory still gave me satisfaction. "I have to admit, if I'd known the action would land me in jail, I probably would have put some elbow into a good swing."

"I know the *mutawwa* power goes in waves," Gerry admitted, "but they're definitely in overdrive." He passed everyone second helpings of meat and vegetables.

"It's true," David Hodgkinson agreed. "With the King out of the country, they're worse than ever. The situation is becoming untenable. Ever since 9/11, they've become more aggressive. It's not just expats who are complaining, either. A lot of Saudis are fed up with their antagonistic behaviour."

As head of Saudi British Bank, David had numerous sources to provide insights into the deteriorating situation. No one needed special sources, however, to feel the increase in tensions.

A call from a Saudi friend a few days later reinforced our conclusion that expats weren't the only ones concerned about the growing intrusiveness of the *mutawwa*.

"I had dinner last night with the chief of police. He told me they had jailed their first Canadian woman – for prostitution! He didn't know the name of the person so I asked him to find out immediately. He made a couple of phone calls and confirmed my worst fears. It was you! I came to your defence and told him what a terrible mistake they had made. You are like my family. I have been personally insulted by what happened. What *did* happen?"

I gave Mohammed the details and assured him that no harm had come to me.

"It's simply another notch in my belt of Saudi escapades," I said lightly. On a more serious note, I added, "Those good women that I met in jail deserve respect, not persecution for crimes they didn't commit. They shouldn't be treated in such a manner."

"You're right, of course," Mohammed agreed. "But I'm particularly offended that you were treated in such a manner. Those crazy religious people are out of control. Something has to be done to stop them before they ruin the country."

"All the Saudis I know say it's wrong the way some *mutawwa* misrepresent Islam. Why don't you strengthen your voices? The Chinese philosopher Confucius said, 'If you don't change the road you're travelling on, you'll probably end up where you're going.'"

Mohammed didn't have an answer. I wondered if he'd ever have the courage to have a voice.

* * * *

"I'm beginning to think our departures are bad luck for Saudi Arabia. The last time we left, the country was on the verge of war. This time Al-Qaeda is on the offensive. There seems to be a message that we should stay put – purely to keep the Kingdom safe, of course."

We were driving home from a farewell dinner at the Canadian Embassy. Exceptionally, both Prince Bandar and his wife Princess Masha'el had accepted the invitation. It was almost unheard of for Saudi men and women to attend a public social event together. They had paid us a high compliment indeed. This fun evening with good friends deepened our sadness at leaving.

"You're grasping at straws, sweetheart." Sean chose to ignore the impishness of the comment. "We're leaving. Try to focus on the positive aspects of that reality. Think of our unknown future as one of your magical mystery tours."

Sean's contract ended in December 2002.

"Stay on for as long as you want," Prince Bandar offered, showing typical generosity and sensitivity. "Take whatever time you need to tie up all your loose ends,"

My loose ends included dissolving Design Arabia and Flavours of Arabia. I couldn't sell the businesses in such a depressed environment. This meant having to dispose of a lot of stock. As tempting as it was to make the process drag on forever, we asked for an extension of only a month, until the end of January.

Relinquishing the way of life we had known for most of our married life would present us with a whole new set of challenges. We'd been pampered with cars, homes, paid school fees and holidays. Now we'd have no such perks. Worse, we'd have no income, tax-free or otherwise. Without this safety net, I felt as though we were stepping into an abyss. We hadn't expected to be unemployed so early in our careers. Sean had received a couple of job offers in new locations but he preferred to take a prolonged break from work pressures. Although I supported him in this indulgence, I felt adrift without A Long-Term Plan.

Until life offered us a new direction, we would spend winters at our apartment in a fishing village in Mallorca, Spain, and summers at our home on Bantry Bay, Ireland. The destinations sounded idyllic but could we sustain a holiday-style existence, perhaps for the rest of our lives? Could we easily adjust to such a different lifestyle?

"Do you think we'll forget our social skills?" I asked Sean one evening as we filled large, black plastic bags with things we'd leave behind.

He had the decency not to roll his eyes.

"We're retiring, not leaving the fold of humanity. We'll make new friends and have new interests."

"Yes," I replied with a mock anguish, "but the dress code will be jeans and a woolly sweater and we'll probably be discussing whether or not the spate of bad weather will ruin the crops or be bad for fishing! I'll be scraping dirt from under my nails instead of putting polish on top of them!"

"You do like drama, don't you, Kathy?" Sean sighed. "We'll get on just fine socially. You'll be picking up people in restaurants and supermarkets in no time," he joked. "The big adjustment for you will be the weather."

This was an understatement. I thrived in the sunshine and dry heat of the desert.

"It scares me that I'll eventually adapt to grey skies and weeks of rain. How utterly dreary. But I have a much more serious concern: how will I possibly survive without a maid?"

Wonderful Marlen had run our home with hyper efficiency for almost 10 years. Her absence would be an emotional loss and a housekeeping disaster. We'd had maids or houseboys for most of our married lives. Now the relentless career of housewife had caught up with me. I was unqualified for the job.

I stood in front of open cupboard doors, deciding what to keep and what to give away.

"One thing for sure, the moon won't be quite as interesting to me after we leave," I said absently, adding more items of clothing to the leave-behind bag.

"Why do you think that?" Sean frowned. "It's the same moon in Europe as it is here."

"Same moon, different effect. The Foundation pays me according to the lunar *hijri* calendar. The phase of the moon tells me how close I am to payday. Moon gazing definitely won't have the same attraction once I'm not on salary."

Carrying an armload of winter clothes to an open suitcase, I continued, "Not all the adjustments will be negative, of course. We'll no longer have to worry about prayer times and maniac *mutawwa* interrupting our shopping!"

"And I won't have to constantly check my rearview mirror to make sure no one is trying to pass me – in the breakdown lane!"

"We'll be able to read newspapers and magazines without black marks all over them," I added, warming to the exercise.

Our faces smiled at the banter but our hearts were heavy.

"We're just trying to make ourselves feel better, aren't we?" I said with a catch in my voice.

Sean crossed the room to give me a hug.

"It'll get worse before it gets better," he whispered into my hair, "but it will get better."

* * * *

We watched the movers work with speedy efficiency. Suddenly all the boxes had been squeezed into the 20-foot shipping container that sat in the driveway. The vehicle departed with our possessions. The house looked empty and we felt drained.

"It's been a great ride, hasn't it?" Sean said. He poured himself the remains of his last bottle of scotch and topped up my glass of Perrier. We sat together in the living room reflecting on our Saudi years. "We've been privileged to witness some of the fastest, most remarkable progress that history has ever seen."

"You've had a major role in that progress," I said proudly. "Your projects included the largest airport in the world at the time, huge underground command and operations facilities and then Riyadh's first skyscraper and multi-use commercial complex. Those are pretty significant contributions."

"Those jobs traced the growth of Riyadh: from responding to basic needs to enjoying sophisticated luxuries. We arrived in a country steeped in the old ways. Few people had TVs or telephones. The outside world was still outside. In little more than one generation, an underdeveloped oasis has matured into a world capital."

"How I rebelled at the prospect of going to a distant desert outpost! I wanted to go anywhere else but Saudi Arabia!" I laughed at the memory. "Everything we heard about the place was so unfavourable! My inclination to wait for a more female-friendly assignment nearly caused us to pass up the opportunity of a lifetime. If nothing else, I've learned that even in a desert – real or allegorical – life can be rich if you make an effort."

We sat quietly remembering our nearly 24 years in Riyadh.

"It's not just Riyadh that's changed," I said, breaking our contemplative silence. "I arrived as a young, inexperienced mother, the wife of Sean Cuddihy. I'm leaving as a grandmother and a person in my own right: a businesswoman, PR consultant and writer. Do you think those achievements came about because of all the hurdles in Saudi or in spite of them?" I added gave Sean a playful nudge.

Sean gave me one of Those Looks.

"Sometimes I think the whole appeal of this place for you has been the thrill of breaking rules. You certainly pushed the boundaries."

"True," I agreed, "but look at the rewards. I discovered a wonderful new world. How different my Saudi experience would have been if I'd always – ever – accepted 'no' as an answer."

"You're right," Sean laughed. "You often left me speechless with your naïve daring but you *did* made things happen. The only thing you didn't accomplish," he added mischievously, "was getting a Saudi driving license. But then, no other woman has achieved that either!"

Sean paused for a moment and drained his glass.

"I've changed, too, from the person I was when we arrived. Not least," he chuckled, "because I'm leaving as the husband of Kathy Cuddihy."

Sean's comment made me grateful, yet again, for such an understanding husband. Although not always inclined to encourage my endeavours, he never stood in my way.

"This whole Saudi experience has been a blessing," I said with a lump in my throat. "I wouldn't have missed it for the world."

Sean and I held each other's hands, each of us lost in our own memories. Then we went upstairs to finish packing, close the suitcases and turn the page on this grand adventure. Perhaps this wasn't goodbye, just farewell. Would we ever return? The only possible answer was a heartfelt *insha'allah*.